SECOND HELPINGS

from

Union Square Cafe

SECOND HELPINGS

from

Union Square Cafe

Danny Meyer
and
Michael Romano

Photographs by
Duane Michals

HarperCollinsPublishers

SECOND HELPINGS FROM UNION SQUARE CAFE. Copyright © 2001 by Danny Meyer and Michael Romano. All rights reserved. Printed in Japan. No part of this book may be used or reproduced in any manner whatsoever without written permission except in the case of brief quotations embodied in critical articles and reviews. For information, address HarperCollins Publishers Inc., 10 East 53rd Street, New York, NY 10022.

HarperCollins books may be purchased for education, business, or sales promotional use. For information, please write: Special Markets Department, HarperCollins Publishers Inc., 10 East 53rd Street, New York, NY 10022.

FIRST EDITION

Designed by Joel Avirom
Design assistants: Meghan Day Healey and Jason Snyder

Printed on acid-free paper

Library of Congress Cataloging-in-Publication Data

Meyer, Danny.
   Second helpings from Union Square Cafe/Danny Meyer & Michael Romano. —1st ed.
     p. cm.
   Includes index.
   ISBN 0-06-019647-5
   1. Cookery. 2. Union Square Cafe. I. Romano, Michael. II. Title.

TX715 .M6215 2001
641.5—dc21   2001016565

01 02 03 04 05 ❖/TOP 10 9 8 7 6 5 4 3 2 1

To our friend and partner
Paul Bolles-Beaven

———

I toast you with these ancient wishes:
Good food, good friends, good conversation,
And when you've drunk your last libation,
May someone else then do the dishes.

CONTENTS

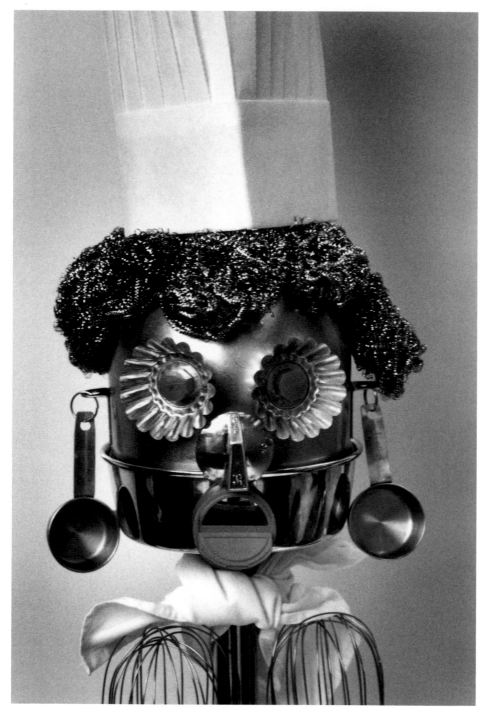

ARCHIMBOLDO'S
CHEF-D'OEUVRES

ACKNOWLEDGMENTS

Adding a monumental project like writing a cookbook to the already hectic day of running a busy restaurant like Union Square Cafe can only mean one thing: Help needed! While our primary goal was to write a book you'd enjoy using and owning, an equal goal was to make certain that the process would neither disrupt the consistent operation of Union Square Cafe nor prevent us from spending cherished time with family and friends. You can be sure there are plenty of people on whose patience, hard work, and support we depended, and to whom we owe our enthusiastic gratitude:

Our family of Union Square Cafe staff members, whose passion for hospitality and excellence is as keen as ever and remains the true secret of our success.

Our legion of Union Square Cafe guests, who continue to challenge us to reach, stretch, and improve, and who are as loyal when we trip as when we triumph.

The Union Square community—a fabulously vital New York neighborhood of creative residents, book publishers, ad firms, Off-Broadway theaters, dynamic schools, greenmarket farmers, architects, restaurateurs, high-tech types, and lots of kids—who collectively form the most vibrant backdrop imaginable for a restaurant like USC.

Our suppliers and purveyors, on whose dedication to quality we depend for every ingredient that goes into a Union Square Cafe meal.

Our partners, chefs, and general managers—Paul Bolles-Beaven, Floyd Cardoz, Tom Colicchio, Richard Coraine, Steven Eckler, Randy Garutti, Kerry Heffernan, Nick Mautone, Mark Maynard-Parisi, and David Swinghamer— who are responsible for each of our restaurants, every day, and who willingly shrugged off our repeated refrain of "Can't make that meeting—there's another cookbook deadline."

Susan Friedland, our editor and dear friend, was on our side every step of the way, and always is. Her confidence in the project and her one-of-a-kind sense of humor kept us cooking and writing. We benefited mightily from the gift of her openness in freely sharing honest convictions. We especially dedicate the recipe for *Bollito di Vitello* to Susan. She deserves all the credit for helping us write her favorite USC recipe in a way that can actually succeed brilliantly in a very small home kitchen.

Susan Lescher and Robert Lescher, whose unwavering belief in Union Square Cafe and persistent encouragement finally persuaded us to write a second cookbook.

Victoria Burghi's yummy, refreshingly straightforward desserts are the perfect way to end a meal at Union Square Cafe, and her recipes grace this book.

Jenny Zinman, Vanessa Stich, Dayna Ryan, Michelle Haberli, and Bridget Watkins—behind-the-scenes heroes of this effort—whose spirited encouragement, imposed discipline, and extraordinary organizational support allowed us to nail (almost) every deadline.

Joel Avirom's magical blend of professionalism and creativity is responsible for the look of our book. Sue Llewellyn's keen eyes helped us mind the details.

Dan Silverman, Ken Callaghan, Mark Gandara, and Deborah Arriaga—leaders of the Union Square Cafe kitchen, keep it humming with unparalleled consistency every day, and pulled more than their collective weight during the writing of the book. Karen Ann King makes sure USC's wine list continues to provide plenty of wonderful complements for our cooking.

Thanks to Stephanie Lyness and David Nussbaum for their perseverance, diligence, excellence, and care in home testing every recipe in this book—and whole lot more that didn't quite make the cut.

Thanks to Jim Berrien, Mary Jane Berrien, Anne Bolles-Beaven, Paul Bolles-Beaven, William Bolles-Beaven, Yasmine Delawari, Ari Ellis, Morgan Entrekin, Paul Gottlieb, Alexandra Gray, Michelle Haberli, Dan Halpern, Jacques Pépin, Scott Poticha, Andrew Rasiej, Alain Sailhac, Duncan Sokolov,

André Soltner, Roger Straus, Robin Wagner, Jennifer Rudolph Walsh, Deborah Yates, and Jenny Zinman, all friends of Union Square Cafe who had absolutely *no* idea what they were getting into when they graciously accepted our unconventional invitation to model for Duane Michals's photographs in *Second Helpings*.

About those photographs . . . Union Square Cafe succeeds as a purveyor of warm, familiar comfort, generous flavors, and delicious food. How, then, we wondered, to reflect the mood and style of the restaurant in photographs for *Second Helpings*? After considering several food photographers, at last we went in an unusual direction. Duane Michals is a longtime friend of Union Square Cafe who, we knew, had just about no experience or interest in photographing food. Duane knows USC's food well, but as he does with almost everything else that surrounds him, he's more interested in observing what's going on *beyond* the main event—in this case, restaurant life. As a survival tool, we've always approached the restaurant business with our own healthy sense of humor and irony, thus Duane was a perfect collaborator. Duane's witty photo essays illustrate restaurant life beyond the food. He allowed us to poke fun at ourselves and at the things we do and see every day in the restaurant business. Duane's stories won't help you know that you prepared the recipes the right way, but if they make you smile while you're cooking, they will have added a wonderful ingredient to the finished product.

      Audrey Heffernan Meyer, my perfectly matched mate and the brilliant mother of my four kids deserves a huge thank-you for saying yes to this project, even against her better judgment. And here's a wish for Hallie, Charles, Gretchen, and Peyton Meyer: Don't grow up too quickly, but when you do, I hope this book will bring you lots of joy!

In loving memory of Mary Ann Romano, Michael's mother, who taught him that giving love and giving good food were one and the same, and to John Romano and Juliette, Tom, and Siobhan Taaffe, Michael's loving family, who keep Mary Ann's memory alive.

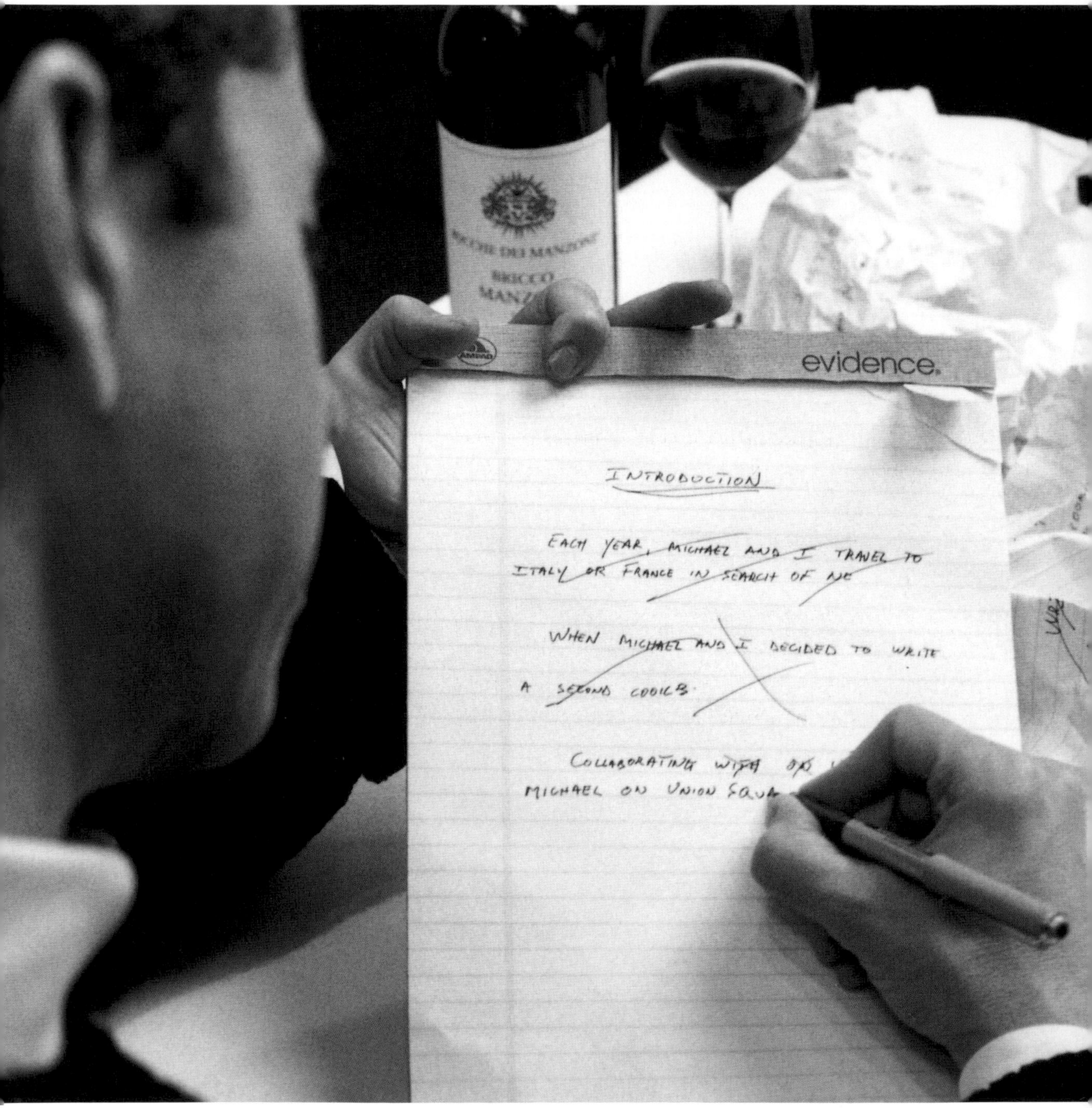

INTRODUCTION

Each year, Michael and I travel to Italy and France—usually independently, due to our schedules, but always in hungry pursuit of fresh inspiration for our menu and wine list. Having each been brought up with a very western European sensibility about the kitchen and table, we continually look to our early influences to help rekindle the culinary flame that first lit our desires to be in the restaurant business.

Over the course of a dozen years working together, Michael and I have taken just four of these food-finding journeys together—three times to Italy and once to France. Since it's rare for us to take precious time away from home and work, it's always critical that we arrange a trip carefully, with clear objectives and usually a very fast pace. There's a lot of joy in the planning and anticipating—similar to the feeling of picking a special wine from the cellar to pour and enjoy with a very good friend: It's always exciting before you pull the cork, but there's no way of knowing if the bottle will actually deliver. When it does, the sharing magnifies the magic.

For most of our trips, we'll budget about six or seven days, designing a gastronomically grueling itinerary that includes lunch and dinner each day and requires us to sleep on a different pillow in a different town each night. Of the twelve to fourteen meals we'll eat (not counting breakfasts), three are generally return trips to favorite places that have inspired us on earlier trips, one or two are at a vineyard or private home, and eight are at restaurants we've never tried but have read or heard great things about. When we travel together, a lot of time is spent side by side in the car, plenty of hours are passed across from each other at the table, and any free moments are used to scour fresh food markets, visit winemaker friends, see important sights, and walk or jog.

Though this is an extraordinary way to spend a week, we invariably return home feeling tired, puffy, overwhelmed, and even a little let down. It's rare that more than half the meals reveal the new ideas we had hoped to discover, and from the standpoint of either food, wine, or hospitality, some of the restaurants leave us scratching our heads. But we've never regretted one of those trips. Even if culinary highlights are scarce, we always make good use of the gift of concentrated time away from the day-to-day routine of running the restaurant.

Michael and I debated where to go for our most recent trip almost up to the day of departure. The stakes somehow seemed higher than ever for a lot of reasons. For one thing, Union Square Cafe was approaching its fifteenth birthday and seemed thirsty for a spirited injection of fresh ideas. For another, Michael and I had committed to meeting our deadline for writing this cookbook, and we had been woefully unsuccessful at making enough time to work on it together. When we wrote our first book, *The Union Square Cafe Cookbook,* there was one restaurant and I had one child. This time around, there were three additional restaurants (Gramercy Tavern, Eleven Madison Park, and Tabla) and four young children. Still, we chose to write it, and were stubborn about writing it ourselves. Time was short, and we had to make it count. I *needed* a return trip to Italy. There's something about that country that draws me back and then back again, and when I go too long without it, I feel a deep sense of hollowness. It's the animated people, the robust food, the deeply brooding history, the cypress-studded landscape, and exquisite architecture. It's my just-off-the-airplane espresso, the familiar feel of colorful lire in my hands, and the excitement of digging into my first bowl of pasta.

I was going to go to Italy, with or without Michael, because I had to. I argued that we could accomplish our usual culinary goals plus spend all of our downtime working on the cookbook. Knowing how these trips go, and with an impossible schedule of his own to rearrange, Michael was skeptical. I shocked myself by suggesting that the trip could succeed if, instead of doing the busman's holiday "another-day-another-town" routine, we spent the *entire* week in Rome. There would be just one hotel, no city-to-city driving, lots of walking, and an abundance of good *trattorie*. Knowing my peripatetic nature, Michael was in shock when he heard me say "one week: one city," and he finally agreed to peel away from New York to join me for the last four days of my week in Rome. We'd feverishly write each morning, break for lunch, write all afternoon, go out for dinner, and then sleep.

The morning Michael arrived, we meandered to Piazza Sant'Eustacchio by way of the Pantheon. It was my fourth visit to the Pantheon in three days and my third visit to the excellent coffee bar Camilloni di Sant'Eustacchio for cappuccino and *cornetti*. Michael asked me where I had eaten so far, and I let him know that my two best meals had been return visits to places he knew— La Taverna da Giovanni and Al Moro. Though I hadn't unearthed any new ideas, all the old standards tasted exactly as they had more than twenty years earlier, when I lived in Rome. In fact, strolling down *via* after *via*, I had inspected scores of menus, and just as I remembered from over two decades ago, almost every *trattoria* served the exact same roster of dishes it always had. Where was the creativity? Where were the fresh ideas? What was there to learn? Why had I chosen to spend the entirety of this one precious week in Rome?

The answer was not apparent until we'd had two disappointing meals— regrettably, Michael's first two in Rome. Though I now let on that I had an itch to spend a day or two outside the Eternal City, we both agreed to stay a little longer in Rome before throwing in the towel. There was plenty of work to do on the cookbook, the city was especially beautiful, thanks to the complete scrubbing it had been given for the Millennium Jubilee, and after all, there were still many restaurants left on our list. You could also do a lot worse than to be in Rome in balmy April. Rather than try something new, the next day we decided to play it safe by dining at the two restaurants that I had most enjoyed before Michael's arrival. Things began to perk up. At Al Moro we lunched on *spaghetti al Moro,* the house's peppery version of carbonara, and on a brilliant stew of fava beans, spring vegetables, olive oil, and herbs. For dinner we returned to La Taverna da Giovanni. Giovanni's family was my Italian family when I lived in Rome in the late 1970s and early 1980s as a tour guide, student, and later as an apprentice cook. The embracing welcome we got from Mimmo, Claudio, and Mamma was joyous and genuine.

In Mimmo's arms, familiar plates of antipasti arrived, one by one, each simple, pure, and delicious. Marinated bean salad, roasted peppers, prosciutto, *mozzarella di bufala,* marinated fried zucchini, celery and parsley salad, and so on. For pasta, we enjoyed *spaghetti alle vongole, bombolotti "al modo mio,"* and *bucatini all'Amatriciana.* As *secondi* we ate veal saltimbocca and, for the second night in a row, *coda alla vaccinara,* the traditional Roman butchers' method of braising oxtails. They were the best oxtails I'd ever had, succulent and rich with deep layers of soul-satisfying flavor. Claudio proudly invited us into the kitchen— midmeal—to learn how he had made the *coda.* His secret ingredient was chocolate. We downed a simple, straightforward red wine from Abruzzo, and left Giovanni's after enjoying a glass of *centerbe*—the potent, green *digestivo* ostensibly made by monks from one hundred herbs. Mimmo made us promise to return again before leaving Rome.

The next morning, following a run through the Borghese Gardens, I met Michael for the cappuccino, pastry, and apricot nectar that would fuel our work on the cookbook. I had lost my urge to leave Rome, having convinced myself that even if every succeeding meal was a bust, our dinner the night before was the reason I had come to Rome. Finally, I understood what had drawn me there so powerfully in the first place. The traditional Roman *trattoria* was at the heart of why I opened Union Square Cafe in 1985. As the best Roman *trattorie* and family-run restaurants always have, we've tried to distinguish Union Square Cafe's food by its simplicity, consistency, and straightforward flavors; its hospitality, by warmth and generosity; and its atmosphere, by a convivial, full house of animated guests with robust appetites.

In every respect, Rome exists for the purpose of savoring what is old and what is good. It was one of those forehead-slapping moments for me when I realized that in a perfect world, that's what I had always wanted for Union Square Cafe. Of course, this is New York, not Rome, and we're an American, not Italian, restaurant. One of the things we've learned is that to keep a restaurant vital, you've got to propose a menu that successfully balances the tightwire of having enough new items (to make people feel excited about returning) with enough dependable mainstays (to assure they'll *want* to return). It's a fine line: too much change feels uncomfortable and makes a restaurant appear inconsistent, and not enough of it makes the place feel lackluster and uninspiring.

So our menu does change, and it does so with lots of multicultural influence. When Michael returned seven years ago from a culinary tour of India, he brought back an excitement and curiosity that ended up on plates at Union Square Cafe. The response from our guests was so positive that we decided to launch a new restaurant, Tabla, which celebrates the marriage of American cooking with Indian spices.

The continuous blending of dynamic change with reliable consistency has been a winning formula for Union Square Cafe. In the seven years since we wrote *The Union Square Cafe Cookbook,* we've developed scores of new recipes without abandoning old favorites. The selection here is culled from the most successful crowd-pleasers of those new recipes; the ones our guests request over and over again. We have also chosen dishes with a careful eye toward what will work best in the home kitchen. The book offers recipes of varying degrees of ease. Not every recipe is a snap (though many are), but we're confident after exhaustive testing in home kitchens that every one *works* and will deliciously reward the cook's efforts.

The past several years have been remarkable ones for Union Square Cafe: the *New York Times* renewed our three-star rating, we won James Beard Awards for Outstanding Restaurant and Outstanding Wine Service, and the restaurant was voted New Yorkers' number one favorite for five consecutive years in the Zagat survey. In an era that has seen an unparalleled explosion of new restaurants—and good ones—we're especially proud of our achievements.

We're pleased to share these recipes with you; they are, after all, the real reason people keep returning so enthusiastically to Union Square Cafe. We wish you the same success at home.

NOTES ON EQUIPMENT AND INGREDIENTS

Years of cooking have taught us that there is no substitute for good ingredients and that good cooking is greatly aided by proper equipment. We recommend using well-constructed, heavy-bottomed pans, preferably made of tin or stainless steel–lined copper, stainless steel, cast iron, enameled cast iron, or black steel. Good pans, like good knives, may cost a little more at the outset, but they return a lifetime of service if given reasonable care. It's a one-time investment, and you should buy the best you can afford.

Olive oil is the preferred cooking fat at Union Square Cafe. Over the years we've found endless ways to use the different qualities and characteristics of olive oil in our cooking, including, as you'll find in this book, deep-frying in extra-virgin olive oil. Generally, when a recipe calls for cooking with olive oil, try a good-quality, pure olive oil, or nonpremium extra virgin, and reserve your prized boutique extra-virgin oil for salads or for drizzling over cooked vegetables, fish, and meat.

For certain recipes, Italian red wine vinegar is called for. We prize its slightly higher acidity level (7.5 percent as opposed to 5 or 6 percent of other vinegars) and unique flavor.

Another vinegar we call for fairly often is balsamic vinegar. It is an Italian vinegar from the northeastern region of Emilia-Romagna. Balsamic is made from the juice of Trebbiano grapes, which is cooked according to a very precise recipe and then matured in a complex and painstaking process that involves aging the vinegar in barrels of different types of wood. There is a broad range of "balsamic" vinegar available in today's market. At the most basic (and inexpensive) level, the vinegar will be somewhat thin and sharp with a trace of sweetness, which may or may not have come from adding sugar. As you progress up the scale to finer, more aged products (six-, twelve-, or twenty-year-old vinegars are not uncommon), the quality improves dramatically. Finally, there is *aceto balsamico tradizionale,* the finest expression of the balsamic vinegar–maker's art, aged from 60 to 100 years and sold in very small bottles for very high prices. This last product is not really meant to be used as an ingredient in salad dressing: it is at its best drizzled sparingly over simmered white beans, grilled meat or fish, a wedge of aged Parmigiano-Reggiano, or even fresh strawberries. It is a gustatory marvel and should be experienced at least once. When balsamic is called for in this book, it refers to a well-made vinegar from the middle category, as we have described.

Panko is a prepared Japanese bread crumb available in Asian food markets. Because it is coarsely cut, it lends a wonderful texture to the food it coats. You can substitute homemade fresh bread crumbs.

Verjus is the juice of unripened grapes. It is not fermented and therefore does not contain alcohol, and it is wonderful in sauces where the acidity of vinegar might be excessive. If you cannot find verjus in your market, substitute a blend of 4 parts white grape juice to 1 part white wine vinegar.

In many of our recipes, you will come across Aleppo pepper. We discovered this wonderful seasoning years ago in a Middle Eastern market near the restaurant, and have loved using it ever since. Aleppo is a very ancient town in northern Syria, and Aleppo pepper is a sun-dried, ground red chili with an enticingly smoky aroma, a medium heat level, and a rich, round taste. Use it wherever you might use crushed red pepper flakes. If you cannot find Aleppo pepper, substitute crushed red pepper or cayenne, using about half the amount called for.

Fleur de sel is a sea salt from France, only recently exported to this country. The name, which literally means "flower of salt," refers to the finest grade of sea salt. These delicate, almost powderlike crystals of snow-white salt are hand harvested from atop the salt beds, only when weather conditions permit. *Fleur de sel* has an exquisite taste, and is incomparable when sprinkled over grilled, sautéed, or roasted meats, fish, or vegetables. Some cooks even include it in desserts. Like fine balsamic vinegar, it is best used for finishing dishes, rather than as the main seasoning.

Several of our dessert recipes call for vegetable oil spray to coat a cookie sheet, pie tin, or cake pan. We use it for the convenience and ease it offers in our high-volume kitchen—it enables us to quickly and evenly apply a lubricating layer of fat to the pan. You'll find it equally convenient at home, but you can achieve the desired effect with a paper towel or brush dipped lightly in oil or melted butter.

Finally, the unusual spices and spice blends we call for in some of the recipes, such as curry leaves, black cumin, and garam masala, offer interesting and tasty glimpses into some of the more exotic cuisines of the world.

SECOND HELPINGS
from
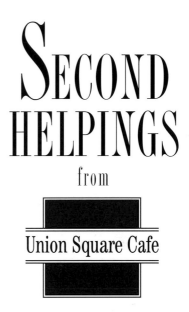
Union Square Cafe

ON EATING
SHELLFISH WITH A
SELFISH CELL PHONE

Portobello Crostini

SERVES 4

These crostini (or toasts) are fun to make and simply rely on a colorful combination of peppers, mushrooms, and Taleggio—a creamy cow's-milk cheese from Italy's Lombardy region. They are assembled on ciabatta, a mildly salty Italian bread whose soft interior "cracks and crevices" make it an ideal foundation for toppings. You can serve the crostini as a passed hors d'oeuvre, a plated appetizer, or as a lunch main course, accompanied by soup and salad. If you're unable to find ciabatta, substitute slices of any good sourdough or crusty country bread.

1 red bell pepper
1 yellow bell pepper
4 medium portobello mushrooms, stems removed
    and caps rubbed clean
½ cup Anchovy Dressing (see page 10)
4 slices ciabatta, or another rustic bread, ½ to ¾
    inch thick and at least 2½ inches wide
2 garlic cloves, peeled and split lengthwise
¾ pound Taleggio, crust removed, and sliced ¼
    inch thick

1. Preheat the oven to 375 degrees F.

2. Roast and slice the peppers: Spear the peppers with a kitchen fork or skewer and hold them over an open flame until charred. Alternatively, cook the peppers under the broiler until their skins blacken. Placed the charred peppers in a paper bag or in a tightly covered container until they are cool enough to handle. Rub off the skins (never

Wine Suggestions:
Try to find a fruity Italian white like Soave Classico, arneis, or Lombardy's Franciacorta Bianca.

run them under water, which washes away the flavorful oils), split the peppers lengthwise, and discard the stems and seeds. Cut each pepper lengthwise into eight 1-inch-wide strips and set aside.

3. Lay the mushrooms on a baking sheet and brush them with 2 to 3 tablespoons of the anchovy dressing. Roast the mushrooms in the oven until tender, 20 to 30 minutes. Then, while they are still warm, cut each mushroom on a sharp bias into 4 wide slices. Cover and set aside.

4. Toast the bread slices and rub one side of each piece with half a clove of garlic.

5. Preheat the broiler.

6. To assemble the crostini, atop each piece of bread alternate four slices of the warm mushrooms with layers of the roasted pepper strips. Cover each crostino with one-quarter of the cheese slices.

7. Lay the crostini on a baking sheet and broil until the cheese is melted and bubbly. Drizzle the remaining anchovy dressing over the crostini and serve hot.

Chicken Liver Crostini

SERVES 8 TO 16

Any traveler lucky enough to visit central Tuscany knows that almost
every trattoria meal there is likely to begin with a passed plate of toasts
topped with savory chicken liver spread. Not every crostino is created
equal, however. Caring cooks work hard to arrive at a spread with the
proper texture—neither too coarse nor overly pureed, and with layers of
flavor to accent and brighten the fresh liver taste. After lots and lots of
experimenting, Michael hit on this version of *crostini di fegatini,* which
we recommend serving warm, either on their own or as part of an antipasto
plate, as we do at Union Square Cafe. After you try this recipe, you're likely
to think everything else is just chopped liver.

1 cup olive oil

¼ cup coarsely chopped pancetta

½ cup chopped onion

3 fresh sage leaves

3 juniper berries

½ teaspoon capers, drained

2 anchovy fillets

8 ounces chicken livers (about 5 medium),
    trimmed of fat, rinsed, and patted dry

½ teaspoon kosher salt

⅛ teaspoon freshly ground black pepper

¼ cup white wine

½ cup Chicken Stock (page 315)

2 tablespoons butter

1 fresh baguette, at least 12 inches long, sliced on
    a diagonal into thirty-two ¼-inch-thick slices

Wine Suggestions:

Try a refreshing and
bright white to contrast
with the rich liver flavor.
We'd suggest going
with a Tuscan Vernaccia
di San Gimigniano, a
sparkling prosecco from
the Veneto, or a crisp
sauvignon blanc from
almost anywhere.

1. Heat 1 tablespoon of the olive oil over medium heat in a 10-inch skillet. Add the chopped pancetta and cook until the fat is rendered, 2 to 3 minutes. Add the onion and cook until softened, but not colored, 2 to 3 minutes. Add the sage leaves, juniper berries, capers, and anchovy fillets and cook an additional 2 minutes.

2. Season the chicken livers on both sides with the salt and pepper. Add to the skillet and cook, stirring, for 2 minutes. Add the wine, bring to a simmer, and reduce until almost dry. Pour in the stock and simmer until reduced by about one-half and thickened. Swirl in the butter.

3. Transfer the contents of the skillet to the bowl of a food processor and pulse to a chunky puree.

4. Wash and dry the skillet. Place over medium heat, pour in ½ cup of the oil, and bring it almost to the smoking point. Add as many baguette slices as will fit into the skillet, and cook until the croutons are golden brown, but still soft in the center, 15 to 30 seconds each side. Adjust the heat as necessary if the croutons brown too fast or not fast enough. Transfer the cooked croutons to a plate lined with paper towels. Repeat to cook all of the croutons, adding more oil to the skillet as needed.

5. Spread the warm chicken liver mixture onto the croutons and serve immediately. As an alternative, transfer the warm chicken liver mixture to a bowl and serve the toasts on the side.

Cornmeal-Crusted Ricotta Fritters

SERVES 4

We serve these fritters atop bitter greens to make a marvelously satisfying salad with a balanced contrast of flavors, textures, and temperatures. You can also enjoy any of the salad's component parts on their own. The ricotta fritters—crunchy on the outside and creamy within—make a wonderful passed hors d'oeuvre or accompaniment to sliced Italian meats like mortadella, prosciutto, and salami. The salad, with its tangy anchovy vinaigrette, is a winner, with or without the fritters.

RICOTTA WEDGES

15 ounces whole-milk ricotta cheese

5 large eggs

½ cup grated Pecorino Romano

Kosher salt

Freshly ground black pepper

1 teaspoon extra-virgin olive oil, plus extra for the
    cake pan or mold

½ cup all-purpose flour

½ cup cornmeal

1 cup olive oil

ANCHOVY DRESSING

2 tablespoons anchovy paste

2 tablespoons Italian red wine vinegar

½ teaspoon finely minced garlic

½ cup extra-virgin olive oil

2 tablespoons grated Pecorino Romano

Kosher salt

⅛ teaspoon freshly ground black pepper

SALAD

4 cups mixed arugula and frisée, trimmed, rinsed, and dried

Wine Suggestions:
This calls for a fruity, crisp white. Try a dry riesling from Germany or Alsace, or any youthful white from Italy's Trentino–Alto Adige.

1. Wrap the ricotta in cheesecloth and tie with a string at the top, to make a bundle. Place in a strainer set over a bowl and allow it to drain for at least 2 hours, or overnight, in the refrigerator.

2. Preheat the oven to 250 degrees F. Lightly oil an 8-inch cake pan or soufflé mold.

3. In a large bowl, beat 3 of the eggs until well blended. Add the drained ricotta, the pecorino, 1 teaspoon salt, and ⅛ teaspoon pepper; stir until well combined. Scrape the mixture into the oiled pan and spread evenly.

4. Make a *bain-marie* by placing the pan inside a larger baking dish or roasting pan and filling the outer dish with enough hot water to come three-quarters of the way up the sides of the inner pan. Carefully place the *bain-marie* in the center of the oven and bake until the ricotta is just set, but still creamy, about 70 to 75 minutes. Let cool, then cover and refrigerate until completely chilled. The fritters can be made to this point up to 2 days ahead.

5. Make the dressing by whisking together all the ingredients in a small bowl, making sure to completely dissolve the anchovy paste. Set aside.

6. In a small bowl, lightly beat the remaining 2 eggs with the teaspoon of extra-virgin olive oil. Combine the flour and the cornmeal on a plate and season with the remaining ½ teaspoon salt and a pinch of pepper. When the ricotta is chilled, cut it into 8 wedges and carefully lift each one out with a rubber spatula. Gently dip each into the egg mixture, and dredge in the flour-cornmeal mixture. Set aside on a plate.

7. Heat the olive oil in a large heavy-bottomed skillet over medium heat until the oil begins to shimmer. Add the coated ricotta wedges in a single layer and fry until the coating is set and lightly browned, about 1 minute for each side. Set the fritters aside on an absorbent paper towel.

8. Toss the greens with the dressing and divide among 4 plates. Arrange 2 warm ricotta wedges atop each mound of greens and serve immediately.

Baked Stuffed Littleneck Clams

SERVES 4

This recipe is a delightful departure from the usual garlicky baked-clam norm, marrying toasted hazelnuts, crunchy celery, and refreshing citrus. When broiling clams or any shellfish, prevent them from tipping over by evenly sprinkling a baking sheet with a ¼-inch layer of kosher salt or coarse sea salt, and nesting the shells in the salt.

24 littleneck clams, well scrubbed
¼ cup white wine
4 tablespoons (½ stick) butter, softened
1 celery stalk, peeled and minced (about ½ cup)
2 tablespoons chopped shallots
2 tablespoons toasted, peeled, and chopped
    hazelnuts
⅛ teaspoon freshly ground black pepper
Pinch of cayenne
1 teaspoon grated orange zest plus juice of 2
    oranges (about 1 cup)
1 tablespoon chopped fresh parsley
¼ to ⅓ cup panko (Japanese bread crumbs)

1. Combine the clams and wine in a pot large enough to hold all of the clams comfortably. Cover, bring to a simmer, and cook until the clams open, 5 to 8 minutes. Pour the clams into a colander set in a large bowl. Reserve the broth and allow the clams to cool.

2. Heat 1 tablespoon of the butter in a 9-inch skillet over medium heat. Add the celery and shallots and stir to cook, without coloring, for 3 minutes.

Wine Suggestions:
As a complement to the citrus notes, California or New Zealand sauvignon blanc will work beautifully here.

Stir in the hazelnuts, black pepper, and cayenne. Add the reserved clam broth and the orange juice. Simmer until the liquid is almost entirely evaporated, stirring occasionally to avoid sticking. Scrape the mixture into a bowl, stir in the orange zest and parsley, and allow to cool for at least 15 minutes in the refrigerator. Finish the stuffing by folding in the remaining 3 tablespoons of butter with a small rubber spatula.

3. Pry away and discard the top shell from each clam. Place each clam in its bottom shell on a plate and set aside.

4. Preheat the broiler with the rack set on the middle shelf.

5. Spoon about 1 teaspoon of the stuffing over each clam, spreading it evenly to the edge of the shell. Sprinkle each stuffed clam with about ½ teaspoon of the panko.

6. Arrange the clams on a baking sheet and broil until golden brown on top, 2 to 4 minutes. Transfer carefully to a platter and serve hot.

Steamed Clams and Arugula

SERVES 4

This is a kissing cousin to the traditional recipe you'd use to make a "white clam" sauce for pasta. We've adopted it as a sensational accompaniment for garlic-rubbed toast and peppery arugula. Once you've scrubbed your clams, the recipe is a breeze to prepare, and we recommend serving it as a rustic late summer or early autumn appetizer. For added richness, whisk a tablespoon or two of sweet butter into the broth just before serving.

2 tablespoons olive oil

¼ cup chopped shallots

1 tablespoon minced garlic, plus 2 cloves, split

½ teaspoon Aleppo pepper

¼ cup white wine

32 littleneck or 24 cherrystone clams,
    well scrubbed

4 (1-inch) slices of sourdough, whole wheat,
    or peasant bread

Extra-virgin olive oil for drizzling

4 firmly packed cups arugula, trimmed,
    washed, and dried

1 tablespoon sliced fresh basil

1 tablespoon chopped fresh parsley

1.   Combine the oil, shallots, minced garlic, and Aleppo pepper in a pot large enough to hold all of the clams comfortably. Stir gently over medium heat without browning the ingredients, about 2 minutes. Add the wine and clams, cover, bring to a simmer, and cook until the clams open, 5 to 8 minutes. Set aside.

Wine Suggestions:
Serve this with a crisp, refreshing white, like sauvignon blanc, dry riesling, or pinot grigio. Prosecco, the lightly sparkling wine from Italy's Veneto region, would also be delightful.

2. While the clams are cooking, grill or toast the bread until golden brown. Immediately rub each warm piece of toast with a garlic half. The garlic will "melt" into the bread and give it an intense flavor. Transfer the *bruschette* to a serving plate, drizzle the tops generously with extra-virgin olive oil, and set aside.

3. Arrange the arugula among 4 bowls. Remove the clams from the broth with a slotted spoon and divide them evenly to top the arugula in the bowls. Return the broth to a simmer, stir in the herbs, and immediately pour over the clams and arugula. Serve the bruschette on the side, to mop up the herb broth.

Eggplant "Meatballs"

SERVES 6

Forming eggplant and fresh mozzarella into *polpettine*—Italian for "meatballs"—makes an enormously versatile and delicious dish that is satisfying as a passed hors d'oeuvre or as an appetizer accompanied by tomato sauce (try with the spicy Arrabbiata sauce on page 94). These meatless *polpettine* also work wonderfully as an unexpected twist on spaghetti and meatballs.

1 large eggplant (about 1¼ pounds)
1 tablespoon olive oil
3⅓ cups fresh bread crumbs
⅔ cup grated Pecorino Romano
1 tablespoon coarsely chopped fresh parsley
1 large egg yolk
Kosher salt
Freshly ground black pepper
¼ pound fresh mozzarella, cut into
        18 (½-inch) cubes
1½ quarts vegetable or olive oil for deep-frying

Wine Suggestions:

The *polpettine* are great with a rustic red wine like Valpolicella, Salice Salentino, or Sangiovese di Romagna. Or try them with a fruity white like Franciacorta Bianca or Vernaccia di San Gimigniano.

1. Preheat the oven to 375 degrees F.

2. Rub the eggplant with 1 tablespoon of olive oil and prick in several places with the tines of a fork. Roast until soft, about 1 hour and 15 minutes. Make a shallow slit in the skin the length of the eggplant, and place the eggplant, slit side down, in a colander set over a bowl. Place a weight (such as a small plate weighted with a can) over the eggplant and let sit for at least 1 hour to drain.

3. Halve the eggplant lengthwise, scoop out the flesh, and puree in a food processor until smooth. Transfer the puree to a large bowl. Add 1⅓ cups of the bread crumbs, the pecorino, parsley, egg yolk, ¼ teaspoon salt, and ⅛ teaspoon pepper, stirring until well combined.

4. Place the remaining 2 cups of bread crumbs in a large bowl.

5. Spoon out about 1 tablespoon of the eggplant mixture and, with wet hands, roll it between your palms into a round slightly smaller than a Ping-Pong ball. Press in one cube of the mozzarella and then reshape the ball. The cheese should be entirely enclosed. Gently roll the eggplant in the bread crumbs, re-forming into a ball if necessary, and set on a cookie sheet. (If you find that the eggplant mixture is too soft to hold its shape during the rolling process, add some more bread crumbs.)

6. Pour the oil for deep-frying into a 6-quart heavy-bottomed, straight-sided saucepan. The oil should be 1¼ to 1½ inches deep, and the pan no more than a quarter full. This prevents any bubbling over when frying the *polpettine*. Heat the oil to 305 to 310 degrees F on a deep-fat thermometer. (Alternatively, heat 6 tablespoons of oil in a heavy skillet and pan-fry. The *polpettine* may lose their round shape, but will be just as delicious.)

7. Carefully slide as many *polpettine* into the oil as will comfortably fit. Fry, turning occasionally with a slotted spoon, until the coating is well browned and the cheese is melted, about 3 minutes. Transfer the *polpettine* to paper towels to drain. Serve immediately.

When I dine, and a cell phone rings,
it makes me mean and scheme revenge.
But my plotting soon is bollixed,
when this outré phonaholic
turns to me to say, "How do you do?
This call's for you."

Suppli al Telefono

SERVES 4

Suppli al Telefono—Italian for "telephone cords"—are cheese-filled rice balls, so named since each delicious bite pulls with it a long, gooey string of mozzarella. In Rome, they're enjoyed as a quick snack; it's easy to find platters stacked full of them in almost every *tavola calda*—the city's wonderful takeout food shops. Michael fondly remembers holiday family gatherings where *suppli* always made an appearance as part of the antipasto course. At the restaurant, we serve them as an appetizer accompanied by an arugula salad, simply dressed with lemon, olive oil, and a bit of salt. *Suppli al Telefono* can be made from leftover risotto; they're a big hit with kids (and adults) since they're so much fun to eat. Once you've learned to make them, experiment with such different flavoring ingredients as chopped mushrooms, sliced asparagus, or peas.

1 tablespoon butter

1 cup chopped onion

1 teaspoon minced garlic

1 cup arborio rice

2 cups Chicken Stock (page 315)

1¾ teaspoons kosher salt

⅛ teaspoon freshly ground black pepper

Heaping ¼ teaspoon Aleppo pepper

1 (¼-inch-thick) slice prosciutto (4 ounces), minced

2 ounces fresh mozzarella, finely diced (⅓ cup)

1 tablespoon minced fresh oregano

2 large eggs

2 cups panko (Japanese bread crumbs) or coarse fresh bread crumbs

1 cup olive oil

2 lemons, quartered

Wine Suggestions:

Suppli call for a simple, light house wine. Use a Soave Classico, Frascati, or almost any fresh Italian white. Dolcetto d'Alba, Valpolicella, and Chianti are good choices among reds.

1. Heat the butter in a 2-quart saucepan over low heat. Add the onion and cook until softened, but not colored, 3 to 4 minutes. Add the garlic and cook 30 more seconds. Add the rice and stir to coat with the butter. Then add the stock, salt, and black and Aleppo peppers. Bring to a boil, reduce the heat, cover, and simmer 15 minutes. Uncover and stir constantly for the final 2 minutes of cooking to develop the creaminess of the rice. Transfer the rice to a large platter or cookie sheet, spread out evenly and let it cool completely.

2. Combine the prosciutto, mozzarella, and oregano in a small bowl.

3. Line a cookie sheet with parchment paper or aluminum foil. Using a wet tablespoon, scoop out 16 heaping tablespoons of rice and place them on the cookie sheet.

4. Wet your hands and pick up one of the mounds of rice, placing it, rounded side down, in the palm of one hand. Use the thumb of your other hand to make an indentation in the rice. Fill the indentation with a rounded teaspoon of the cheese-prosciutto mixture. Place a second mound over the first, rounded side up, and press the two together between the palms of your hands to completely enclose the filling. Shape the rice into a ball. Repeat with the remaining rice to make 7 more balls.

5. Lightly beat the eggs in a medium bowl. Pour the panko into another medium bowl. Dip the rice balls into the egg and then roll them in the panko until they are completely coated. Place the coated rice balls on the cookie sheet until ready to cook. They can be refrigerated, covered, for several hours.

6. Heat the oil in a 10-inch skillet over medium-high heat until shimmering. Place 4 of the rice balls in the pan and cook, turning occasionally, until golden brown, 5 to 6 minutes. Transfer the finished rice balls to a plate lined with paper towels while you fry the rest. Serve hot, with lemon wedges.

USC's Fried Calamari, Part II

SERVES 4

The idea for this recipe came to us by accident while we were preparing to cook Union Square Cafe's original fried calamari for a group of Italian food journalists at a culinary exposition in Verona. Though we had faxed ahead to assure that all of our ingredients would be on hand (the only one they said they couldn't provide was graham cracker crumbs), unaccountably, someone had forgotten to stock our kitchen with vegetable oil for frying. With just over an hour to go before our fried calamari appetizer was to be served, we went on a mad hunt throughout the convention hall, begging each artisanal olive oil producer to part with a half-liter bottle of prized extra-virgin olive oil. After a remarkable show of typical Italian generosity, we had filled our basket with about 18 very good bottles of oil, and one by one, we poured them into a large kettle, in which we proceeded to fry our calamari. They had never been better.

Unlike our original recipe, these require no graham cracker crumbs. Instead, they rely on excellent olive oil for flavor, and club soda to guarantee an unbelievably light, tender texture. They're perfectly wonderful with a sprinkling of sea salt and fresh lemon juice, or you can serve them as we do, atop some romaine leaves lightly dressed with anchovy vinaigrette. The key to success with this dish is to cook the calamari in small batches; if the pan gets too crowded, the coating won't be as crisp.

1 pound fresh, cleaned calamari
2 cups club soda or seltzer
4 cups extra-virgin olive oil
2 cups all-purpose flour
Kosher salt
2 lemons, quartered

Wine Suggestions:
Choosing a wine with this dish is "*very*" easy! Try a simple coastal white, such as *ver*dicchio, *ver*mentino, or *ver*naccia, with the calamari.

1. Cut the calamari crosswise into ¼-inch rings. If the tentacles are large, halve or quarter them lengthwise. Put the calamari into a medium bowl, pour in the club soda or seltzer, and refrigerate for 15 minutes.

2. Preheat the oven to 200 degrees F.

3. Pour the oil into a heavy-bottomed, straight-sided 3-quart saucepan, about 8 inches in diameter. The pan should be not more than one-quarter full, or the oil may bubble over when the calamari are frying. Heat the oil to 325 degrees F on a deep-fat thermometer.

4. While the oil is heating, put the flour into a bowl. Remove a small handful of calamari from the soda and put it into the bowl with the flour. Toss to coat the calamari with the flour. Transfer the calamari to a mesh strainer and shake lightly to shed excess flour. Slide the calamari into the hot oil, and stir gently with a slotted spoon to separate the rings. Fry until the coating is crisp and very lightly colored, 45 seconds to 1 minute. Remove with a slotted spoon to a plate lined with paper towels. Sprinkle immediately with salt. Keep the cooked calamari warm in the oven, uncovered, while you continue frying. Check and maintain your oil temperature and repeat with the remaining calamari. (You'll need to do several batches.) Serve hot with lemon quarters.

THE THREE MUSKETEERS

SOUPS

Lemongrass Vichyssoise

———

Sweet-Hot Beet Soup

———

Spicy Corn Chowder

———

Lentil Soup with Portobello Mushrooms
and Spinach

———

Butternut Squash and Bean Soup

———

Chilled Melon and Vodka Soup

———

Minestra di Ceci

———

Minestra di Farro

———

Lemongrass Vichyssoise

SERVES 4

In the heat of summer, a refreshing, chilled bowl of vichyssoise is a great way to start a meal. The clean potato-onion flavor and satiny texture are irresistible. As a winning twist on this classic soup, we've found that an infusion of the crisp, citrus flavors of lemongrass counterbalance perfectly the richness of vichyssoise.

2 stalks lemongrass
1 cup half-and-half
2 tablespoons butter
1 cup chopped onion
2 cups well rinsed and chopped leeks, white part only
Kosher salt
Freshly ground white pepper
1 large or 2 medium Idaho potatoes
4½ cups Chicken Stock (page 315)
1 tablespoon chopped fresh chives

1. Cut off the root ends of the lemongrass and discard. Trim the tops of the stalks at the point at which they begin to branch. Reserve the trimmings. Peel away the outer layers until you reach the smooth, pale green inner core. Reserve the outer layers. Split the inner core lengthwise and mince finely; you should have about ½ cup.

2. Rinse the reserved lemongrass trimmings and outer layers. Coarsely chop them and transfer to a small saucepan; add the half-and-half. Bring to a simmer, remove from the heat, and let stand, covered, to infuse while you prepare the rest of the soup.

Wine Suggestions:
A light, citrusy sauvignon blanc from California or New Zealand would be great with the vichyssoise.

3. Melt the butter in a 2-quart saucepan over medium-low heat. Add the minced lemongrass, the onion, and leek and cook until the onion and leek soften, 4 to 5 minutes. Midway through the cooking, season with 1 teaspoon salt and ⅛ teaspoon white pepper.

4. Peel and coarsely chop the potatoes. Reserve in a bowl of cold water to prevent discoloration.

5. Drain the potatoes and add to the pan. Add the stock, bring to a simmer, cover, and cook until the potatoes are tender, about 20 minutes. Working in batches, transfer the mixture to a blender and puree until very smooth. Pass both the soup and the infused half-and-half through a fine-mesh strainer into a soup tureen. Stir well to combine, and refrigerate until well chilled. Taste and adjust the seasoning, if needed. Ladle into chilled soup bowls and sprinkle with chives.

Sweet-Hot Beet Soup

Serves 6

This crimson soup is like a meatless Indian version of borscht with layers of flavors that reveal themselves, one by one, with each spoonful. Our recipe is fairly mild on the piquancy scale, but by upping the amount of ground Thai chilies from ¼ to ½ teaspoon, you can deliver a more potent punch. Using vegetable stock gives the soup a nice sweetness; if you prefer to use water, try adding another 1½ teaspoons honey. We'd suggest following this with another Indian-flavored dish, like Sautéed Shrimp Goan Style (page 132), or braised lamb shanks. Feel free to prepare the soup a day or two in advance.

2 pounds medium beets

1½ tablespoons vegetable oil

2 cups sliced onion

1 jalapeño pepper, seeded and chopped

1½ tablespoons peeled and minced
    fresh ginger

2 teaspoons cumin seeds, freshly ground

1 tablespoon coriander seeds,
    freshly ground

½ teaspoon ground turmeric

Rounded ¼ teaspoon ground Thai chilies

3 tablespoons basmati rice

2 teaspoons kosher salt

⅛ teaspoon freshly ground black pepper

6 cups Vegetable Stock (page 318) or water

½ cup coconut milk

⅔ cup crème fraîche or heavy cream

1 tablespoon honey

1 tablespoon fresh lemon juice

½ teaspoon garam masala (see Note)

¼ cup washed and dried cilantro leaves

Wine Suggestions:

Here's another good opportunity to bring out a wine with lots of ripe fruit like New Zealand sauvignon blanc or an Alsatian tokay–pinot gris, muscat, or gewürztraminer.

SECOND HELPINGS FROM UNION SQUARE CAFE

1. Preheat the oven to 400 degrees F.

2. Trim the beets, leaving a ½- to 1-inch stem. Rinse the beets and wrap in aluminum foil. Roast until the tip of a paring knife can easily pierce the beets, about 1 hour and 10 minutes. When the beets are cool enough to handle, trim the ends, and peel off the skins. Slice the beets. Place them in the bowl of a food processor and pulse, scraping down the sides often, until they are very finely chopped but not pureed. Set aside.

3. Heat the oil in a 3-quart saucepan over low heat. Add the onions and cook, stirring often, until they are wilted and translucent but not browned, 7 to 8 minutes. Add the jalapeño and the ginger and cook for an additional 2 minutes. Add the ground cumin, coriander, turmeric, and chili and cook, stirring, 3 more minutes.

4. Stir in the rice, salt, and pepper. Add the stock or water, bring to a boil, reduce the heat, and simmer, covered, until the rice is very tender, about 20 minutes.

5. Puree the soup in a food processor in batches, if necessary, and return to the pan. Stir in the coconut milk, crème fraîche or cream, and the chopped beets. Return the soup to a simmer. Stir in the honey, lemon juice, and garam masala, and adjust the seasoning to your taste. Ladle the soup into warm bowls and garnish with cilantro leaves.

Note: Garam masala is a complex spice blend that is available in Indian and Middle Eastern markets. It's often called for in Indian recipes, and you can experiment by using it as a seasoning for pot roast, pork chops, lamb stew, or braised chickpeas. To make your own, combine 9 whole cloves, 10 green cardamom seeds, 1 tablespoon of whole black peppercorns, ½ stick cinnamon, 2 tablespoons of coriander seeds, 1 tablespoon of cumin seeds, and 1 bay leaf in a small skillet. Warm over low heat, shaking the pan often, until the spices become fragrant and darken just slightly, 4 to 5 minutes. Transfer to a bowl and mix in ⅛ teaspoon of ground nutmeg. Cool completely; then grind to a powder in a spice grinder. Store tightly covered.

Spicy Corn Chowder

SERVES 4

This is a fabulous variation on classic corn chowder—it's seasoned with ginger, cumin, turmeric, and jalapeño peppers. Using small rounds of sliced fingerling potatoes in place of the more traditional dice adds both flavor and visual interest.

4 cups fresh corn kernels (cut from 4 to 5 ears);
    corncobs cut into 2-inch pieces and reserved

1 cup heavy cream

2 cups milk

2 tablespoons butter

½ cup diced onion

½ cup well washed and diced leek, white part only

1½ tablespoons ground cumin

Pinch of ground turmeric

1 jalapeño pepper, seeded and chopped

1 tablespoon minced fresh ginger

1½ teaspoons kosher salt

⅛ teaspoon freshly ground white pepper

1 cup sliced (⅛-inch-thick rounds) fingerling or
    small new potatoes (about 12 ounces)

1 cup Vegetable Stock (page 318) or Chicken
    Stock (page 315)

2 tablespoons snipped fresh chives

1. Combine half of the corn kernels, the cut-up corncobs, the cream, and milk in a 2-quart saucepan. Bring to a boil, reduce the heat, and simmer for 10 minutes. Remove from the heat, and use tongs to remove and discard the corncobs. Puree the corn and cream mixture

Wine Suggestions:
Champagne, Vouvray *pétillant*, or any good sparkling wine goes beautifully with this chowder.

in a blender in as many batches as necessary. Pass the mixture through a fine-mesh strainer and into a large bowl, and set aside.

2. Melt the butter over low heat in a 3-quart saucepan. Add the onion and leek and cook, stirring occasionally, until tender but not browned, about 5 minutes. Stir in the cumin, turmeric, jalapeño, ginger, salt, and pepper and cook for 3 more minutes. Add the remaining corn and the potatoes and cook, stirring, for 3 minutes. Remove from the heat.

3. Add the reserved pureed corn mixture to the saucepan with the vegetables. Pour in the vegetable or chicken stock, bring to a simmer, and cook gently, partially covered, until the potatoes are tender, about 10 minutes. Ladle the soup into bowls, sprinkle with chives, and serve.

Lentil Soup with Portobello Mushrooms and Spinach

SERVES 8 TO 10

Here is an immensely satisfying and easy-to-prepare soup that is partly pureed, partly chunky, and entirely chock-full of flavor. Though the soup is vegetarian, the combination of portobello mushrooms and lentils delivers a "meaty" flavor. Serve a bowl of this hearty soup as a starter, or as an ample main course accompanied by some garlic bread.

12 ounces portobello mushrooms, stems removed
    and caps rubbed clean
3 tablespoons butter
1 cup chopped onion
1 cup peeled and chopped carrot
1 cup peeled and chopped celery
1 bay leaf
2 teaspoons fresh thyme leaves
1 cup peeled, seeded, and diced tomato
1 tablespoon plus 1 teaspoon kosher salt
¼ teaspoon freshly ground black pepper
¼ teaspoon Aleppo pepper
1½ cups brown lentils, picked over and rinsed
10 cups Vegetable Stock (page 318) or water
6 packed cups stemmed and chopped spinach
¼ cup finely grated Parmigiano-Reggiano
3 tablespoons extra-virgin olive oil

Wine Suggestions:
The earthy, meaty mushroom flavor makes this a made-in-heaven match for mature pinot noir, sangiovese, or cabernet franc. It's also wonderful accompanied by a glass of good-quality Manzanilla sherry.

1. Thinly slice the mushroom caps and then cut the slices crosswise into thirds. (You should have about 6 cups of sliced mushrooms.)

2. Melt the butter in a large soup pot over medium heat. Add the onion, carrot, celery, bay leaf, and thyme. Cook until the vegetables are softened, but not colored, 8 to 10 minutes.

3. Raise the heat to medium-high, add the portobellos, and cook, stirring occasionally, until they give up and then reabsorb their liquid, 3 to 5 minutes.

4. Add the tomato and cook until the mixture is juicy, 2 to 3 minutes.

5. Stir in the salt, black and Aleppo peppers, and the lentils. Add the stock or water; bring to a boil, reduce the heat, cover, and simmer until the lentils are tender, about 45 minutes.

6. Scoop out 1 cup of the lentils with a slotted spoon (some of the vegetables will cling to the lentils) and puree in a blender or food processor until smooth. Return the puree to the pot and stir to combine.

7. Stir in the spinach, bring the soup to a simmer, and continue cooking until the spinach wilts, 1 to 2 minutes. Adjust the seasoning to your taste.

8. Ladle the soup into a warm serving tureen or individual soup bowls. Sprinkle each serving with Parmigiano-Reggiano and drizzle with olive oil. Serve piping hot.

Butternut Squash and Bean Soup

This unlikely combination of dried beans with root vegetables and sage makes a richly textured *potage* with a subtle backbone of peppery heat. Try to find dense, rather firm parsnips. If you encounter any spongy, woody sections, cut them out and discard before adding the parsnips to the soup.

1 pound dried borlotti (cranberry or October) beans

8 cups water

2 bay leaves

2 tablespoons kosher salt

CROUTONS

2 cups rustic or sourdough bread cubes (½-inch, crusts removed)

3 unpeeled garlic cloves, smashed

¼ teaspoon salt

Pinch of freshly ground black pepper

1 tablespoon olive oil

1 teaspoon chopped fresh sage leaves

¼ cup plus 2 tablespoons extra-virgin olive oil

1 cup diced (½-inch) onion

1 cup diced (½-inch) carrots

1 cup sliced celery (stalks cut in half lengthwise and then cut into ½-inch slices)

1 cup diced (½-inch) parsnip

1 teaspoon minced garlic

2 firmly packed tablespoons sliced fresh sage leaves

3 cups peeled and diced (½-inch) butternut squash

⅛ teaspoon freshly ground black pepper

⅛ teaspoon Aleppo pepper or dried red pepper flakes

1 teaspoon honey

Wine Suggestions:
Try a Vouvray (sec or demi-sec), a Tuscan chardonnay, or an Austrian white like grüner veltliner.

1. Soak the beans overnight, or for at least 6 hours, in enough cold water to cover. Drain and transfer to a large pot or Dutch oven. Add the water and bay leaves. Bring to a boil, reduce the heat, and simmer, covered, until almost tender, 45 to 50 minutes. Add 1 tablespoon of the salt and cook 10 more minutes.

2. Make the croutons: Preheat the oven to 350 degrees F. Spread the bread cubes on a baking sheet and bake until golden brown, 5 to 10 minutes. Transfer the cubes to a large bowl and toss with the garlic, salt, pepper, oil, and sage. Let stand 30 minutes.

3. Meanwhile, heat the oil in a second large pot or Dutch oven over medium heat. Add the onion, carrot, celery, parsnip, garlic, and sage and cook until the vegetables have softened but are not colored, about 10 minutes. Add the squash and cook for 10 more minutes. Season with the remaining tablespoon of salt, and the black and Aleppo peppers. Remove from the heat and set aside.

4. Spoon 1 cup of the cooked beans along with ¼ cup of their cooking liquid into a blender and puree until smooth. Using a rubber spatula, scrape the puree into the pan with the vegetables. Add the whole beans with their cooking liquid, the bay leaves, and honey, and simmer until the vegetables are completely tender, about 10 more minutes. Taste and adjust the seasoning if desired.

5. Serve the soup in warm bowls, topped with the croutons.

Chilled Melon and Vodka Soup

SMALL CAPS: Serves 6

For years people have used melon in savory ways, seasoning it with table salt or accompanying it with slices of prosciutto. In this delightfully refreshing and simple recipe, ripe melon is pureed along with aromatic spices, lime juice, and a dash of vodka. It's a light and fun way to begin dinner on a hot summer night.

1 (6-pound) honeydew melon, seeds and rind
    removed, cut into large chunks
¼ teaspoon ground coriander seed
¼ teaspoon ground cardamom
¼ teaspoon powdered ginger
Pinch of kosher salt
¼ cup fresh lime juice
¼ cup vodka

Puree the melon as finely as possible in a food processor and pass through a fine-mesh strainer, pressing with a ladle to push through as much of the pulp as possible. Stir in the remaining ingredients and continue stirring until well combined. Cover and chill. Ladle into bowls and serve.

Minestra di Ceci

In the heart of Tuscany's Chianti Classico region, each family, it seems, has its own cherished recipe for this marvelous chickpea soup. In our version, slow-roast tomatoes, rosemary, and pecorino cheese add depth and lots of lingering flavor to every mouthful. You can make the soup up to several days in advance. Just make sure to store it well covered and refrigerated, and, so that it won't become mushy, don't add the pasta until you're ready to enjoy the soup. Drizzle your very best olive oil over the top just before serving.

2 cups dried chickpeas

4 (5-inch) branches fresh rosemary, leaves chopped
    (about 3 tablespoons), stems reserved

½ cup parsley stems

1 bay leaf

6 whole black peppercorns

1 (2-inch) square Pecorino Romano rind,
    coarsely chopped (optional)

3 tablespoons extra-virgin olive oil

1 medium white onion, coarsely chopped

2 small carrots, peeled and coarsely chopped

1 large celery stalk, coarsely chopped

6 garlic cloves, sliced

½ teaspoon dried red pepper flakes

6 cups water

½ cup Oven-Dried Tomatoes (page 319)
    or sun-dried tomatoes, chopped

2½ teaspoons kosher salt

½ cup ditalini pasta

¼ teaspoon freshly ground black pepper

2 tablespoons grated Pecorino Romano

2 tablespoons chopped fresh parsley leaves

Wine Suggestions:
Chianti Classico, Vino Nobile di Montepulciano, or any wine made from sangiovese grapes goes hand in hand with this soup.

1. Soak the chickpeas overnight, or for at least 6 hours, in enough cold water to cover.

2. Make an herb bundle: in a small piece of cheesecloth, place the rosemary and parsley stems, the bay leaf, peppercorns, and pecorino rind, if using. Close the bundle by tying with a piece of kitchen twine.

3. In a 3-quart saucepan, heat 1½ tablespoons of the oil over medium heat. Add the onion, carrots, celery, garlic, chopped rosemary, and red pepper flakes and cook until the vegetables are softened, but not browned, about 10 minutes. Drain the chickpeas and add them to the pan along with the herb bundle, the water, and the tomatoes. Bring to a boil, reduce the heat and simmer, covered, for 50 minutes. Season with 1½ teaspoons of the salt and continue cooking until the chickpeas are tender, about 10 more minutes.

4. Remove and discard the herb bundle. Scoop out 1 cup of the chickpeas with a slotted spoon and reserve. (It's okay that some of the vegetables will cling to the chickpeas.) In a blender or food processor, puree the remaining chickpeas and vegetables with their cooking liquid, in batches if necessary, until smooth. Return the puree to the saucepan and set aside.

5. Bring 1½ quarts of water to a boil with the remaining 1 teaspoon of salt. Add the ditalini and cook until *al dente*, about 8 to 10 minutes. Drain.

6. To serve, bring the pureed soup to a gentle simmer. Add the reserved chickpeas, the cooked ditalini, and the black pepper and heat for 5 minutes. Adjust the seasoning to your taste. To serve, ladle into

a warm serving tureen or individual soup bowls. Top with the grated cheese and the chopped parsley, and drizzle with the remaining 1½ tablespoons of olive oil. Serve hot.

Note: To store the soup for serving the next day, refrigerate the cooked pasta separately so that it doesn't become soggy. When you're ready to serve, combine the soup and the pasta and heat gently, adding a little water, if necessary, to thin the soup.

Minestra di Farro

SERVES 6

In Tuscany's beautiful walled town of Lucca, each trattoria vies for the most soulful rendition of this porridgelike soup based on farro, an ancient Italian wheat grain. The addition of artichokes and mushrooms lends an earthy richness that creates layers of flavor in this satisfying dish. We serve the *minestra* as an appetizer, but you might enjoy a big bowl of it for a weekend lunch, accompanied by nothing more than a simple green salad and a hunk of crusty bread. It's always a good idea to "pick over" grains to remove the occasional pebble. An easy way to accomplish this is to pour the farro onto one half of a cookie sheet and then slide small amounts of the grains to the other side, closely examining for any debris as you go.

FARRO

1 tablespoon extra-virgin olive oil
½ onion, chopped
1 garlic clove, minced
1½ cups farro, picked over and rinsed
6 cups Chicken Stock (page 315)
1 bay leaf
1 teaspoon salt
⅛ teaspoon freshly ground pepper

MINESTRA

1 lemon
2 large artichokes
2 tablespoons extra-virgin olive oil
¼ cup minced shallots
1 tablespoon minced garlic
3 cups sliced celery (stalks halved lengthwise
    and sliced on the bias)
⅛ teaspoon Aleppo pepper or dried red pepper flakes

Wine Suggestions:

Try pairing this with a fruity white like tocai friulano or arneis from Italy, or the Spanish albariño. You might also try a youthful and forward red like Rosso di Montalcino, Dolcetto, or Barbera d'Alba.

3 cups sliced cremini mushrooms (about 8 ounces)

Kosher salt

Freshly ground black pepper

¼ cup dry vermouth or white wine

⅔ cup chopped canned tomatoes

½ cup Basic Tomato Sauce (page 318) or
   store-bought tomato sauce

2½ cups Chicken Stock (page 315)

1½ teaspoons chopped fresh rosemary

2 tablespoons grated Pecorino Romano

2 tablespoons chopped fresh parsley

1. To cook the farro, heat the oil over medium heat in a 2-quart saucepan.
    Add the onion and garlic and cook until softened and not browned, 2 to
    3 minutes. Add the farro and stir to coat with the oil. Add the stock,
    bay leaf, salt, and pepper; bring to a boil. Reduce the heat and simmer,
    covered, until the stock has been absorbed, about 60 to 70 minutes.
    The farro should be split, fluffy, and tender, but not mushy.

2. While the farro cooks, prepare the artichokes: Squeeze the lemon into a
    bowl of cold water large enough to hold the artichokes. Snap off the
    outer, dark green leaves of an artichoke until you get to the innermost
    core of light yellow leaves. Slice off the top of the core to reveal the
    choke. Cut off the stem and set aside. Trim off all of the dark green
    from the base of the artichoke and trim the base flat. Scrape out the
    choke with the edge of a teaspoon and discard. Place the trimmed base
    in the lemon water to prevent discoloring. Peel the reserved stem down
    to the whitish flesh and add to the lemon water. Repeat with the
    second artichoke. Cut each trimmed artichoke heart in half and then
    cut each half into 8 to 10 thin slices. Slice the stems into thin circles.
    Return the artichokes to the lemon water and set aside.

3. Heat the oil in a 3-quart saucepan over medium heat. Add the shallots
    and garlic and cook until softened, but not browned, 2 to 3 minutes.

Drain the sliced artichokes and add to the pot along with the celery and Aleppo or red pepper flakes, and cook, stirring occasionally, until the vegetables begin to soften, about 5 more minutes. Raise the heat to medium-high, add the mushrooms, and cook until softened, 3 to 4 more minutes, or until any mushroom liquid has evaporated. Season with 1¼ teaspoon salt and ⅛ teaspoon black pepper. Add the vermouth and reduce by half. Add the tomatoes, tomato sauce, and stock; bring to a boil. Reduce the heat and simmer, uncovered, until the vegetables are tender but not falling apart, about 20 minutes. You can prepare the recipe to this point up to 3 days in advance. Store the vegetables and farro separately, tightly covered and refrigerated.

4. To serve, add the rosemary to the vegetable mixture and bring to a boil. Add the cooked farro and continue to boil, stirring occasionally, until the liquid has reduced and the *minestra* has the consistency of a loose risotto. Ladle into warm bowls and top with the grated cheese and parsley.

CHECK MATES

Carrot, Beet, and Watercress Salad

———

Spinach, Fennel, and
Portobello Mushroom Salad

———

Goat Cheese, Beet, and Lentil Salad

———

Frisée Salad with Bottarga and Grapefruit

———

Crabmeat and Endive Salad

———

Michael's Insalata ai Frutti di Mare

———

Carrot, Beet, and Watercress Salad

SERVES 4

Here's our recipe for a colorfully crunchy salad that is a welcome departure when you've had your fill of dainty mesclun—or any other lettuce, for that matter. You could also serve this salad as an appetizer, or as a side dish for roast poultry or grilled fish. Soaking the finely cut raw vegetables in ice water renders them crispy and crunchy.

2 large carrots, peeled and cut into fine matchstick
    julienne (about 1 cup)
1 large beet, peeled and cut into fine matchstick
    julienne (about 1 cup)
½ cup very thinly sliced red onion

PECAN VINAIGRETTE

½ cup pecans
1 tablespoon honey
2 tablespoons plus ½ teaspoon Dijon mustard
1 tablespoon plus 1 teaspoon sherry wine vinegar
¾ teaspoon chopped shallot
¾ teaspoon chopped fresh thyme leaves
⅛ teaspoon kosher salt
⅛ teaspoon freshly ground black pepper
Pinch of cayenne
1 teaspoon plus ¼ cup grapeseed or vegetable oil
¾ teaspoon mustard seeds

6 cups watercress, washed and dried,
    large stems removed

1. Preheat the oven to 350 degrees F.

2. Place the julienned carrots, beets, and sliced onions in a large bowl, cover with ice water, and let stand for 15 minutes. Drain well and dry the vegetables on a paper towel. Set aside.

3. Begin the vinaigrette: Spread the pecans on a cookie sheet and roast until fragrant, about 10 minutes. Chop coarsely.

4. Combine the honey, mustard, vinegar, shallot, thyme, salt, black pepper, and cayenne in a jar.

5. Heat 1 teaspoon of the oil in a small skillet over medium heat until very hot but not smoking. Remove the skillet from the heat, add the mustard seeds, and cover the pan. Shake the skillet, still off the heat, until the seeds sputter and darken somewhat. Add to the jar. Then add the remaining ¼ cup oil and the toasted pecans and shake vigorously to combine.

6. Combine the carrots, beet, red onion, and watercress in a large bowl. Add the vinaigrette and toss. Serve immediately. The salad elements can be prepared in advance, kept separate, and combined just before serving.

Spinach, Fennel, and Portobello Mushroom Salad

SERVES 4

This salad, both delicious and beautifully presented, has become one of our guests' all-time favorites. Happily, we're able to serve it year-round, since its ingredients are always available. The contrast of warm, soft mushrooms with refreshing, crunchy fennel is a key to the salad's success. A useful variation on this recipe is to grill the portobello mushrooms and serve them as a terrific accompaniment to a summer barbecue.

VINAIGRETTE

¼ teaspoon kosher salt

⅛ teaspoon freshly ground black pepper

1 small garlic clove, finely minced

2 tablespoons good-quality, aged balsamic vinegar

¾ cup extra-virgin olive oil

⅔ cup finely grated Parmigiano-Reggiano

SALAD

4 medium portobello mushrooms, stems removed and
    caps rubbed clean

1 medium bulb fresh fennel, green top and tough outer
    leaves removed, and bulb washed thoroughly

6 packed cups stemmed, washed, and dried young
    spinach leaves

24 shards Parmigiano-Reggiano (shaved with a
    cheese slicer or a vegetable peeler)

1. Preheat the oven to 375 degrees F.

2. Combine the vinaigrette ingredients in a jar.
   Close the lid tightly and shake vigorously until
   well combined.

Wine Suggestions:
These are big flavors that need a wine with lots of fruit and enough acid to stand up to the vinaigrette. Try a zinfandel, Côtes du Rhône, or Aglianico del Vulture.

3. Lay the mushrooms on a baking sheet and brush them with 2 tablespoons of the vinaigrette. Roast in the oven until tender, 20 to 30 minutes.

4. While the mushrooms are cooking, prepare the fennel: Trim away the brown root, making sure to leave the bulb intact. Using a mandoline or the slicer attachment of a food processor, slice the entire bulb of fennel lengthwise into paper-thin slices. (If you don't have a mandoline or food processor, cut slices as thinly as possible with a sharp knife.) Arrange the slices, overlapping slightly, around the rims of 4 salad plates.

5. Pour about three-quarters of the vinaigrette into a large salad bowl, add the spinach, and toss well to coat. Mound equal portions of the dressed spinach in the center of each salad plate.

6. While the mushrooms are still warm, slice them very thinly on a sharp bias, and drape the slices lengthwise over the spinach mounds. Top the mushrooms with the Parmigiano shards, drizzle the remaining vinaigrette over the cheese and fennel, and serve.

Goat Cheese, Beet, and Lentil Salad

SERVES 4

This layered salad has become a Union Square Cafe favorite, and it's no wonder: it's an addictively flavorful combination of creamy and crunchy textures in a visually stunning presentation. You don't have to dine out often to notice that chefs love using ring molds to add interest to plate presentations. Rather than buy one, you can easily make one using an empty, washed tuna can from which both top and bottom have been removed. By the way, each of the salad's components stands beautifully on its own. The lentil salad makes a great side dish, and the goat cheese, garlic, and herb mixture can be enjoyed spread on celery, crackers, or crusty bread. It tastes like a homemade version of Boursin. At the restaurant, we use French green lentils, which we prefer for their firm texture and nutty flavor. If they are unavailable, use brown lentils for the salad. Chervil is a traditional component of *fines herbes*, but may be hard to find; if so, omit it.

1 medium beet (6 to 8 ounces)

1 cup green lentils, rinsed

3 cups Vegetable Stock (page 318) or water

1 tablespoon kosher salt

½ cup finely diced carrot

½ cup finely diced celery

3 tablespoons minced shallot

8 ounces fresh goat cheese

¼ cup minced fresh *fines herbes* (equal parts parsley, tarragon, chervil, and chives)

2 tablespoons extra-virgin olive oil, plus extra for drizzling

1 small garlic clove, peeled, mashed, and minced

6 cups mesclun salad mixture

12 chervil sprigs for garnish, or 1 tablespoon chopped fresh parsley

Wine Suggestions:
A ripe but light chardonnay from France's Mâconnais district would fit nicely here. Try St. Veran, Pouilly-Fuissé, or Mâcon-Clessé.

½ teaspoon chopped garlic

1½ teaspoons chopped fresh *fines herbes*

½ teaspoon kosher salt

⅛ teaspoon freshly ground pepper

1 tablespoon sherry wine vinegar

¼ cup plus 2 tablespoons olive oil

1. Preheat the oven to 400 degrees F.

2. Trim the beet, leaving a ½- to 1-inch stem attached. Rinse the beet, wrap it in aluminum foil, and roast until the beet is easily pierced by the tip of a paring knife, about 1 hour and 10 minutes. (This can be done several days ahead if you leave the beet whole in its foil and refrigerate it.) When cool enough to handle, trim the ends and peel off the skin. Halve the beet lengthwise, and cut each half into ¼-inch slices. Set aside.

3. Combine the lentils with the stock or water in a 2-quart saucepan. Bring to a boil, reduce the heat, cover, and simmer for 10 minutes. Stir in the salt, cover, and continue cooking until tender, 30 to 40 minutes longer. Drain, transfer to a bowl, and toss in the diced carrot, celery, and shallot.

4. Combine the goat cheese, *fines herbes*, 2 tablespoons of oil, and garlic in a bowl and stir until smooth. Set aside.

5. Combine the vinaigrette ingredients in a jar. Close the lid tightly and shake vigorously.

6. To assemble the salad, season the lentils with about two-thirds of the vinaigrette. Place the remaining vinaigrette in a bowl, add the mesclun, and toss until evenly coated. Center a 3-inch ring mold or can on a large plate. Spoon ⅔ cup of the lentil mixture into the mold and level it with the back of a spoon. Top with ¼ cup of the cheese mixture, and smooth, until level, with the spoon. Gently lift the mold, leaving a

layered disk of lentils and goat cheese on the plate. On each plate, arrange one-quarter of the seasoned greens around the lentils and cheese. Distribute the beet slices evenly over the greens on each plate. Drizzle the cheese lightly with olive oil, and garnish with chervil sprigs or chopped parsley.

Oops!

Frisée Salad with Bottarga and Grapefruit

SERVES 4

Here's a refreshing and offbeat salad whose unusual components complement one another beautifully. Bottarga (dried tuna or mullet roe) lends a salty punch that is perfectly balanced by the bright and tart citrus vinaigrette. We use freshly squeezed lemon juice in place of vinegar for the dressing. Its fruity acidity is a natural complement to the grapefruit and doesn't overwhelm the bottarga. Try the "lemonette" as well with grilled fish, seafood salads, or chilled asparagus and artichokes.

"LEMONETTE"

2 tablespoons freshly squeezed lemon juice

⅛ teaspoon freshly ground black pepper

¼ teaspoon kosher salt

4½ tablespoons extra-virgin olive oil

SALAD

1 tablespoon vegetable oil

1 cup thinly sliced celery

¾ teaspoon kosher salt

4 packed cups frisée lettuce

2 packed cups arugula

1 cup thinly sliced fennel

¼ teaspoon freshly ground black pepper

2 grapefruits, preferably pink, peeled and sectioned, with pith and pits removed

1 tablespoon Seasoned Bottarga Mixture (see page 252)

1. Combine the "lemonette" ingredients in a jar. Close the lid tightly and shake the jar vigorously to combine.

Wine Suggestions:

You'll want a bracingly fruity white such as Sancerre or a California sauvignon blanc, or perhaps a young Italian white from Sardinia or Friuli-Venezia-Giulia.

2. For the salad, heat the oil in a medium skillet over medium-high heat. Add the celery and ¼ teaspoon of the salt and cook 1 minute, stirring, to soften the celery. Transfer to a plate and allow to cool.

3. Pour the "lemonette" into a large salad bowl. Add the frisée, arugula, fennel, and celery and sprinkle with the remaining ½ teaspoon of salt and the pepper. Toss to coat the lettuces with the "lemonette." Divide the salad among 4 salad plates. Divide the grapefruit among the salads, tucking the sections into the greens. Sprinkle one-quarter of the bottarga mixture over each salad and serve.

Crabmeat and Endive Salad

SERVES 4

For its sweetness and firm texture, it's worth seeking out fresh jumbo lump (rather than flake) crabmeat for this refreshing salad. The dressing is a more delicate version of the one you'd use for crabmeat Louis—fresh tomato water is substituted for ketchup. You can make the dressing a few hours ahead of time, but to preserve the salad's toothsome texture, don't mix it with the fresh crabmeat and endive until just before serving. The salad makes an elegant appetizer or a passed hors d'oeuvre, spooned onto endive spears or toasts.

DRESSING

1 large tomato
½ cup mayonnaise
1½ teaspoons Dijon mustard
2½ teaspoons fresh lemon juice
1 teaspoon Cognac
¼ teaspoon kosher salt
⅛ teaspoon freshly ground black pepper
Pinch of cayenne pepper
1 tablespoon chopped fresh parsley
1 tablespoon snipped fresh chives
1 tablespoon chopped fresh tarragon

SALAD

1½ teaspoons olive oil
1 cup peeled and chopped celery
Kosher salt
2 large Belgian endives
1 pound jumbo lump crabmeat, picked over
   carefully for bits of cartilage
Freshly ground black pepper

Wine Suggestions:
Serve a floral white from Italy's Friuli-Venezia-Giulia district like Müller-Thurgau, sauvignon blanc, tocai friulano, or ribolla gialla.

1. Prepare the dressing: Place a fine-mesh strainer over a medium bowl. Cut the tomato in half crosswise and gently squeeze the halves, cut sides down, into the strainer. Use your fingers or a spoon to scoop out any juice and seeds remaining in the tomato, and strain these as well. You should have about 2 tablespoons of strained "tomato water" in the bowl. Save the squeezed tomato halves for another use. Add all of the remaining dressing ingredients and whisk well to blend. Set aside.

2. For the salad, heat the oil in a medium skillet over medium-high heat. Add the celery and cook for 1 minute, just until the celery is still crunchy but no longer raw. Season with ¼ teaspoon salt, and set aside in a large bowl to cool.

3. Cut away and discard ¼ inch of stem from the endives. Peel off and reserve 12 large outer leaves. Cut the remaining endive cores crosswise into ¼-inch slices and add them to the bowl with the celery. Add the crabmeat and dressing, season with ⅛ teaspoon salt and ⅛ teaspoon pepper, and stir gently with a rubber spatula to combine. Arrange 3 endive spears in a spoke pattern, with the tips facing out, on each of 4 chilled serving plates. Mound equal amounts of the salad in the center of each plate and serve.

yikes!

Michael's Insalata ai Frutti di Mare

SERVES 6

This seafood salad is simple to assemble and far better than what you're likely to find in a store. They won't be quite as sweet, but feel free to substitute littleneck clams for the cockles, or sea scallops for the bay scallops. Most important, begin with pristinely fresh seafood and finish with the best extra-virgin olive oil you can find.

3 tablespoons olive oil

18 medium-to-large shrimp in the shell, rinsed

Kosher salt

1½ teaspoons minced garlic

1 tablespoon chopped fresh parsley

8 ounces bay scallops (or sea scallops, cleaned and cut into pieces the size of bay scallops)

7 ounces cleaned squid, bodies cut into rings, tentacles split lengthwise

1 cup peeled, split, thinly sliced celery

Freshly ground black pepper

18 mussels, debearded and scrubbed

36 cockle clams, scrubbed to remove sand

¼ cup fresh lemon juice

¼ cup plus 3 tablespoons best-quality extra-virgin olive oil

2 tablespoons fresh basil, cut into ribbons

⅛ teaspoon cayenne

9 cups frisée lettuce, coarsely chopped, washed, and dried

1. In a large skillet, heat 1 tablespoon olive oil over high heat. Add the shrimp and cook 1 minute, stirring. Add ¼ teaspoon salt and ½ teaspoon of the garlic and continue stirring until the shrimp

Wine Suggestions:
Almost any fresh, fragrant white wine will do here, but we'd grab a cold bottle of muscadet, tocai friulano, Vermentino di Sardegna, or even your favorite rosé.

are cooked through, about 1 more minute. (The garlic should not brown.) Stir in 1 teaspoon parsley and transfer the shrimp to a bowl, with any liquid in the pan.

2. Heat another tablespoon of olive oil in the same skillet over high heat. Add the scallops and squid, ½ teaspoon salt, ½ teaspoon garlic, and stir until the seafood is just cooked through, about 1 minute. Toss in 2 teaspoons parsley and transfer to a second bowl, with the pan juices.

3. Increase the heat to medium-high and add the remaining tablespoon of olive oil to the skillet. Add the celery, ½ teaspoon salt, and ⅛ teaspoon black pepper. Cook, stirring, for 1 minute. Transfer the celery to the bowl with the scallops and squid.

4. Place the mussels and cockles in the skillet along with the remaining ½ teaspoon of garlic. Pour in the accumulated juices from the shrimp, scallops, and squid. Cover and cook over high heat until the shells open, 4 to 5 minutes. Pour the shellfish and the liquid into a large colander placed over a bowl. Allow the juices to drain, then pass the liquid through a fine mesh strainer and reserve.

5. Shell the mussels and cockles, discarding the shells, and put them in the bowl with the scallops, squid, and celery. Shell the shrimp, halve them crosswise, and remove any black veins. Place the shrimp in the bowl with the rest of the shellfish. Then add the reserved cooking liquid along with the lemon juice, extra-virgin olive oil, basil, cayenne, 1¼ teaspoons of salt, and the pinch of black pepper. Toss well, cover tightly, and allow to macerate at least 30 minutes or up to 2 hours at room temperature before serving. The salad can be made up to 2 days ahead of time and refrigerated, tightly covered. For maximum flavor, bring to room temperature before serving.

6. To serve, divide the frisée evenly among 6 plates. Spoon portions of the seafood on top, and drizzle the juices over the lettuce.

ORDER ENVY OR "LET'S SHARE"

PASTA AND RISOTTO

Crabmeat-Artichoke Tortelli

———

Sardinian Ravioli

———

Zucchini Fazzoletti

———

Pappardelle al Sugo di Coniglio

———

Fettuccine with Sweet Corn
and Gorgonzola

———

Tagliarini ai Funghi

———

Tagliolini with Cherry Tomatoes
and Arugula

———

Linguine with Clams and Pancetta

———

Spaghetti all'Aragosta

———

Spaghettini con Bottarga

———

Rigatoni with Zucchini, Tomatoes,
and Cream

———

Pennette all'Arrabbiata

———

Spring Risotto

———

Zucchini Risotto

———

Risotto Rosso

———

Risotto with Eggplant, Anchovy,
and Mint

———

Sheep's-Milk Ricotta Gnocchi

———

Crabmeat-Artichoke Tortelli

SERVES 6 AS AN APPETIZER, 4 AS A MAIN COURSE

Here's the recipe for one of the all-time favorite pasta dishes we've ever
served at USC. The essential flavors of fresh crabmeat, artichokes, roasted
tomatoes, and butter would complement one another wonderfully in almost
any guise, and here they're rolled into the fresh rings of pasta dough known
as tortelli. Clearly, it's a labor of love to make your own tortelli from scratch,
so if time is short, use the delicious crabmeat-artichoke mixture as a topping
for spaghetti, stuffed into cooked artichoke bottoms, or simply spread onto
toasts to make crostini.

TORTELLI

⅔ batch Fresh Pasta Dough (page 319),
    made with 1⅓ cups flour, ½ teaspoon salt,
    2 eggs, and water as needed

1 lemon

1 large artichoke

2 tablespoons olive oil

Kosher salt

Freshly ground black pepper

2 tablespoons plus 1 teaspoon chopped shallots
    (about 2 shallots)

¾ teaspoon minced garlic

⅓ cup plus 1 tablespoon chopped Oven-Dried Tomatoes
    (page 319)

1 tablespoon plus 1 teaspoon chopped fresh oregano

8 ounces fresh lump crabmeat, picked over carefully
    for bits of cartilage

2 tablespoons white wine

1 tablespoon chopped fresh parsley

½ cup semolina or cornmeal

All-purpose flour for sprinkling

Wine Suggestions:
Try a white with floral
accents like Spain's
albariño, or a viognier
from California or France.

TOMATO-BUTTER SAUCE

¾ cup white wine

12 tablespoons (1½ sticks) cold unsalted butter,
  cut into pieces

½ teaspoon kosher salt

⅛ teaspoon freshly ground white pepper

1. Prepare the pasta dough, wrap it in plastic, and let rest at room temperature for at least 30 minutes.

2. Squeeze the lemon into a medium bowl of cold water. Snap off the outer, dark green leaves of the artichoke until you get to the innermost core of light yellow leaves. Slice off the core to reveal the choke. Cut off the stem and set aside. Trim off all of the dark green from the base of the artichoke and trim the base flat. Scrape out the choke with a small spoon and discard. Place the trimmed base in the lemon water to prevent discoloring. Peel the dark green skin from the stem down to the whitish flesh and add the peeled stem to the bowl.

3. Drain the artichoke base and stem and slice thinly. Heat 1 tablespoon of the oil in a medium skillet over medium-low heat, add the artichoke slices to the pan, and cook until tender, but not browned, 4 to 6 minutes. Midway through the cooking, season with ⅛ teaspoon salt and a pinch of pepper. Transfer the cooked artichoke to a cutting board and chop finely.

4. Add the remaining tablespoon of oil to the skillet and place over medium heat. Add the shallots and cook until softened, about 1 minute. Add the garlic and cook 15 seconds. Stir in the chopped artichoke, the chopped oven-dried tomatoes, the oregano, ¼ teaspoon salt, and a pinch of pepper. Cook for 2 minutes, stirring to combine. Remove the pan from the heat and set aside 3 tablespoons of the mixture for the tomato-butter sauce. Return the pan to the heat, add the crabmeat and stir, breaking it up with a spoon. Pour in the wine and cook until it has evaporated. Stir in the parsley, ½ teaspoon salt, and ¼ teaspoon pepper. Transfer the mixture to a bowl and refrigerate until completely cool.

5. Sprinkle the semolina or cornmeal on a cookie sheet. Using cold water, prepare 2 damp, not wet, kitchen towels.

6. Cut the pasta dough in half; wrap 1 half in plastic and set aside. Pass the remaining dough half through the widest setting on a manual or electric pasta machine onto a lightly floured surface. Decrease the setting one notch and pass the dough through again. Decrease once again, and pass the dough through. Fold the flattened dough into thirds, folding the two ends in toward the center, as you would to fold a letter. Flatten the dough with your fingers, return the machine to its widest setting, and pass the dough through again, feeding one of the two open ends through the rollers. Repeat this process 5 or 6 times, lightly sprinkling the strip of dough with flour every now and then, until the dough becomes silky and elastic.

7. Roll the dough through the machine on decreasing settings until just 2 notches before the finest setting. Roll the dough through this setting 3 or 4 times until you have a strip of dough that is 33 to 34 inches long and very smooth and elastic.

8. Cut the strip of dough in half crosswise to make two 16- to 17-inch strips. Set one strip on the floured work surface, out of your way, and cover with one of the damp towels. Spread out the second damp towel on the work surface in front of you, and place the second strip of dough on top. Carefully brush off any flour. Cut the strip in half lengthwise, and then 4 times crosswise to create 10 squares, each about 2½ inches square.

9. With lightly floured hands, transfer one of the squares from the towel to a clean surface, turning it over so that the damp side faces up, and positioning the square so that one corner is pointing up, like a diamond. Spoon a mounded teaspoon of the crabmeat and artichoke filling into the middle of the square. Form the tortelli: Bring the bottom corner of the square up to meet the top corner to enclose the filling in a triangular shape. Press the edges together. Then gently lift up the left

and right corners of the triangle and pinch them together, twisting slightly to seal. As you finish each of the tortelli, place it on the semolina-lined cookie sheet. Repeat with the remaining filling and pasta squares to make about 35 more tortelli. The tortelli can be made in advance. Refrigerate them for up to 1 day or freeze for up to 2 weeks. If you do freeze them, you must also freeze the reserved 3 tablespoons of artichoke-tomato mixture, which will become part of the sauce. Do defrost the artichoke-tomato mixture, but *don't* defrost the tortelli before cooking.

10. To make the sauce: Pour the wine into a 2-quart saucepan, place over medium heat, and reduce to about 2 tablespoons. Add the butter, a few pieces at a time, whisking constantly, until the sauce is thick and creamy. Do not boil, or the sauce may separate. Whisk in the reserved 3 tablespoons of artichoke-tomato mixture, salt, and pepper. Remove from the heat.

11. Bring 4 quarts of water to a boil in a large pot and add 2 tablespoons salt. Add the tortelli all at once and cook until the pasta is tender, 5 to 6 minutes, or 2 minutes longer if frozen.

12. Drain the pasta well in a colander. Arrange 6 hot tortelli on each of 6 warm serving plates. Spoon equal amounts of the butter sauce over each plate of tortelli and serve immediately.

Sardinian Ravioli

SERVES 10 AS AN APPETIZER, 5 AS A MAIN COURSE

We've enjoyed many versions of these ravioli in Sardinia, where cooks make clever use of the island's profusion of sheep's-milk products. At their best, the ravioli are as light and fluffy as down pillows. There's just enough black pepper to add bite to the mild cheese filling. It's best to cook fresh ravioli within 6 hours of making them, but you can successfully freeze ravioli. Don't defrost frozen ravioli: just add 1 or 2 minutes to their cooking time.

Fresh Pasta Dough (page 319)

SHEEP'S-MILK CHEESE FILLING

1 cup mascarpone

8 ounces ricotta salata, grated (about 2 cups)

1 large egg

1 teaspoon butcher-ground or coarsely ground
   black pepper

BROWN BUTTER

6 tablespoons butter

2 teaspoons fresh lemon juice

¼ teaspoon salt

Pinch of freshly ground black pepper

All-purpose flour for sprinkling

¼ cup coarse semolina or cornmeal

1 egg, beaten

¼ cup grated Pecorino Romano

1. Make the pasta dough and let rest for at least 30 minutes, or refrigerate, tightly wrapped in plastic, overnight.

Wine Suggestions:
Try to find a bottle of Sardinia's cannonau red, or enjoy the ravioli with zinfandel, Rioja, or cabernet franc. A good white wine match would be Vernaccia di San Gimigniano or a Tuscan Galestro.

2. Combine all of the filling ingredients in a food processor and process until completely smooth.

3. Lightly flour the work surface. Cut the pasta dough into quarters; wrap 3 of the quarters in plastic and set aside. Begin stretching the dough: pass 1 dough quarter through the widest setting on a hand-cranked or electric pasta machine. Decrease the setting a notch and pass the dough through again. Continue by decreasing one more notch and passing the dough through once again. Fold the strip of dough in thirds, as you would a letter. Flatten the dough with your fingers, return the machine to its widest setting, and begin passing the dough through the machine once again, narrow end first. Lightly dust the dough with flour every now and then if gets sticky, and repeat the entire stretching process 5 or 6 more times, until the dough feels silky and elastic. Finish by rolling the dough through the machine, decreasing the setting a notch each time until you reach one notch before the finest setting. Roll the dough through this final setting one or two more times, stretching it gently as you pull it through. The sheet of dough should be smooth and elastic and measure about 30 inches long, 5 inches wide, and $\frac{1}{16}$ inch thick.

4. Sprinkle a sheet pan with the coarse semolina or cornmeal. Set aside.

5. Lay the sheet of dough on the lightly floured work surface and square off the ends with a large kitchen knife. Brush half the length of the strip (15 inches) with the beaten egg. Onto that half, using a spoon or a pastry bag fitted with a large open tip, spoon or pipe the ricotta cheese filling into 2 rows of 5 mounds each. Each mound should be a heaping teaspoonful, and the mounds should be evenly spaced from one another and from the edges of the dough. Fold the other half of the sheet over the filled side, carefully matching the edges. Using your fingers, press gently around the mounds of filling to release the air and to seal the sheets of dough closely around the filling.

6. Cut out 10 ravioli by using a 2½-inch round cookie cutter (or cut square ravioli with a knife). Place the ravioli on the prepared sheet pan.

7. Repeat steps 4 to 6 with the remaining dough and filling to make 30 more ravioli. You can freeze them at this point.

8. For the brown butter, melt the butter over medium heat in a small, heavy-bottomed saucepan. Skim and discard the foam that rises to the surface as the butter heats, and cook gently until the butter turns a light brown and smells nutty, about 4 or 5 minutes. Pour the butter through a fine-mesh sieve or tea strainer and into a small skillet, leaving behind the darkened milk solids. Add the lemon juice, salt, and pepper; set aside.

9. Bring 4 quarts water to a boil in a large pot and add 2 tablespoons of salt. Carefully place 16 (or more) ravioli in the water, lower the heat so that the water returns to a gentle simmer, and cook until the edges of the pasta are tender, about 4 to 5 minutes. (Frozen ravioli will take 1 or 2 minutes longer.)

10. Warm the brown butter over medium heat. Using a slotted spoon, carefully transfer the cooked ravioli to a colander to drain. To serve, place ravioli on heated plates or on a warm platter. Spoon the brown butter over the ravioli, sprinkle with the grated pecorino, and serve immediately.

Zucchini Fazzoletti

A *fazzoletto* is a fresh flat pasta shape whimsically named for its resemblance to a silk handkerchief. *Fazzoletti* can be folded or laid flat on a plate, served atop or beneath a thick sauce, or enjoyed simply napped with brown butter and a sprinkling of grated cheese. At the restaurant we sauce the pasta with a looser version of our Zucchini Puree with Marjoram (page 206), and add an extra note of elegance by "stamping" each *fazzoletto* with its own fresh zucchini blossom, rolled into the dough during its final passes through the pasta crank.

⅔ batch Fresh Pasta Dough (page 319) made with
    1⅓ cups flour, 2 eggs, ½ teaspoon salt, and water
    as needed
¾ cup Chicken Stock (page 315)
Kosher salt
Freshly ground black pepper
1 cup all-purpose flour
½ batch Zucchini Puree with Marjoram
4 tablespoons (½ stick) butter
¼ cup grated Parmigiano-Reggiano

1. Make the pasta dough, wrap it in plastic, and let rest for 30 minutes.

2. Make the zucchini puree, but add an additional ¾ cup chicken stock to the zucchini mixture before pureeing. Then puree as usual; the puree will have the consistency of a thick sauce. Return the sauce to the pan and stir in ¼ teaspoon of the salt and a pinch of pepper. Set aside.

Wine Suggestions:

This dish calls for a delicate, flowery white like Pigato from Liguria or a wine made from the chasselas grape, such as Switzerland's Épesses or Dézaley.

3. Sprinkle ½ cup of the flour over each of 2 cookie sheets.

4. Cut the pasta dough in half; wrap 1 half in plastic and set aside. Pass the remaining dough half through the widest setting on a manual or electric pasta machine onto a lightly floured surface. Decrease the setting one notch and pass the dough through again. Decrease once again, and pass the dough through. Fold the flattened dough into thirds, folding the two ends in toward the center as you would to fold a letter. Flatten the dough with your fingers, return the machine to its widest setting, and pass the dough through again, feeding one of the two open ends through the rollers. Repeat this process 5 or 6 times, lightly sprinkling the strip of dough with flour every now and then, until the dough becomes silky and elastic.

5. Now pass the dough through the machine on decreasing settings until you have rolled it through the finest setting. You'll have a long strip about 5 inches wide. Flour the work surface and lay the pasta strip on the surface. Using a large knife, trim the ends of the strip so that they are straight. Cut the pasta strip crosswise into 4 equal rectangles, or *fazzoletti*. Place the *fazzoletti* in a single layer on one of the cookie sheets. Repeat the process with the remaining pasta dough, cutting 4 more *fazzoletti* and placing them in a single layer on the second floured cookie sheet.

6. Bring 4 quarts water to a rolling boil and add 2 tablespoons of salt.

7. Bring the zucchini-marjoram sauce to a simmer; cover and set aside.

8. Combine the butter, ⅓ cup water, ½ teaspoon salt, and a pinch of pepper in a very large skillet. Bring to a boil to melt the butter and swirl to combine the ingredients. Remove from the heat.

9. Add the *fazzoletti* to the boiling pasta water and cook until tender, about 3 minutes. Drain the cooked *fazzoletti* and immediately add them to the skillet. Return the skillet to medium heat and toss the *fazzoletti* gently to coat with the butter. Spoon about ¼ cup of the zucchini sauce onto each of 8 serving plates, spreading the sauce to cover the bottom of each plate. Using a pair of tongs, place a *fazzoletto* on top of each pool of sauce, draping the pasta so that it looks like a handkerchief. Sprinkle with the Parmigiano-Reggiano and serve.

Pappardelle al Sugo di Coniglio

SERVES 6 AS AN APPETIZER, 4 AS A MAIN COURSE

This is Union Square Cafe's version of a Tuscan classic, in which wide-ribbon pappardelle noodles are sauced with a hearty, slow-cooked *sugo* of braised rabbit, pancetta, and tomatoes. The recipe is superb with homemade pappardelle (see page 319), but works beautifully with dried noodles as well. Ask your butcher to cut the rabbit into 10 similarly sized pieces for even braising. Since it is unlikely that you'll buy anything less than a whole rabbit, this recipe makes enough sauce for 12 servings. If you're preparing the dish as an appetizer for 6, freeze half the sauce for the next time you make the dish.

1 rabbit (about 3 pounds), cut into 10 pieces

¼ cup olive oil

1 large onion, half of it thinly sliced, the other
    half minced

2 celery stalks, one sliced, the other minced

1 head garlic, unpeeled, quartered, plus 1 teaspoon
    minced

6 fresh basil leaves, plus 1 tablespoon sliced fresh basil

1 small sprig fresh thyme, roughly chopped

Kosher salt

Freshly ground black pepper

1 cup white wine

2 cups Chicken Stock (page 315) or broth

6 ounces pancetta, chopped (1 cup)

½ cup minced carrots

3 cups Basic Tomato Sauce (page 318) or store-bought
    tomato sauce

½ cup grated Parmigiano-Reggiano, plus more
    for sprinkling

1 pound dried pappardelle (or mafaldine or trenette)

1 tablespoon chopped fresh parsley

Wine Suggestions:

Here's a good spot to bring out a favorite Tuscan red. We'd suggest a well-made Morellino di Scansano, Vino Nobile di Montepulciano, or a well-made Chianti Classico Riserva.

1. Preheat the oven to 450 degrees F.

2. Combine the rabbit, 2 tablespoons of the olive oil, the sliced onion and celery, quartered head of garlic, whole basil leaves, thyme, 1½ teaspoons salt and ¼ teaspoon pepper in a small roasting pan. Toss with your hands to coat everything with the oil. Arrange the ingredients in the roasting pan so that the rabbit pieces are atop the vegetables. Roast in the oven until the rabbit begins to brown, about 30 minutes.

3. Pour the wine over the rabbit in the roasting pan and continue cooking for 10 minutes.

4. Reduce the oven heat to 350 degrees F. Pour the chicken stock over the rabbit in the roasting pan, cover with aluminum foil, return to the oven, and braise until the rabbit is tender, about 1 hour. Remove the rabbit from the braising liquid with a slotted spoon, transfer to a platter, cover, and let cool.

5. Strain the braising liquid into a bowl, pressing well on the solids to extract all the liquid; reserve.

6. When the meat is cool enough to handle pull it off the bones and chop it finely, feeling carefully for, and discarding, any small bones. Set aside the meat and strain any juices accumulated on the platter into the braising liquid.

7. Heat the remaining 2 tablespoons of oil in a large saucepan over medium heat. Add the pancetta and cook to render the fat, about 3 minutes. Reduce the heat to very low, add the minced onion, celery, garlic, and carrots and cook slowly until very soft, about 10 minutes. Stir in the chopped rabbit meat. Add the reserved braising liquid, the tomato sauce, and sliced basil to the pan, and simmer very gently, uncovered, for 30 minutes. Remove from the stove and stir in the cheese. Set aside half the sauce for future use (refrigerate for up to 5 days or freeze) and cover the saucepan.

8. Bring 4 quarts of water to a boil in a large pot and add 2 tablespoons salt.

9. Cook the pappardelle until *al dente* and drain in a colander. Toss in the pan with the remaining sauce over medium heat until the pasta is coated, and then transfer to a serving platter or individual bowls. Sprinkle with parsley and cheese and serve.

Fettuccine with Sweet Corn and Gorgonzola

SERVES 6 AS AN APPETIZER, 4 AS A MAIN COURSE

This has long been a late-summer pasta staple at Union Square Cafe. We encourage you to make your own fresh fettuccine (see page 319) as we do at the restaurant, but for ease, you'll be more than satisfied using a good-quality dried egg fettuccine. For the sauce, we've borrowed a *truc* from classic corn chowder recipes, steeping corncobs with white wine and cream, to lend a richly complex, sweet corn flavor. The addition of roasted tomatoes, Gorgonzola, and pancetta completes one of our very favorite pasta sauces.

2 large ears sweet corn

1 tablespoon olive oil

2 ounces pancetta, diced (about ½ cup)

½ cup sliced shallots

1 tablespoon coarsely chopped garlic

½ cup white wine

2 cups heavy cream

Kosher salt

2 tablespoons Gorgonzola cheese

⅛ teaspoon freshly ground black pepper

12 Oven-Dried Tomatoes, cut in half lengthwise (page 319)

½ cup sliced (on the diagonal) scallions, white and green parts

⅓ cup sliced basil leaves

1 pound egg fettuccine

Wine Suggestions:

This works well with fruity whites like tocai friulano or chardonnay, or with a youthful red like Barbera d'Alba or Valpolicella Classico.

1. Cut the kernels off the corncobs by standing each corncob on its flat end on a cutting board or in a roasting pan, and slicing down against the cob. Set the kernels aside. Cut the cobs into 2-inch sections.

2. Combine the oil and pancetta in a 2-quart saucepan and cook over medium-high heat to render the fat and crisp the pancetta, about 5 minutes. Remove the pancetta with a slotted spoon and set aside. Discard all but 1 tablespoon of the fat.

3. Reduce the heat to medium. Add the shallots, garlic, and corncobs and cook until the shallots are softened but not browned, about 3 minutes. Pour in the wine and reduce until almost dry. Add the cream and simmer very gently for 5 minutes. Remove from the heat, cover, and let the sauce steep for at least 15 minutes.

4. Bring 4 quarts of water to a boil in a large pot and add 2 tablespoons salt.

5. Strain the sauce through a fine-mesh strainer into a straight-sided skillet or saucepan large enough to hold all the pasta. Place over medium heat and whisk in the cheese in small pieces. Season with 1 teaspoon of salt and the pepper. Add the pancetta, corn kernels, tomatoes, scallions, and basil. Bring to a simmer, turn off the heat, cover, and set aside.

6. Cook the fettuccine in the boiling water until *al dente,* and drain in a colander. Add the drained pasta to the sauce and toss until the pasta is well coated. Transfer to a platter and serve hot.

Tagliarini ai Funghi

Thoroughly Tuscan in its conception, the slow cooking of chopped mushrooms yields a simple-to-make sauce with layers of earthy flavor. At the restaurant, we use as many as four mushroom types—including seasonal wild varieties— to maximize flavor and textural interest, but you'd enjoy the recipe even if you were to use just one type of mushroom. We pair the sauce with homemade, "eggy" tagliarini pasta, whose "little cut" shape is like a narrow version of fettuccine. If you choose not to use fresh pasta, we'd recommend a dried egg noodle like fettuccine, tagliatelle, or pappardelle. Follow this pasta with steak or pork, served with lots of greens.

Fresh Pasta Dough (page 319)

¼ cup packed dried porcini mushrooms

1¾ pounds assorted mushrooms (such as white, shiitake, portobello, and cremini), stems trimmed, and cleaned

¼ cup plus 1 tablespoon extra-virgin olive oil

2 tablespoons minced garlic

⅛ teaspoon dried red pepper flakes

Kosher salt

⅛ teaspoon freshly ground pepper

½ cup dry white wine

½ cup all-purpose flour, plus extra for dusting

1 cup crème fraîche or heavy cream

¼ cup chopped fresh parsley

1. Make the pasta dough, wrap in plastic, and let rest for 30 minutes, or refrigerate overnight.

Wine Suggestions:

Here's a good opportunity to bring out a pinot noir, Chianti Classico Riserva, or a cabernet franc–based wine such as Saumur-Champigny or Chinon.

2. Soak the dried mushrooms in enough hot water to cover for 30 minutes. Strain, discard the water, and finely chop the mushrooms. Set aside.

3. Working in 3 or 4 batches, pulse the fresh mushrooms in the bowl of a food processor until they are evenly chopped, but not pureed. Combine with the chopped porcini mushrooms and set aside.

4. Combine the olive oil with the garlic in a sauté pan large enough to eventually hold the mushrooms and the pasta, and place over medium heat. Cook until the garlic is softened but not browned, about 2 or 3 minutes. Stir in the pepper flakes and cook for 30 seconds. Raise the heat to high, add all of the chopped mushrooms, and cook until their liquid has evaporated, but the mushrooms are still moist, about 10 minutes. Season with 2 teaspoons salt and the pepper.

5. Add the wine and continue to cook, stirring often, until the wine is reduced to almost a glaze. Taste and adjust the seasoning, if necessary; cover and set aside.

6. Lightly flour the work surface and sprinkle the ½ cup flour on a cookie sheet. Cut the pasta dough into quarters; wrap 3 of the quarters in plastic and set aside. Begin stretching the dough: pass 1 dough quarter through the widest setting on a hand-cranked or electric pasta machine. Decrease the setting a notch and pass the dough through again. Continue by decreasing one more notch and passing the dough through once again. Fold the strip of dough in thirds, as you would a letter. Flatten the dough with your fingers, return the machine to its widest setting, and begin passing the dough through the machine once again, narrow end first. Lightly dust the dough with flour every now and then if it gets sticky, and repeat the entire stretching process 5 or 6 more times, until the dough feels silky and elastic. Finish by rolling the dough through the machine, decreasing the setting a notch each time until

you reach two notches before the finest setting. Roll the dough through this final setting one or two more times, stretching it gently as you pull it through. The sheet of dough should be smooth and elastic and about 30 inches long.

7. Cut the dough into thirds (three 10-inch lengths). Then cut the lengths into ¼-inch-wide strips, using the appropriate attachment on the pasta machine. You can also cut the pasta by hand by lightly flouring both sides of each 10-inch sheet of pasta, folding it into thirds like a letter, and cutting ¼-inch strands. Sprinkle the cut pasta lightly with flour, wrap it around your fingers to make a nest, and place each nest on the cookie sheet. Repeat the process of rolling and cutting all of the dough. You should have 3 nests.

8. Bring 4 quarts of water to a boil and add 2 tablespoons of salt.

9. Add the crème fraîche or cream to the mushroom mixture and bring to a boil over medium-high heat. Keep warm over very low heat. Cook the pasta in the boiling water until just done, but not mushy, about 3 minutes. Drain and transfer to the pan with the mushroom sauce and bring to a boil, tossing to coat the pasta with the sauce. Sprinkle with parsley and serve hot.

Tagliolini with Cherry Tomatoes and Arugula

SERVES 6 AS AN APPETIZER, 4 AS A MAIN COURSE

This is another recipe whose simplicity makes it imperative to use excellent ingredients when they're in peak season. It's a combination of hot pasta and room-temperature tomato salad that is both refreshing and utterly satisfying. At the restaurant, we use the cherry tomato salad with homemade tagliolini—sort of a narrow fettuccine shape, for which we've provided the recipe. If you don't feel like making pasta from scratch in the warm salad days when tomatoes are in season, by all means use a good-quality store-bought fresh pasta or dried linguine or fettuccine.

Fresh Pasta Dough (page 319)
2 pints ripe cherry tomatoes, stemmed and washed
½ teaspoon minced garlic
½ teaspoon Italian red wine vinegar
¼ cup extra-virgin olive oil
Kosher salt
Freshly ground black pepper
¾ cup thinly sliced red onion
¼ cup fresh basil leaves
½ cup all-purpose flour, plus extra for dusting
4 packed cups coarsely chopped arugula

1. Make the pasta dough, wrap it in plastic, and let rest for 30 minutes.

2. Meanwhile, halve 1½ cups of the tomatoes and set aside.

Wine Suggestions:
Use a rosé or a white with bracing acidity and good fruit. Sauvignon blanc, chenin blanc, or riesling would do well.

3. Puree the remaining 2½ cups of tomatoes in a food processor and strain into a large bowl. Whisk in the garlic and vinegar, and then the olive oil, pouring in a thin stream. Season with 1½ teaspoons salt and ⅛ teaspoon pepper. Fold in the halved tomatoes, red onion, and basil and set aside.

4. Sprinkle the flour on a jelly roll pan. Cut the pasta dough into quarters; wrap 3 of the quarters in plastic and set aside. Pass 1 dough quarter through the widest setting on a hand-crank or electric pasta machine on a lightly floured board. Decrease the setting and pass the dough through again. Decrease once again, and pass the dough through. Then fold the flattened dough in thirds, folding the two ends in toward the center as you would to fold a letter. Flatten the dough with your fingers, turn the machine to the widest setting, and pass the dough though the machine again, feeding one of the two open ends through the rollers. Repeat this process 5 or 6 times, passing the dough strip lightly through the flour every now and then, until the dough is silky and elastic.

5. Now roll the dough through the machine on decreasing settings until just two notches before the finest setting. Roll the dough through this setting several times until it is very smooth and elastic. Cut the dough in thirds (three 10-inch lengths). Then cut the lengths into thin (¼-inch) strands, using the appropriate attachment on the pasta machine or a sharp chef's knife. Roll the tagliolini around your fingers to make a nest, and then toss gently with flour on the jelly roll pan. Repeat to roll and cut all of the dough. You should have 3 nests.

6. Bring 4 quarts of water to a boil and add 2 tablespoons salt. Cook the pasta in the boiling water until *al dente*. Drain the pasta well, add it to the bowl with the sauce, and toss gently to coat. Adjust the seasoning to your taste. Divide the arugula between 6 warm pasta bowls, top with the pasta, and serve.

Linguine with Clams and Pancetta

SERVES 6 AS AN APPETIZER, 4 AS A MAIN COURSE

Here's Union Square Cafe's variation on the classic *linguine alle vongole,* in which pancetta serves as a wonderful complement for fresh clams. We use tiny, sweet cockle clams, but if they're hard to find, any small, fresh hard-shell clam will do.

2 tablespoons kosher salt
1 tablespoon extra-virgin olive oil
4 ounces pancetta, cut into ½-inch pieces
40 cockle clams, scrubbed
12 ounces dried linguine
½ teaspoon chopped garlic
½ teaspoon Aleppo pepper or dried red pepper flakes
¼ teaspoon freshly ground black pepper
1 tablespoon fresh basil leaves, sliced into thin ribbons
1½ tablespoons chopped fresh parsley
1 cup bottled clam juice
2 tablespoons unsalted butter

1. Bring 4 quarts of water to a boil in a large pot and add the salt.

2. Combine the oil and pancetta in a deep 9-inch skillet and cook over medium-high heat to render the fat and crisp the pancetta, 3 to 5 minutes. Remove the pancetta with a slotted spoon and set aside.

3. Add the cockles to the skillet, cover, and cook until the cockles open, about 5 minutes. Transfer the cockles to a bowl with a slotted spoon and set aside. Reserve the skillet and any juices it contains to finish the recipe.

Wine Suggestions:
This dish is reminiscent of the Italian seashore, and goes well with any light, fresh white like verdicchio, Frascati, or vermentino.

SECOND HELPINGS FROM UNION SQUARE CAFE

4. Plunge the linguine into the boiling water, cook, stirring occasionally until almost *al dente,* and drain.

5. When the linguine is cooked, return the pancetta to the pan along with the garlic, the Aleppo and black pepper, the basil, parsley, and clam juice and bring to a boil. Add the butter and the pasta and cook over medium-high heat, stirring occasionally, until the sauce has reduced to a lightly thickened broth around the pasta. Toss in the cockles along with all of their liquid. Transfer the pasta to a warm platter, pour over any remaining sauce, and serve immediately.

Spaghetti all'Aragosta

Here's a new Union Square Cafe favorite that beautifully captures the seaside essence of lobster flavor, infusing it into an intense tomato sauce that works well with spaghetti or linguine. We serve this as an appetizer, but it would work equally well as a satisfying main course, accompanied by broccoli rabe, spinach, or a big green salad. The recipe makes enough sauce for 12, so you'll have the choice of doubling the amount of pasta you cook or reserving half the sauce for another time, well covered and refrigerated or frozen.

2 (28-ounce) cans peeled whole tomatoes
3 (1¼-pound) live lobsters
¼ cup olive oil
2 tablespoons extra-virgin olive oil
1½ teaspoons minced garlic
1 teaspoon Aleppo pepper
Kosher salt
4 cups peeled, seeded, and diced ripe fresh tomatoes
½ teaspoon freshly ground black pepper
2 tablespoons sliced fresh basil
1 pound spaghetti
2 tablespoons chopped fresh parsley

1. Puree the canned tomatoes with their juice in a blender. Pass through a strainer to remove the seeds and set aside.

2. Place a lobster, belly side down, on a cutting board and hold it firmly at its midsection. Place the point of a large kitchen knife about midway down the head of the lobster, blade side facing toward the head. With one strong motion, pierce downward

Wine Suggestions:
This dish takes us right to the Italian coast, and it would be hard to go wrong with the vinous trilogy of vermentino, vernaccia, and verdicchio—each of which has the refreshingly crisp fruit to complement the lobster and tomato sauce.

and then slice forward with the knife, splitting the top portion of the lobster's head and killing it instantly. Separate the tail from the body and remove the claws. Cut the tail crosswise into 4 even pieces, and set aside with the claws. Split the head and remove only the gritty sack. Split the head in half again crosswise and set it aside separately from the tail and claws. Repeat with the remaining 2 lobsters.

3. Heat 2 tablespoons of the olive oil in a soup pot over high heat until smoking. Add the lobster heads and sauté until the shells turn red, 3 to 4 minutes. Transfer to a plate and set aside. Pour the remaining 2 tablespoons of olive oil in the pot, and heat until smoking. Add the tails and claws, and sauté until the shells turn red, 2 to 3 minutes. Add the reserved tomato puree, reduce the heat to low, and simmer for 8 minutes. Remove the tails and claws from the sauce and set aside. Return the sautéed lobster heads to the sauce and simmer slowly for 30 minutes, stirring occasionally.

4. Meanwhile, combine the 2 tablespoons of extra-virgin olive oil, the garlic, and Aleppo pepper in a 3-quart saucepan. Place over low heat and cook until the garlic begins to sizzle. Add 1 teaspoon salt and the fresh tomatoes. Increase the heat to medium and cook, stirring occasionally, for 20 minutes.

5. Remove the lobster meat from the tails and claws, discard the shells, cut the meat into small pieces, and set aside.

6. Set the lobster-tomato sauce and the fresh tomato sauce aside when they have finished cooking. Using kitchen tongs, remove the pieces of lobster head from the lobster-tomato sauce and place them in a colander or a conical strainer set over a bowl. Press on the heads with a wooden spoon to extract all the juices. Add the juices back to the sauce and discard the heads. Add the fresh tomato sauce to the soup pot containing the lobster-tomato sauce, bring to a simmer over low heat, and season with 1 teaspoon salt and the black pepper. If the sauce

appears thin or watery, reduce for a few minutes until it thickens to a tomato-sauce consistency. Stir in the chopped lobster meat and the basil and allow to heat through, about 45 seconds. Remove the pot from the stove and ladle out half the sauce to reserve, frozen, for 5 to 6 weeks.

7. Bring 4 quarts of water to a boil and add 2 tablespoons of salt. Cook the spaghetti to just before the *al dente* stage and drain. Transfer the drained pasta to the soup pot, place over medium heat, and continue cooking in the sauce, stirring well, until the pasta is *al dente*. Transfer to a warm platter and serve, sprinkled with the chopped parsley.

Spaghettini con Bottarga

SERVES 6 AS AN APPETIZER, 4 AS A MAIN COURSE

In Sardinia, the nutty, saline flavor of bottarga, combined with garlic and a hint of tomato, makes an unforgettable pasta dish, so well loved that Sardinians enjoy some version of it almost daily. Many years ago, when we introduced this dish to guests at Union Square Cafe and told them that it was essentially *spaghettini all'aglio e olio* with the addition of a little bit of bottarga (sun-dried tuna or mullet roe), many politely asked us to "hold the roe." Fortunately, dozens of other diners had faith and took us up on the suggestion. They subsequently became part of a legion of USC bottarga aficionados who now grow sad each time we give the dish a hiatus from our menu.

BREAD-CRUMB TOPPING

¼ cup fresh bread crumbs
½ teaspoon minced garlic
1 teaspoon olive oil
⅛ teaspoon kosher salt
Pinch of freshly ground black pepper

Wine Suggestions:
Sardinian whites are perfect with this dish. Try vermentino or vernaccia, and if you can't find those, use any crisp, fruity white from one of Italy's coastal regions.

PASTA

Kosher salt

2 tablespoons extra-virgin olive oil

¼ cup Seasoned Bottarga Mixture (see page 252)

¼ cup chopped Oven-Dried Tomatoes (page 319),
   or 2 tablespoons tomato puree

1 tablespoon chopped fresh oregano

12 ounces dried spaghettini

¼ teaspoon freshly ground black pepper

1. Preheat the broiler. Combine the bread-crumb topping ingredients in a small bowl and mix well. Spread the mixture on a cookie sheet and broil until golden brown, about 1 minute. Reserve.

2. In a large pot, bring 4 quarts of water to a boil and add 2 tablespoons salt.

3. In a large skillet over moderate heat, stir together the olive oil, bottarga mixture, chopped tomatoes, and oregano. Remove from the heat and reserve until the pasta is cooked.

4. Plunge the spaghettini into the boiling water and cook, stirring occasionally, until *al dente*. Just before draining the pasta, ladle ½ cup of its cooking water into the skillet and bring the contents of the skillet to a simmer over medium-high heat. Drain the pasta, add to the skillet, and toss to coat the pasta thoroughly. Season with the pepper. Transfer the pasta to a warm platter, sprinkle with the toasted bread-crumb mixture, and serve immediately.

Rigatoni with Zucchini, Tomatoes, and Cream

SERVES 6 AS AN APPETIZER, 4 AS A MAIN COURSE

The success of this very simple tomato, basil, and zucchini sauce is dependent on just a few excellent ingredients—all of which are perfectly ripe and abundant in late summer. The addition of a drop of cream rounds out the flavor. Serve this as an appetizer and follow with Chicken Saltimbocca (page 150) or Michael's Garlic-Lemon Steak (page 163).

3 pounds ripe tomatoes, cored and cut into large chunks

¼ cup olive oil

1 pound small to medium zucchini, washed, split
    lengthwise, and cut crosswise on the diagonal
    into ¾-inch slices

Kosher salt

½ teaspoon minced garlic

3 tablespoons thinly sliced fresh basil

½ teaspoon Aleppo pepper

2 tablespoons heavy cream

¼ cup plus 1 tablespoon grated Parmigiano-Reggiano

⅛ teaspoon freshly ground black pepper

12 ounces rigatoni

2 tablespoons chopped fresh parsley

1. Place the tomatoes in a 10-inch skillet over medium heat and cook until they soften and give up some of their liquid, about 10 minutes. Pass the tomatoes through a food mill set over a bowl and reserve. Alternatively, pulse the tomatoes in a food processor and then pass them through a strainer. Rinse and dry the skillet.

Wine Suggestions:
Almost any wine made from the sangiovese grape would be delicious with the rigatoni. From Tuscany, try Rosso di Montalcino, Morelino di Scansano, or Carmignano.

2. Heat the oil in the same skillet over high heat until smoking. Add the sliced zucchini and cook, stirring often, until softened and lightly browned, about 5 minutes. Season with ⅛ teaspoon of the salt. Using a slotted spoon, transfer the zucchini to a plate and set aside.

3. Reduce the heat to medium. Add the garlic, basil, and Aleppo pepper. Stir to cook for 30 seconds. Add the tomato puree, bring to a boil, and simmer over low heat until the sauce has reduced by about one-half and the tomato flavor has intensified, 10 to 15 minutes. Stir in the cream, 3 tablespoons of the cheese, 1¼ teaspoons of salt, and the black pepper. Fold in the zucchini and set aside.

4. Bring 1 gallon of water to a boil and add 2 tablespoons of salt. Cook the pasta in the boiling water until *al dente,* and drain. Return the sauce to a simmer over a medium flame and add the pasta, stirring to coat. Transfer the pasta to a warm bowl, sprinkle with the remaining 2 tablespoons of cheese and the parsley, and serve.

Pennette all'Arrabbiata

SERVES 6 AS AN APPETIZER, 4 AS A MAIN COURSE

This is our adaptation of *penne all'Arrabbiata*—quill-shaped pasta with "angry" tomato sauce, so named for its fierce kick of hot pepper. We've layered this sauce with three different kinds of heat: jalapeño to provide fresh chili fire, Middle Eastern Aleppo for its deep smoky notes, and freshly ground black pepper for its bracing bite. You can temper the heat somewhat by omitting the jalapeño seeds. You can use penne for this recipe, but we prefer the smaller pennette, which soak up a bit less of the hot sauce with each forkful.

1 (28-ounce) can peeled whole tomatoes in juice
¼ cup olive oil
1 teaspoon chopped garlic
2 large jalapeño peppers, seeded and minced,
    plus the seeds of 1 jalapeño
1 teaspoon Aleppo pepper
1 tablespoon sliced fresh basil
2 cups peeled, seeded, and diced fresh tomato
    (2 to 3 large tomatoes)
2 teaspoons coarse sea salt
½ teaspoon freshly ground black pepper
Kosher salt
12 ounces pennette or penne
½ cup finely grated Pecorino Romano

1. Puree the canned tomatoes with their juice in a food mill and set aside.

2. Heat the oil in a 3-quart saucepan over medium heat. Add the garlic, jalapeño and Aleppo peppers, and basil; cook for 1 minute without browning

Wine Suggestions:
For white, choose a young, crisp Vernaccia di San Gimigniano or Frascati. "Red-wise," pick a ripe Southern Italian, like Montepulciano d'Abruzzo or almost any rustic offering from Italy's sunny Apulia region.

the ingredients. Add the diced tomatoes, sea salt, and black pepper. Simmer for 10 minutes, stirring occasionally. Add the pureed tomato and continue simmering, stirring occasionally, until the sauce has reduced and thickened, 20 to 25 minutes. Taste and adjust the seasonings. Set aside.

3. Bring 1 gallon of water to a boil and add 2 tablespoons of salt. Cook the pasta until *al dente* and drain in a colander.

4. Combine the cooked pasta with the hot sauce and half the cheese in a large skillet over medium heat, and toss well until the pasta is piping hot and evenly coated with sauce. Transfer to a serving bowl, sprinkle with the remaining cheese, and serve.

Spring Risotto

SERVES 4 TO 6

Risotto is an excellent vehicle for seasonal ingredients that go well together, and here are three that sing of spring. You'll have no trouble finding asparagus, but if you can't get your hands on ramps—the baby wild leeks whose very brief season makes them elusive and difficult to find—substitute an equal amount of spring onions or leeks. The same holds true for the morels. Their woodsy flavor and spongy texture are ideal for this dish, but other mushrooms would also provide delicious results. As fresh products of the earth, spring ingredients often bring with them unwanted sand or dirt. It's worth going to the extra effort of washing them thoroughly. To clean morels, split them in half lengthwise and place them in a large bowl of cool water. Swish them around well and lift them out of the water with your hands. Repeat with fresh water as many times as necessary, until there are no more grains of dirt or sand in the bowl. Work quickly to avoid "waterlogging" the morels, and place them immediately on paper towels to dry.

5 to 6 cups Chicken Stock (page 315)

3 tablespoons olive oil

1 pound asparagus, washed, tough ends snapped off,
    tips cut off in 1-inch lengths, stalks cut into ¼-inch-
    thick rounds

¼ pound morel mushrooms, split or quartered,
    depending on size, and washed (about 2 cups)

¾ cup washed and sliced ramps, spring onions, or leeks
    (white part only)

Kosher salt

Freshly ground black pepper

2 tablespoons minced shallots

1 teaspoon minced garlic

1¾ cups arborio rice

Wine Suggestions:

Wines with earthy sweetness pair beautifully with the risotto. Try an Oregon pinot noir or a Côte Chalonnaise Burgundy like Rully, Mercurey, or Givry. Just as delicious would be a Rioja, Barbaresco, or, for a white, Vouvray.

1½ cups white wine

2 tablespoons butter

½ cup finely grated Parmigiano-Reggiano

1. Bring the chicken stock to a simmer in a saucepan.

2. In an 8-inch (3-quart), heavy-bottomed saucepan, heat 2 tablespoons of the olive oil over high heat. Add the asparagus and cook, stirring, until softened, 2 to 3 minutes.

3. Reduce the heat to medium. Add the morels and ramps, onions, or leeks and cook until softened 3 to 4 minutes. Season with 1 teaspoon salt and ⅛ teaspoon pepper. Using a slotted spoon, remove the asparagus, ramps, and morels from the pan and reserve.

4. Add the remaining tablespoon of olive oil to the pan. Add the shallots and garlic and cook until softened but not colored, about 1 minute. Add the rice and stir with a wooden spoon to coat with the oil.

5. Add the wine, bring to a simmer, and stir constantly until the rice has absorbed the wine.

6. Ladle ½ cup of hot chicken stock into the pan and stir until it is absorbed. Continue with the rest of the stock, adding ½ cup at a time and letting each addition become absorbed completely into the rice before adding more liquid. The constant stirring allows the rice to release its starch into the cooking liquid, resulting in the characteristic risotto creaminess. The grains of rice should be *al dente*. Count on approximately 20 to 25 minutes for the rice to cook.

7. When the rice is *al dente* and creamy, fold in the reserved asparagus, morels, and ramps or onions, and heat through. Stir in the butter, 2½ teaspoons of salt, ⅛ teaspoon of pepper, and ¼ cup of the Parmigiano. Spoon the risotto into a serving bowl or individual bowls, sprinkle with the remaining cheese, and serve immediately.

Zucchini Risotto

In summer, when zucchini and their blossoms are readily available, we're always looking for delicious ways to bring out their subtle, nutty flavor. Here, we hope you enjoy the play on gremolata—in which we've added zucchini blossoms to the classic Milanese trio of lemon, garlic, and parsley traditionally used as a topping for osso buco. Look for zucchini blossoms that are large, firm, unblemished, and just partially opened.

1 recipe Zucchini Puree with Marjoram (page 206),
    completed through step 1 (not pureed)

ZUCCHINI BLOSSOM "GREMOLATA"
1 tablespoon extra-virgin olive oil
½ cup peeled, seeded, and diced tomato
6 to 8 zucchini blossoms, stemmed
¼ teaspoon crushed and minced garlic
¼ teaspoon grated lemon zest
1½ teaspoons coarsely chopped fresh parsley
¼ teaspoon kosher salt
Pinch of freshly ground black pepper

RISOTTO
5 to 6 cups Chicken Stock (page 315)
2 tablespoons olive oil
2 tablespoons minced shallots
1 teaspoon minced garlic
1¾ cups arborio rice
¾ cup white wine
Kosher salt
Freshly ground black pepper
2 tablespoons butter
½ cup finely grated Parmigiano-Reggiano

Wine Suggestions:
Try a good Provençal rosé or a fragrant and delicate white such as Liguria's Pigato, Lombardy's Franciacorta Bianca, or viognier.

1. Cover the warm zucchini and marjoram mixture and set aside.

2. Prepare the "gremolata": Heat the oil over medium-high heat in a small skillet. Add the tomato and cook, stirring, 30 seconds to soften. Add the zucchini blossoms, garlic, lemon zest, parsley, salt, and pepper. Cook until the blossoms wilt and melt into the tomato, 30 seconds to 1 minute longer. Transfer to a small bowl, cover, and set aside.

3. Bring the chicken stock to a simmer in a 2-quart saucepan.

4. In an 8-inch (3-quart), heavy-bottomed saucepan, heat the olive oil over medium heat. Add the shallots and garlic and cook until softened, but not colored, about 1 minute. Add the rice and stir with a wooden spoon to coat with the oil.

5. Add the wine, bring to a simmer, and cook, stirring constantly, until the rice has absorbed the wine.

6. Ladle ½ cup of hot chicken stock into the pan and stir until it is absorbed. Continue with the rest of the stock, adding ½ cup at a time and letting each addition become absorbed completely before adding more liquid. The constant stirring allows the rice to release its starch into the cooking liquid, resulting in the characteristic risotto creaminess. The grains of rice should be *al dente*. Count on approximately 20 to 25 minutes for the rice to cook.

7. When the risotto is *al dente,* season with 2½ teaspoons of salt and ⅛ teaspoon of pepper, fold in the reserved zucchini mixture, and stir until it is thoroughly incorporated. Swirl in the butter and the cheese, and spoon the risotto into warm bowls. Top evenly with the reserved Zucchini Blossom "Gremolata" and serve.

Risotto Rosso

SERVES 4 TO 6

This risotto is winy, meaty, creamy, and crunchy all at once, and if you close
your eyes, we promise you'll be transported to a cozy, rustic *albergo* in the
countryside of Northern Italy. If you can't find fennel sausage, just use a good,
sweet Italian sausage and add ¼ teaspoon of fennel seeds while sautéing.

4 to 5 cups Chicken Stock (page 315)
¼ cup olive oil
4 cups stemmed and quartered radicchio leaves
Kosher salt
Freshly ground black pepper
8 ounces sweet fennel sausage, removed from casing
2 teaspoons minced shallot
1 teaspoon minced garlic
1¾ cups arborio rice
3 cups red wine
2 tablespoons butter
⅓ cup grated Parmigiano-Reggiano
2 tablespoons chopped fresh parsley

1. Bring the chicken broth to a simmer in a small
    saucepan.

2. Heat 2 tablespoons of the oil in a 3-quart, heavy-
    bottomed saucepan or large skillet over medium-
    high heat. Add the radicchio leaves and cook,
    stirring, until just wilted, 4 to 5 minutes. Season
    with ¼ teaspoon of the salt and a pinch of the
    pepper. Remove from the pan and set aside.

Wine Suggestions:

It would be hard to go
wrong with almost any
Italian red, but a standout
for us would be USC's
favorite house wine,
the Piemontese Bricco
Manzoni. Likewise,
Barolo, Valpolicella,
or Vino Nobile di
Montepulciano would
drink beautifully with
the risotto.

3. Lower the heat to medium. Add the remaining 2 tablespoons of oil. Add the sausage and cook until it is well broken up and has lost its raw appearance, 3 to 4 minutes. Remove the sausage and set aside; discard all but 2 tablespoons of the fat from the pan. Add the shallot and garlic and cook until softened but not browned, about 1 minute. Add the rice, season with 1 teaspoon of the salt, and stir with a wooden spoon until the rice is well coated with the oil.

4. Raise the heat to medium-high. Add ¾ cup of the wine, bring to a boil, and cook the rice, stirring constantly with a wooden spoon until the wine is absorbed. Add the remaining wine in 3 more increments, letting each be absorbed completely into the rice before adding more wine.

5. Ladle ½ cup of the simmering broth into the saucepan and stir until it is absorbed. Continue with the rest of the broth, adding ½ cup at a time and letting each addition be absorbed completely into the rice before adding more liquid. The constant stirring allows the rice to release its starch into the cooking liquid, resulting in the characteristic risotto creaminess. Count on approximately 20 to 25 minutes for the rice to be cooked *al dente*. Along with the final ladleful of broth, add the sautéed radicchio and sausage, and continue stirring until heated through.

6. Swirl in the butter, half of the cheese, 1 teaspoon of salt, and ¼ teaspoon of pepper. Spoon onto a warm platter or into individual bowls, sprinkle with the remaining Parmigiano and the chopped parsley, and serve immediately.

Risotto with Eggplant, Anchovy, and Mint

SERVES 4 TO 6

Here's a risotto variation whose bold flavors remind us of the food of Rome's Jewish quarter. Anchovies, pecorino, and mint wake up the subtle, musky eggplant, which almost melts right into the creamy rice. As a starter, this risotto would be a natural before lamb or chicken, or enjoy it as a main course accompanied by a simple salad of bitter greens like arugula, dandelion, or radicchio.

Kosher salt
1 or 2 medium eggplants, unpeeled, cut into
    ½-inch dice (4 cups)
⅓ cup plus 2 tablespoons extra-virgin olive oil
6 cups Chicken Stock (page 315)
2 tablespoon minced shallots
1 teaspoon garlic
5 anchovy fillets, minced
1¾ cups arborio rice
1 cup white wine
3 tablespoons chopped fresh mint
3 tablespoons butter
½ cup grated Pecorino Romano
⅛ teaspoon freshly ground pepper

1. Combine 1 quart of cold water and 2 tablespoons of salt in a large bowl. Add the diced eggplant and let soak for 30 minutes. Drain well in a colander.

2. In a large sauté pan, heat ⅓ cup of the oil over medium-high heat until very hot, and add the drained eggplant. If your sauté pan is not large

Wine Suggestions:
To soften the bitterness of eggplant, pick a red wine with ample tannins and fruit. Try a Montepulciano d'Abruzzo or Sardinian cannonau from Italy, or from France, a syrah or grenache-based wine from Provence or the Rhône Valley.

SECOND HELPINGS FROM UNION SQUARE CAFE

enough to hold all the eggplant in one layer, do this step in more than one batch. Cook the eggplant until well browned and tender, 8 to 10 minutes. Stir often during the last half of cooking, and reduce the heat as needed to keep the eggplant from burning. Transfer to a dish and set aside.

3. In a small saucepan, bring the chicken stock to a simmer.

4. Combine 2 tablespoons of oil, the shallots, garlic, and anchovies in a 3-quart, heavy-bottomed saucepan or skillet. Place over medium heat and stir to cook, without coloring, about 2 minutes. Add the rice and 1 teaspoon of salt, and stir with a wooden spoon until the rice is coated with the oil. Add the wine and bring to a boil over medium-high heat; cook the rice, stirring constantly, until it absorbs the wine.

5. Ladle ½ cup of the simmering broth into the saucepan and stir until it is absorbed. Continue with the rest of the broth, adding ½ cup at a time and letting each addition become absorbed completely into the rice before adding more liquid. The constant stirring allows the rice to release its starch into the cooking liquid, resulting in the characteristic risotto creaminess. Count on approximately 20 to 25 minutes for the rice to be cooked *al dente*.

6. Fold in the eggplant and cook until heated through, about 30 seconds. Add the mint, swirl in the butter and half the cheese, and season with ½ teaspoon of salt and the pepper. Spoon the risotto onto a warm platter or into individual bowls, sprinkle with the remaining pecorino, and serve immediately.

Sheep's-Milk Ricotta Gnocchi

SERVES 6 TO 8

This recipe is a delicious variation on the traditional potato gnocchi. The sheep's-milk ricotta and mascarpone, lightly bound with egg and a touch of flour, create cloudlike puffs, beautifully complemented by a green and white sauce with a gently acidic edge of lemon and verjus—the juice of unripened grapes. Even if you are using them immediately, you might want to consider lightly freezing the gnocchi, as this makes them easier to handle while cooking.

GNOCCHI

15 ounces sheep's-milk ricotta, or cow's-milk ricotta,
    drained in a colander for at least 1 hour

¼ cup mascarpone

2 large eggs

½ cup grated Pecorino Romano

½ cup grated Parmigiano-Reggiano

Kosher salt

Pinch of freshly ground pepper

Pinch of freshly grated nutmeg

½ cup plus 2 tablespoons all-purpose flour,
    plus extra for dusting

LEMON-SPINACH SAUCE

1 lemon

1½ tablespoons butter

1 medium onion, thinly sliced

1 celery stalk, sliced

½ cup verjus or dry white wine

2 cups heavy cream

½ teaspoon kosher salt

Wine Suggestions:
A youthful sauvignon blanc like Sancerre or Pouilly Fumé would be an ideal partner for the gnocchi, as would a pinot bianco or Müller-Thurgau from Friuli-Venezia-Giulia.

⅛ teaspoon freshly ground pepper

Pinch of freshly grated nutmeg

1 packed cup stemmed spinach leaves, cut into
    ½-inch strips

¼ cup plus 2 tablespoons grated Pecorino Romano

1. Make the gnocchi: Combine the ricotta and mascarpone in a food
    processor and process until smooth. Add the eggs, the two grated
    cheeses, the salt, pepper, and nutmeg, and blend until smooth. Transfer
    the mixture to a large bowl. Gently fold in the flour in 2 batches with
    a rubber spatula just until the flour is incorporated and the dough has
    the consistency of a stiff mousse. To avoid tough gnocchi, don't
    overwork the dough.

2. Sprinkle a cookie sheet with flour.

3. Spoon the dough into a pastry bag fitted with a ¾-inch plain tip
    (#808). Squeeze out a 1-inch cylinder of dough and cut it onto the
    cookie sheet, forming evenly spaced rows of gnocchi. This is easily
    done by dipping a paring knife in warm water, then slicing down cleanly
    through the dough with the blade pressing against the pastry tip. Once
    you've cut all the gnocchi, refrigerate until ready to cook. (The gnocchi
    can also be frozen at this point. To do this, first freeze them on the
    cookie sheet, then store in zip-top bags. Do not defrost before cooking.)

4. Make the sauce: Grate the zest from the lemon and squeeze 2 tablespoons
    of juice. Reserve the zest and juice separately.

5. Melt the butter in a 2-quart saucepan (large enough to eventually hold
    the gnocchi) over medium heat. Add the onion and celery and cook
    until wilted, but not browned, about 4 minutes. Add the verjus or white
    wine and the reserved lemon juice. Bring to a boil and reduce until
    almost dry, about 10 minutes. Add the cream and boil, reducing until
    it coats the back of a spoon, about 10 to 12 minutes. Strain the sauce

into a bowl, and season with the salt, pepper, and nutmeg. Stir in the reserved lemon zest and set aside.

6. Bring 4 quarts of water to a boil and add 2 tablespoons of salt. Gently transfer the gnocchi to the water and boil until they are completely cooked through and firm to the touch, 5 minutes. Remove with a slotted spoon and drain in a colander.

7. Return the sauce to the saucepan and bring to a simmer over medium heat. Add the spinach and cook until wilted, about 2 minutes. Add the gnocchi and heat through, tossing gently to coat with the sauce. Spoon into warm bowls and top with the cheese. Serve immediately.

My dear, never volunteer
To share your food with gourmand rakes,
They'll take your steak
and haricots verts,
Then leave you with a plate that's bare.

SIMPLY IRRESISTIBLE

GRILLED SALMON WITH LENTIL
AND BEET VINAIGRETTE

———

STRIPED BASS WITH TOMATO-CAPER SAUCE

———

ROASTED HALIBUT PUGLIESE STYLE

———

CHILI AND SAGE–RUBBED SALMON

———

SICILIAN-STYLE SALMON

———

PARMIGIANO-CRUSTED GROUPER

———

HALIBUT CONFIT

———

RED SNAPPER WITH COGNAC SAUCE

———

MONKFISH SCARPARIELLO

———

SAUTÉED SHRIMP GOAN STYLE

———

SEA SCALLOPS WITH CITRUS-YOGURT MARINADE

———

SOFT-SHELL CRABS WITH TOMATO NAGE

———

GRILLED LOBSTER WITH BRUSCHETTA SAUCE

———

ROASTED LOBSTER WITH CORN AND CHANTERELLES

———

INDIAN "BOUILLABAISSE"

———

SALT-BAKED CHICKEN

———

CHICKEN LAMBRUSCO

———

CHICKEN SALTIMBOCCA

———

PAN-ROASTED CHICKEN
WITH COGNAC-PEPPERCORN SAUCE

———

POUSSIN AL MATTONE

———

ROAST QUAIL

———

ROAST TURKEY WITH APPLE-CIDER GRAVY

———

ROAST GOOSE

———

MICHAEL'S GARLIC-LEMON STEAK

———

ITALIAN BEEF STEW

———

OVEN-BRAISED SHORT RIBS

———

Bollito di Vitello

Herb-Roasted Rack of Veal

Roman-Style Braised Oxtails

Chicken-Fried Venison

Baked Lamb Chops

Olive-Stuffed Lamb

Roast Rack of Lamb

Lamb Stew alla Romana

Spice-Rubbed Pork Tenderloin

Sage-Fried Rabbit

Calf's Liver with Bacon and Sage

Trippa alla Trasteverina

Eggplant-Spinach Rollatine

Grilled Salmon with Lentil and Beet Vinaigrette

SERVES 4

Sweet beets and earthy lentils play a starring role in this immensely satisfying sauce/vinaigrette for grilled salmon fillets. A touch of honey, some red wine, and a little balsamic vinegar give it a beautifully balanced sweet-sour flavor that also works well with grilled shrimp or lobster. Roasting the beet provides a more concentrated beet flavor for this recipe, but if you're in a hurry, the beet can be boiled in a quarter of the time. Use lightly salted water and be sure to cool the beet in its cooking liquid. Since the recipe calls for just 1 tablespoon of bottled clam juice, use the rest in a batch of lemony Bloody Marys, or add it to a warmed mixture of olive oil, garlic, red pepper flakes, and bread crumbs for a quick and simple pasta sauce.

1 small beet, trimmed of greens (1½ to 2 ounces),
    and rinsed
¼ cup green lentils, preferably lentilles du Puy,
    picked over and rinsed well
Kosher salt
1 cup red wine
1 tablespoon honey
1 tablespoon bottled clam juice
2 tablespoons chopped shallot
1 tablespoon aged balsamic vinegar
¼ cup plus 1 tablespoon extra-virgin olive oil
1 teaspoon chopped fresh dill
Freshly ground black pepper
4 (6-ounce) skinless salmon fillets

1. Preheat the oven to 400 degrees F.

Wine Suggestions:

For whites, go with a riesling or ripe sauvignon blanc from New Zealand or South Africa. A good red choice would be any of the Loire Valley cabernet francs: Chinon, Saumur-Champigny, or Bourgueil.

2. Rinse the beet, wrap it in aluminum foil, and roast until it can be easily pierced by the tip of a paring knife, about 60 to 70 minutes. When cool enough to handle, trim the ends and peel off the skin. Cut the beet into ¼-inch dice and set aside.

3. Combine the lentils and water in a small saucepan, bring to a boil, reduce the heat, and simmer, covered, for 15 minutes. Add ¼ teaspoon of the salt and continue cooking until the lentils are tender, 10 to 15 more minutes.

4. Combine the wine and the honey in a 2-quart saucepan and simmer over moderate heat until reduced to ¼ cup. Add the clam juice, return to a simmer, and immediately pour the hot wine mixture into a mixing bowl, using a scraper to transfer all the liquid.

5. Whisk in the shallot and the balsamic vinegar, and then the ¼ cup of the olive oil in a thin stream. Gently stir in the lentils, diced beets, and dill. Season with ¼ teaspoon of salt and ⅛ teaspoon of pepper. Set aside.

6. Preheat a grill or grill pan until very hot.

7. Drizzle the remaining 1 tablespoon of oil over the salmon and turn to coat. Sprinkle with salt and pepper to taste and grill over high heat until just cooked through, 4 to 5 minutes per side.

8. Spoon the lentil sauce (either warm or at room temperature) evenly over 4 plates. Place a cooked salmon fillet atop the sauce on each plate and serve.

Striped Bass with Tomato-Caper Sauce

SERVES 4

Striped bass fillets are quickly oven-stewed in a zesty tomato sauce with capers and anchovy—similar to Puttanesca sauce, but without the olives. Serve the fish with spinach or escarole as well as a simple rice or potato dish to sop up the abundant and delicious sauce. Feel free to replace the striped bass with red snapper or sea bass.

TOMATO-CAPER SAUCE

1 pound fresh, ripe tomatoes, cored and chopped

1 (14½-ounce) can Italian plum tomatoes

¼ cup plus 2½ tablespoons extra-virgin olive oil

½ teaspoon minced garlic

¼ cup diced onion

¼ cup diced celery

½ teaspoon dried red pepper flakes

½ tablespoon tomato paste

½ tablespoon sliced fresh basil

2 tablespoons white wine

1½ tablespoons anchovy paste

1½ tablespoons drained capers

½ tablespoon chopped fresh parsley

½ teaspoon kosher salt

¼ teaspoon freshly ground black pepper

4 (6-ounce) skinless fillets striped bass or red snapper

1. In a 2-quart saucepan, combine the fresh tomatoes with the canned tomatoes and their juice. Cook over medium heat for 15 minutes, or until the

Wine Suggestions:
Any crisp, fragrant white or rosé will do, but to capture the seaside essence of this recipe, try to use one made along Italy's coast.

tomatoes are quite soft. Pass the tomatoes through a food mill and into a large bowl to remove all seeds and skin.

2. Rinse and dry the saucepan. Add 1½ tablespoons of the oil and the garlic and cook over medium heat until the garlic is softened, but not colored, about 1 minute. Add the onion and celery and continue cooking until the vegetables are softened, but not brown, 3 to 4 minutes. Add the pepper flakes, tomato paste, and basil and cook for 1 minute. Stir in the wine and cook for 1 minute. Pour in the pureed tomatoes, bring to a boil, reduce the heat, and simmer until the sauce thickens, about 30 minutes. Remove from the heat and set aside.

3. In a small skillet, warm 1 tablespoon of the olive oil over medium heat. Add the anchovy paste and the capers and cook gently for 2 to 3 minutes, stirring often. Add to the sauce along with the parsley, salt, and pepper. Stir until mixed. Adjust the seasoning to your taste.

4. Preheat the oven to 400 degrees F.

5. Prepare the fish: Heat the remaining 2 tablespoons of olive oil over high heat in an ovenproof skillet large enough to hold all the fillets. Season the fillets with salt and pepper, add them to the pan with skinned sides facing up, and brown on one side, 2 to 3 minutes. Turn the fillets, pour off any fat from the pan, and spoon the sauce over the fish. Bake in the oven until the fish is just cooked through, 6 to 8 minutes. Serve immediately.

Roasted Halibut Pugliese Style

SERVES 4

If you grew up with some version of a baked fish casserole, this wonderful recipe with anchovies and potatoes will be a welcome revelation. In Apulia, there is a great tradition of layering seafood and vegetables into the clay casseroles known as *tielli,* where their flavors marry during the long, slow cooking. Here, halibut is flavored with the rich, winy cooking liquid of artichokes as well as a sprinkling of tangy Pecorino Romano cheese. This is an immensely satisfying recipe that works well as a one-dish meal, needing only a salad to make it a complete dinner.

1 lemon

4 large artichokes

2 quarts water

¼ cup chopped fresh parsley leaves, stems reserved

¼ cup sliced fresh basil leaves, stems reserved

1 bay leaf

Kosher salt

2 pounds small Yukon Gold or Red Bliss potatoes, unpeeled, washed

¼ cup plus 1 tablespoon extra-virgin olive oil, plus extra for oiling the casserole

¼ cup thinly sliced garlic

2 cups sliced Vidalia or white onions

¼ teaspoon freshly ground black pepper

1 teaspoon Aleppo pepper or ½ teaspoon dried red pepper flakes

1 cup white wine

1 cup Chicken Stock (page 315)

1 cup grated Pecorino Romano

4 (6-ounce) skinless halibut fillets, ¾ inch thick

Fine sea salt

Wine Suggestions:

Find a white from Southern Italy like Fiano di Avellino or Trebbiano d'Abruzzo, or a well-made *rosato* (rosé) from Sicily or Tuscany.

1. Squeeze the lemon into a bowl of cold water large enough to hold the artichokes; reserve the lemon halves. Snap off the outer, dark green leaves of the artichokes to expose the innermost core of light yellow leaves. Slice off and discard the cores, revealing the chokes. Cut off the stems and peel the dark green skin down to the whitish flesh. Rub the peeled stems with 1 of the lemon halves, slice each stem crosswise into thin rounds, and place the rounds in the lemon water. Trim off all of the dark green from the hearts of the artichokes. Scrape out the chokes with a small spoon. Rub each of the artichoke hearts with the remaining lemon half, split each heart in half, and cut each half into 8 to 10 thin slices. Place the slices in the bowl with the sliced stems and reserve.

2. Pour the water into a large saucepan, place over medium-high heat, and add the reserved parsley and basil stems, the bay leaf, and 1 tablespoon of kosher salt.

3. Slice the potatoes into ⅛-inch-thick rounds and add them into the saucepan. Bring to a boil, reduce the heat, and simmer until the potatoes are just tender but not falling apart, about 30 minutes. Carefully drain the potatoes, discard the herbs, and set aside.

4. While the potatoes are cooking, combine 3 tablespoons of the oil with the garlic in an 8-inch (3-quart) saucepan. Place the pan over medium-low heat and cook until the garlic is softened but not browned, 1 to 2 minutes. Add the onion and cook, stirring, until softened but not colored, 3 to 4 minutes. Drain the sliced artichokes well and add to the saucepan. Stir in the chopped basil and parsley, 1½ teaspoons of kosher salt, and the black and Aleppo peppers. Increase the heat to medium-high, and cook for 3 minutes. Add the wine and boil to reduce by half. Add the stock, return to a boil, reduce the heat, and simmer, partially covered, until the artichokes are tender, about 20 minutes. Set aside.

5. Heat the oven to 400 degrees F.

6. Lightly oil a 3-quart casserole. Spread half of the potatoes over the bottom of the casserole. With a slotted spoon, lift half of the artichokes out of their liquid and spread evenly over the potatoes. Sprinkle with half of the pecorino. Season the fish on both sides with sea salt and black pepper. Place the fillets atop the sliced artichokes and potatoes. Cover the fish with the remaining artichokes. Spread the remaining potatoes over the artichokes in as flat a layer as possible, and pour the artichoke cooking liquid over the potatoes. Sprinkle the potatoes with the remaining pecorino and drizzle with the remaining 2 tablespoons of oil. Place the casserole in the oven and bake, uncovered, until the fish is just cooked through, 20 to 25 minutes. Remove the casserole from the oven.

7. Turn the oven to its broiler setting. Place the casserole under the broiler and brown the potatoes for 2 to 3 minutes. Present the casserole, spoon out individual portions, and serve hot.

Chili and Sage–Rubbed Salmon

SERVES 4

Union Square Cafe guests are constantly challenging us to serve salmon in new and different guises, and here's one of the most popular ones we've done to date. Salmon is rich and meaty enough to stand up to the assertive chili rub; the trick to this dish is to cook the salmon gently enough to prevent the spices from burning. At the restaurant, we use New Mexico chili powder, which we prize for its fruity, smoky aroma and mild heat level. Buy it if you see it. The salmon is best accompanied by our Green Tomato Chutney (page 260) and a steaming bowl of buttered rice.

CHILI PASTE

1 tablespoon olive oil

2 medium garlic cloves, thinly sliced

1 tablespoon coriander seeds, finely ground

1 teaspoon cumin seeds, finely ground

3½ tablespoons chili powder

¼ teaspoon freshly ground black pepper

1 tablespoon thinly sliced fresh sage leaves

½ cup verjus, apple cider, or 8 tablespoons white grape juice mixed with 2 tablespoons white wine vinegar

SALMON

4 (6-ounce) skinless salmon fillets

2 tablespoons olive oil

Kosher salt

1. Make the paste: Combine the oil and garlic in a small, heavy-bottomed saucepan. Place over low heat and cook until the garlic just barely begins to brown around the edges, 1 to 2 minutes. Add the ground coriander and cumin, and cook 1 minute,

Wine Suggestions:
Champagne or any good sparkling wine would be ideal here. The bubbles and acidity will put out the chili paste fire and cut right through the richness of the salmon. You'd also do well with a young, fruity rosé.

stirring constantly. Stir in the chili powder and black pepper and cook, stirring, 2 minutes longer. Add the sage and verjus, bring to a simmer, and cook until reduced and thickened to a paste, 1 to 2 more minutes. Remove from the heat, transfer to a bowl, and cool completely before using.

2. Use your fingers to coat the salmon all over with the cooled chili paste. Cover and refrigerate for 2 hours.

3. Wipe the paste from the salmon.

4. Heat the oil over medium heat in a skillet large enough to hold all the salmon fillets. Sprinkle the salmon fillets with salt, place them in the pan, and cook gently until well browned and just cooked through, 3 to 4 minutes per side. Transfer the salmon to warm plates and serve immediately.

Sicilian-Style Salmon

SERVES 4

This is Union Square Cafe's version of a classic Sicilian recipe that combines tomatoes, raisins, olives, and almonds in perfect balance. Homemade salmon broth is the depth-providing foundation for a fabulous sauce that will win raves from your guests. Call your fishmonger up to a day ahead and ask him to save you half the frame of a salmon. Beyond the colorful sauce itself, good accompaniments for the salmon are spinach, green beans, red Swiss chard, and Bottarga-Mashed Potatoes (page 252).

Wine Suggestions:
A fruity white with good acidity like pinot bianco, sylvaner, or sauvignon blanc works well with the salmon, as would a well-made rosé from Italy, Spain, or Provence.

Salmon Broth

½ tablespoon olive oil

½ small onion, chopped

1 medium carrot, scrubbed and chopped

1 celery stalk, chopped

1 small bay leaf

5 fresh parsley stems

5 fresh basil stems

6 whole peppercorns

20 coriander seeds

½ salmon frame, rinsed and chopped coarsely

½ teaspoon coarse sea salt

⅛ teaspoon freshly ground black pepper

1 cup verjus

½ cup reserved juice from 1 (14-ounce) can peeled
tomatoes (see below)

Salmon

2 tablespoons golden raisins

¼ cup verjus

½ cup green olives, pitted and diced

¼ cup extra-virgin olive oil

½ cup diced onion

½ cup peeled and chopped celery

¾ teaspoon minced garlic

1 (14-ounce) can peeled tomatoes, drained, seeded,
and diced

2 tablespoons sliced whole almonds

1 tablespoon drained capers

¾ teaspoon grated orange zest

1 bay leaf

1 tablespoon sliced fresh basil leaves

1 tablespoon chopped fresh parsley leaves

½ teaspoon kosher salt

⅛ teaspoon freshly ground black pepper

4 (6-ounce) skinless salmon fillets

1. Make the broth: Heat the oil in a 3-quart saucepan over medium heat. Add the onion, carrot, celery, bay leaf, parsley, basil, peppercorns, and coriander seeds and cook until the vegetables are soft, but not colored, about 10 minutes. Raise the heat to high, add the salmon frame, and cook for 2 minutes, stirring. Season with the salt and pepper. Add the verjus and the reserved tomato juice. Bring to a boil, reduce the heat, cover, and simmer for 30 minutes. Strain the broth through a fine-mesh strainer, pressing well on the solids. Set aside and reserve. The broth can be made up to 1 day in advance, covered, and refrigerated, or frozen for several months.

2. Prepare the salmon: Combine the raisins and the verjus in a small saucepan and bring to a simmer over low heat. Immediately remove from the heat and set aside to plump the raisins. When cooled to room temperature, strain, reserving the raisins and adding the verjus to the salmon broth.

3. Heat 2 tablespoons of the olive oil in a 2-quart saucepan over medium heat. Stir in the onion and celery and cook until softened, but not colored, about 5 minutes. Add the garlic and cook for 30 seconds. Add the tomatoes and cook for an additional 2 minutes. Add the plumped raisins, blanched olives, almonds, capers, orange zest, and bay leaf and simmer, uncovered, until the vegetables are cooked through, but retain their texture, 12 to 15 minutes. Stir in the basil and parsley, season with the salt and pepper and set aside.

4. In a skillet large enough to hold the salmon fillets, heat the remaining 2 tablespoons of the oil over medium-high heat until smoking. Sprinkle the salmon fillets with salt and pepper, place them in the pan, and cook until browned and just cooked through, 3 to 4 minutes per side.

5. Transfer the salmon to a platter, discard the oil from the skillet, and then wipe it clean with a paper towel. Cover the fish loosely with foil to keep warm.

6. Combine the broth and the cooked vegetables in the skillet and bring to a boil over high heat. Cook until the broth has reduced to a syrupy consistency and coats the vegetables. Spoon the hot vegetables over the salmon and serve.

Parmigiano-Crusted Grouper

SERVES 4

Though the combination of grouper and Parmigiano-Reggiano may seem a bit out of the ordinary, the two get along just fine here, with the cheese adding a buttery, nutty flavor, as well as a nice crunchy crust to the fish fillets. To preserve the browned crust, the warm red-pepper vinaigrette gets spooned around the grouper, providing a sweet-and-tart counterpoint to the fish. Serve with Olive-Mashed Potatoes (page 255) or Italian Fries (page 249) and some sautéed spinach or red chard.

RED-PEPPER VINAIGRETTE

2 medium red bell peppers

1 small yellow bell pepper

1 small tomato, cored and roughly chopped

¼ cup sliced shallots and 2 tablespoons minced shallots (about 4 large shallots)

2 tablespoons sliced garlic

1 sprig fresh thyme, plus 1 teaspoon fresh thyme leaves

1 cup white wine

¼ cup red wine vinegar

1 tablespoon tomato paste

1 cup Fish Stock (page 316), reduced to ¼ cup

¼ cup plus 1 tablespoon extra-virgin olive oil

Kosher salt

Freshly ground black pepper

PARMIGIANO-CRUSTED GROUPER

1 cup panko (or fresh bread crumbs)

½ cup grated Parmigiano-Reggiano

Kosher salt

Wine Suggestions:
This versatile dish could be matched with a lively and fruity white like verdicchio or Vernaccia di San Gimigniano, with a well-made rosé, or a red, such as Sangiovese di Romagna or Teroldego Rotaliano.

Freshly ground black pepper

1½ tablespoons butter, melted

4 (6-ounce) skinless grouper fillets (or red snapper or striped bass)

2 tablespoons olive oil

1. Begin the vinaigrette: Core and seed the red and yellow bell peppers. Finely dice 2 tablespoons each of the red and yellow peppers and reserve. Coarsely chop all the remaining pepper.

2. Combine the coarsely chopped pepper in a 2-quart saucepan with the tomato, sliced shallots, garlic, thyme sprig, white wine, vinegar, and tomato paste. Bring to a simmer over medium-low heat and reduce, stirring occasionally until almost dry. Transfer the cooked mixture to a food mill and puree into a large bowl.

3. Wipe out the saucepan and return the puree to the pan. Add the reduced fish stock, bring to a simmer, and cook until the puree is thickened and reduced to about 1 cup. Transfer the puree to a large bowl and make the vinaigrette by whisking in ¼ cup of the extra-virgin olive oil, ¾ teaspoon of salt and ⅛ teaspoon of pepper.

4. Heat the remaining 1 tablespoon of olive oil in a small skillet over medium heat. Add the minced shallot, diced red and yellow peppers, thyme leaves, ½ teaspoon of salt, and ⅛ teaspoon of pepper. Cook, stirring, just until the vegetables become slightly tender, 1 to 2 minutes. Add the mixture to the bowl with the red pepper vinaigrette. Set aside.

5. Preheat the oven to 450 degrees F.

6. To prepare the fish, process the panko in a food processor until it is quite fine. Transfer the bread crumbs to a bowl, and stir in the Parmigiano, ½ teaspoon of salt, ⅛ teaspoon of pepper, and the melted butter.

7. Sprinkle the fillets all over with 1 teaspoon of salt and ¼ teaspoon of pepper. In an ovenproof skillet large enough to hold the fillets in one layer, heat the olive oil over medium-high heat. Add the fillets, skinned sides up, and cook until golden brown, about 3 minutes. Remove from the heat, turn over the fillets, and generously coat the browned sides with the cheese and bread-crumb mixture, pressing the breading onto the fish. Place the skillet in the oven and bake until the fish is cooked through and the breading is golden brown, about 5 minutes. (If the breading hasn't browned sufficiently, place under the broiler for 1 to 2 minutes.) While the fish cooks, gently reheat the vinaigrette; do not let it boil. Transfer the fish to a platter or individual plates, spoon the warm vinaigrette around the fish, and serve.

Halibut Confit

SERVES 4

Poaching halibut in a deep bath of olive oil imbues a rich, Mediterranean flavor to the firm-fleshed white fish, which is perfectly complemented by a quick sauce made from ripe, peak-of-the-season tomatoes. You'll have a lot of olive oil left over after you "confit" the halibut. To use it again, either for this recipe or for deep-frying calamari or other fish, allow the oil to cool, strain, and refrigerate in a tightly covered bottle for up to 2 weeks. As you cook the halibut, keep in mind that you are poaching, not deep-frying, and that the fish should be very gently simmering in the olive oil. Serve with sautéed zucchini or green beans.

¼ cup olive oil
½ cup thinly sliced spring onions (white bulbs and
    green tops) or scallions

Wine Suggestions:
These flavors suggest a Provençal-style wine like Bandol rosé, St. Joseph blanc, or Condrieu. From California, go with a well-made rosé, Sonoma chardonnay, or marsanne.

2 garlic cloves, minced

2 pounds ripe, fresh tomatoes, peeled, seeded, and
    chopped (3 cups)

2 teaspoons coarse sea salt

¼ teaspoon freshly ground black pepper

1½ teaspoons red wine vinegar

¼ cup sliced fresh basil leaves

4 cups extra-virgin olive oil

4 (6-ounce) skinless halibut fillets

Kosher salt

Freshly ground black pepper

1. Heat the ¼ cup oil over medium heat in a 3-quart nonreactive saucepan. Add the spring onions and cook, stirring occasionally, until softened, but not browned, about 2 minutes. Add the garlic and continue cooking for an additional 2 minutes. Add the tomatoes and cook, stirring occasionally, until juicy, 2 to 3 minutes. Stir in the salt, pepper, vinegar, and basil. Simmer for 30 seconds, remove from the heat, and set aside.

2. Pour the 4 cups of olive oil into a pot large enough to hold the halibut fillets in one layer and deep enough so that the oil comes to no more than one-third the way up its sides. Set the pot on the heat, turned to its very lowest setting, and heat the oil to 180 to 190 degrees F on a deep-fat thermometer. Season the halibut with kosher salt to taste on both sides, and sprinkle with pepper on just the underside. Using a spatula, carefully slide the fish into the oil and poach until the halibut is just cooked through, 8 to 9 minutes. Remove from the oil with the spatula, and drain on paper towels.

3. Return the tomato sauce to a simmer. Divide the sauce among 4 deep plates or large bowls. Set the halibut fillets on top of the sauce and serve hot.

Red Snapper with Cognac Sauce

SERVES 4

The simply sautéed red snapper is served with an elegantly assertive French-style sauce made with cognac, pepper, sherry, and cream. This recipe produces a deliciously round and balanced sauce using just chicken stock as the foundation. For added depth of flavor, another option is to make the sauce as we do at the restaurant. Just after cooking the shallots in step 1, toss in a chopped and rinsed fish frame, which will cook along with the other ingredients and bring more intensity to the sauce.

COGNAC SAUCE

1½ tablespoons butter
½ cup sliced shallots
2 garlic cloves, sliced
1 bay leaf
¼ teaspoon whole black peppercorns
½ teaspoon fresh thyme leaves, stems reserved
¼ cup chopped fresh parsley
2 tablespoons dry sherry
2 tablespoons Cognac
2 cups Chicken Stock (page 315)
2 cups heavy cream
1 tablespoon Dijon mustard
1¼ teaspoons kosher salt
⅛ teaspoon freshly ground black pepper
2 teaspoons fresh lemon juice

SNAPPER

2 tablespoons olive oil
4 (6-ounce) red snapper fillets
Kosher salt
Freshly ground black pepper

Wine Suggestions:
The sauce would be nicely complemented with a white Rhône, such as Châteauneuf-du-Pape or Hermitage Blanc. You would also be pleased with a California marsanne, roussanne, or viognier.

SECOND HELPINGS FROM UNION SQUARE CAFE

1. Make the sauce: Melt the butter in a 2-quart saucepan over medium heat. Add the shallots, garlic, bay leaf, peppercorns, thyme stems, and parsley, and cook, stirring occasionally, until the shallots are tender, but not browned, 4 to 5 minutes. Add the sherry and Cognac and reduce until almost dry. Pour in the stock and reduce by three-quarters. Stir in the cream and reduce until the sauce coats the back of a spoon and measures about 2 cups. Whisk in the mustard; then pass the sauce through a fine-mesh strainer. Season with the salt and pepper, thyme leaves, and 1 to 2 teaspoons lemon juice. Cover the sauce and set aside.

2. Heat the oil for the snapper in a 12-inch skillet over high heat. Season the fish on both sides with salt and pepper and sauté, skin side down, for 4 to 5 minutes, pressing the fish occasionally with a spatula to brown the skin evenly. Turn the fish over with a spatula and cook for an additional 1 to 2 minutes.

3. While the fish is cooking, return the sauce to a gentle simmer. Transfer the cooked fillets to a serving platter, spoon over the sauce, and serve.

Monkfish Scarpariello

SERVES 4

This is Union Square Cafe's variation on *pollo scarpariello* (chicken "shoemaker's style"), long a fixture on the menus of New York's Neapolitan Italian restaurants. In our recipe we've exchanged the more traditional chicken for monkfish, but have retained the tangle of sweet peppers, fennel sausage, and mushrooms. Monkfish is a lean, meaty fish that works particularly well here since it can withstand a good sauté without toughening in texture. A big bowl of steamed broccoli or sautéed broccoli rabe, and a platter of Italian Fries (249) would make terrific accompaniments.

1 small red bell pepper

1 small yellow bell pepper

¼ cup olive oil

8 pieces monkfish, 1½ to 2 inches thick, cut across the bone and trimmed of all dark skin (about 2 pounds total weight)

Kosher salt

Freshly ground black pepper

6 ounces fresh sweet fennel sausage, cut on the diagonal into 16 thin slices

2 cups cleaned and thinly sliced white or cremini mushrooms

1 tablespoon plus 1 teaspoon all-purpose flour

1 tablespoon plus 1 teaspoon red wine vinegar (preferably Italian)

1½ cups Chicken Stock (page 315)

½ cup Basic Tomato Sauce (page 318) or good-quality store-bought sauce

1 heaping tablespoon chopped fresh parsley

Wine Suggestions:

Though a nice, crisp white would work, here's a good spot to break a rule and choose red wine with fish. If you're so inclined, try a Barbera d'Alba, Dolcetto d'Alba, or a Chianti Classico—any of which would lend a note of rich juiciness to the dish.

1. Roast and slice the peppers: spear the peppers with a kitchen fork or skewer and hold them over an open flame until charred all over. Place the charred peppers in a paper bag or in a covered container until they are cool enough to handle. (This step facilitates removing the skin.) Rub off the skins (never run them under water, which washes away the flavorful oils), cut the peppers in half lengthwise, and discard the stems and seeds. Cut the pepper halves into ¼-inch-wide strips and set aside.

2. Heat the oil in a large skillet over medium-high heat. Sprinkle the monkfish with 1½ teaspoons of salt and ½ teaspoon of pepper and cook until lightly browned, about 2 minutes on each side. Transfer the fish to a plate and reserve.

3. Add the sausage to the skillet and cook until browned on both sides, about 2 minutes. (Reduce the heat as needed to keep the skillet from burning.) Toss in the mushrooms and cook along with the sausage, stirring until softened, about 2 minutes. Add the peppers and stir in the flour. Cook for 1 minute, stir in the vinegar, stock, and tomato sauce and bring to a simmer, scraping the bottom of the pan to deglaze. Season with ½ teaspoon of salt and a pinch of pepper.

4. Return the fish to the skillet along with any juices that have accumulated on the plate. Cover the skillet and simmer gently, basting the fish occasionally, until it is just cooked through, 8 to 10 minutes. Transfer the monkfish to a warm serving platter. Return the skillet to the heat and reduce the liquid until it thickens to a sauce consistency, about 1 to 2 minutes. Taste and adjust the seasoning. Spoon the sauce, mushrooms, peppers, and sausage over the fish, sprinkle with the chopped parsley, and serve immediately.

Sautéed Shrimp Goan Style

SERVES 4

Practically all the work for this dish takes place long before you flash-sauté the shrimp. During its 2 hours of contact, the spice paste lends loads of complex sweet-hot flavor, which gets absorbed by the shrimp. The paste would also work beautifully as a dry marinade for chicken, spareribs, or pork chops, which can then be seared or grilled. Make sure to serve this with Basmati Rice Pilaf (page 236), and a simple steamed vegetable like broccoli, string beans, or cauliflower.

½ teaspoon whole cloves
¼ teaspoon whole black peppercorns
1 small cinnamon stick
2 teaspoons cumin seeds
3 to 4 small, dried Thai chilies
⅓ cup garlic cloves, roughly chopped
2 inches fresh ginger, peeled and roughly chopped
⅓ cup Champagne or white wine vinegar
1½ tablespoons brown sugar
1½ pounds medium shrimp, shelled and deveined
2 tablespoons vegetable oil
½ teaspoon kosher salt

1. In a spice grinder, grind the cloves, peppercorns, cinnamon, cumin, and chilies to a fine powder and set aside.

2. Mince the garlic and ginger in a small electric chopper or blender. Add the vinegar and process to a puree. Add the reserved spices and the sugar and process to a smooth paste.

Wine Suggestions:
The spices call out for a wine that is generously fruity and relatively low in alcohol and high in fruit. Try a German or Alsatian riesling, or Vouvray. Champagne or an ice-cold beer is also good!

SECOND HELPINGS FROM UNION SQUARE CAFE

3. Combine the shrimp and the spice paste in a large bowl, stirring to coat the shrimp evenly. Cover and refrigerate for 2 hours.

4. Wipe the excess spice paste off each shrimp with the dull edge of a butter knife. Heat the oil in a large skillet over high heat until very hot. Season the shrimp with the salt. Add half of the shrimp to the pan and cook for 1 minute. Turn the shrimp with tongs and continue cooking until the shrimp are almost cooked through, but are still translucent in the center, 30 seconds to 1 minute longer. Transfer to a serving plate and cover with foil. Add the remaining shrimp to the pan and cook in the same way. Serve immediately.

Sea Scallops with Citrus-Yogurt Marinade

SERVES 6

Pristinely fresh, sweet sea scallops are a treat marinated, as they are here, with tangy yogurt, citrus, and Indian spices. The marinade is a snap to put together, and also works quite well with such white fish as halibut, snapper, and bass. Good accompaniments for the scallops would be Spiced Creamed Spinach (page 216) or Basmati Rice Pilaf (page 236). For a real treat, use the leftover marinade as part of the liquid for cooking rice.

MARINADE

¼ cup packed fresh cilantro leaves

2 tablespoons fresh lemon juice

¼ cup fresh lime juice

2 jalapeño peppers, stemmed, seeded, and coarsely
    chopped, plus the seeds from 1 pepper

½ teaspoon Aleppo pepper

½ teaspoon ground cumin

½ teaspoon ground coriander

½ teaspoon turmeric

2 tablespoons mustard oil or vegetable oil

2 garlic cloves, sliced

½ cup plain, whole-milk yogurt

SCALLOPS

24 large sea scallops (about 2¼ pounds)

Kosher salt and freshly ground black pepper

3 tablespoons vegetable oil

Wine Suggestions:

Try a good Alsatian white like riesling, gewürztraminer or tokay pinot gris, or a brightly flavored sauvignon blanc from New Zealand, South Africa, or California.

1. Combine all of the marinade ingredients except the yogurt in the bowl of a food processor and pulse until coarsely chopped. Add the yogurt and process to combine.

2. Place the scallops in a nonreactive bowl or baking dish, pour the marinade over the scallops, and refrigerate for 3 to 4 hours.

3. With a paper towel, wipe the excess marinade from the scallops and sprinkle them with salt and black pepper. Heat the vegetable oil over medium heat in a skillet large enough to hold at least half the scallops in one layer. Place half the scallops in the pan and sauté until golden brown, 3 to 5 minutes. Using kitchen tongs, turn over the scallops and sauté for an additional minute. The scallops should be lightly browned and somewhat firm to the touch. Transfer the cooked scallops to a plate and cover with foil to keep warm. Sauté the second batch of the scallops, adding more oil if necessary. Serve hot.

Soft-Shell Crabs with Tomato Nage

SERVES 4

Local tomatoes and basil arrive at the market toward the end of soft-shell crab season, and the three are wonderful together. Make sure to use the cleaned fresh crabs the day you buy them. The tomato nage is also excellent with sautéed red snapper or sea bass. At the restaurant we accompany the crabs with a colorful medley of sautéed yellow and green zucchini, oyster mushrooms, and roasted onions.

TOMATO NAGE

2 pounds ripe tomatoes, cored and coarsely chopped

4½ tablespoons cold butter

¼ cup sliced shallots

1 tablespoon sliced garlic

3 fresh parsley sprigs, coarsely chopped

3 fresh basil sprigs, coarsely chopped, plus 1 tablespoon sliced basil leaves

2 tablespoons heavy cream

SOFT-SHELL CRABS

⅓ cup all-purpose flour

½ teaspoon kosher salt

⅛ teaspoon freshly ground black pepper

8 medium soft-shell crabs, cleaned

⅓ cup olive oil

1. Puree the tomatoes in a food processor and set aside.

2. Melt 1½ tablespoons of the butter in a 2-quart saucepan over low heat. Add the shallot and garlic and cook until softened, but not colored, about 3 minutes. Add the parsley and basil sprigs and

Wine Suggestions:
Here's a good spot for a chenin blanc like Savennières or Vouvray, or even Champagne or Chablis, whose minerally flavors pair well with the crab.

SECOND HELPINGS FROM UNION SQUARE CAFE

continue cooking for 1 minute. Add the reserved tomato puree and bring to a boil. Reduce the heat and simmer gently for 10 to 15 minutes. You will have about 1⅓ cups of sauce. Strain the sauce into a bowl. Rinse out the pan, and return the strained puree to the clean pan. Bring the sauce to a simmer over medium heat. Whisk in the cream, and then the remaining 3 tablespoons of butter, cut into bits. Stir in the sliced basil and set the nage aside.

3. Preheat the oven to 200 degrees F.

4. To prepare the crabs, combine the flour, salt, and pepper on large plate. Dredge the crabs in the seasoned flour, shaking off the excess. Transfer to another plate.

5. Heat the olive oil in a 10-inch skillet over medium-high heat until it just begins to smoke. Sauté the crabs, 4 at a time, shell sides down, in one layer until the shells turn a reddish brown color, 3 to 4 minutes. Use tongs to turn the crabs and cook for an additional 3 to 4 minutes. Drain on a plate lined with paper towels and keep warm in the oven. Repeat with the remaining crabs.

6. To serve, warm the sauce over medium heat. Ladle the sauce into 4 deep plates or shallow dinner bowls. Arrange 2 crabs on each plate, and serve immediately.

Grilled Lobster
with Bruschetta Sauce

Serves 4

We first put together this simple recipe during the heart of tomato season, when we go through crates and crates of ripe, sweet greenmarket tomatoes to make the topping for USC's Bruschetta Rossa—garlic-rubbed toast topped with tomatoes, basil, and olive oil. The bruschetta topping tastes good with almost anything (if you're brave enough to try it with scrambled eggs), but the addition of lemon zest, tarragon, and chives make it a perfect condiment for grilled lobsters—and a terrific dish for easygoing summer entertaining. Serve extra sauce on the side, and make sure to have plenty of bibs and lobster crackers on hand for enjoying the claw meat. Serve with Roasted Asparagus (page 202) and steamed corn on the cob.

4 (1½-pound) live lobsters

3 large ripe tomatoes, cored

Kosher salt

¼ teaspoon freshly ground black pepper

¼ cup extra-virgin olive oil

2 garlic cloves, peeled and split lengthwise

¼ cup firmly packed fresh basil leaves, washed, dried, and sliced

1 tablespoon chopped fresh parsley

¾ teaspoon chopped fresh tarragon

2 teaspoons chopped fresh chives

¾ teaspoon finely grated lemon zest

Wine Suggestions:
It would be hard to go wrong with any chilled, vibrant white, and a fresh sauvignon blanc from California, New Zealand, or Italy would work quite well.

1. Bring a large pot of water to a boil. Working in batches if necessary, plunge the lobsters into the water, cover immediately, and cook for 2 minutes. Using kitchen tongs, transfer the parboiled lobsters to a colander and let cool. Set aside the pot with the lobster water.

2. Prepare a bowl of ice water large enough to hold the tomatoes. Return the lobster water to a boil, add the tomatoes, and cook for 30 seconds. Remove the tomatoes with a slotted spoon and immediately immerse them in the bowl of ice water. When the tomatoes are cool, peel and halve them crosswise. Use your fingers or a teaspoon to scoop out and discard the seeds. Flatten the tomato halves on a cutting board with the heel of your hand and chop the tomatoes into ½-inch dice. Scrape the tomatoes into a large bowl and add 1 teaspoon of salt, the pepper, oil, garlic, fresh herbs, and lemon zest; stir well to combine. Set the sauce aside.

3. Preheat a charcoal or gas grill to high.

4. Place the cooled lobsters, belly down, on a cutting board and, using a large chef's knife, split them in half lengthwise. Remove the small gritty sack from each head and discard. Baste the lobster tail meat with a few spoonfuls of the oil from the reserved tomato sauce, sprinkle the meat with 1 teaspoon of salt and place the lobsters on the grill, shell sides down. Close the grill, or place a cover over the lobsters, and grill until the lobster tails are cooked through, about 5 minutes. The cooked lobster meat will appear white throughout and feel somewhat firm to the touch. Arrange the cooked lobsters, shell sides down, on a large serving platter or individual plates. Remove the split garlic cloves from the sauce, spoon the sauce over the tails, and serve.

Roasted Lobster with Corn and Chanterelles

SERVES 4

Roasting lobster is traditionally a restaurant technique, but it's one you can easily do at home. The hot oven and olive oil sear the meat, imparting a smoky, almost nutty flavor. We nap the lobster with a decadent sauce made from bourbon, sweet corn, and chanterelles. It makes a wonderful dinner toward the end of summer, when the ingredients are at their best and the slightest chill in the air restores your appetite for something rich.

4 (1½-pound) live lobsters
¼ cup olive oil
3 cups Fish Stock (page 316)
6 tablespoons butter
⅓ cup finely chopped shallots
¼ teaspoon Aleppo pepper
1 pound chanterelle mushrooms, stems trimmed,
    washed, dried, and split lengthwise
Freshly ground black pepper
1½ cups corn kernels (from about 2 ears of corn)
Kosher salt
2 tablespoons bourbon
¼ cup white wine
2 teaspoons chopped fresh tarragon

1. Preheat the oven to 400 degrees F.

2. Place a lobster, belly side down, on a cutting board and hold it firmly at its midsection. Place the point of a large kitchen knife about midway down the head of the lobster at the point where the head and body meet, with the blade side facing toward the

Wine Suggestions:
Here's an opportunity to bring out a buttery California chardonnay, a crisp, minerally Chablis, or even a Savennières from the Loire Valley.

head. With one deliberate motion, pierce downward and then slice forward with the knife, splitting the top portion of the lobster's head and killing it instantly. Then split the lobster completely in half lengthwise. Separate the 2 tail sections from the body and remove the claws. Remove the gritty dirt sack from the head, and split the head and body in half again, crosswise (to create 4 pieces). Reserve the head and body separately from the tail and claws. Repeat with the remaining lobsters.

3. Heat 2 tablespoons oil in a soup pot over high heat. Add the lobster heads and cook, stirring, until they turn red, 3 to 4 minutes. Pour in the fish stock, bring to a boil, reduce the heat, cover, and simmer gently for 20 minutes. Remove from the heat and reserve.

4. While the lobster heads cook, pour the remaining 2 tablespoons oil into a 12-inch, ovenproof skillet. Place the skillet over high heat, and bring the oil to the smoking point. Add the lobster claws, place in the oven, and roast for 15 minutes. Transfer the cooked claws to a plate. Add the split tails to the skillet, shell sides down, and roast until just cooked, 8 to 10 minutes. Transfer to the plate with the claws and set aside.

5. Pour off the oil from the skillet, add 2 tablespoons butter, and melt over medium-high heat. Add the shallots and Aleppo pepper and cook for 30 seconds, stirring. Stir in the chanterelles and ⅛ teaspoon black pepper, cook until the chanterelles are softened but not browned, about 3 minutes. Add the corn, 1 teaspoon salt, and the bourbon, and reduce until dry. Add the wine and reduce until almost dry. Strain the lobster broth into the pan, raise the heat, and boil until reduced and syrupy, 4 to 5 minutes. Add the tarragon and swirl in the remaining 4 tablespoons butter, ¼ teaspoon salt, and ⅛ teaspoon black pepper. Remove from the heat.

6. Shell the lobster meat. Add the lobster pieces to the skillet with the sauce, along with any juices that have accumulated on the plate, and heat over medium heat just until the lobster is warmed through. Arrange 2 pieces of the tail meat and 2 claws on each of 4 dinner plates, and top with the sauce, mushrooms, and corn. Serve immediately.

Indian "Bouillabaisse"

SERVES 8

This is Michael's adaptation of a fragrant fish curry he once savored in India. Adding a few ingredients and juggling the proportions of stock, he transformed it into a wonderful twist on bouillabaisse that's well worth the effort to make at home. Don't be put off by the long list of spices; they are available at a good supermarket, specialty store, or through mail order. You can equip your kitchen for cooking with Indian flavors with a very small investment. When they're in season, we substitute bay scallops for half the shrimp. As a nice accent, garnish the bouillabaisse with a dollop of whole-milk yogurt, seasoned with salt, pepper, and a squeeze of pressed garlic.

2 tablespoons olive oil

40 medium shrimp, shelled, deveined, and split, and
    shells reserved

2 quarts Fish Stock (page 316)

1 tablespoon plus 1 teaspoon chopped fresh gingerroot

4 garlic cloves, chopped

1 teaspoon ground turmeric

1 tablespoon plus 1 teaspoon mustard powder

Pinch of saffron

1 tablespoon finely ground coriander seeds

1½ teaspoons finely ground cumin seeds

2 teaspoons finely ground Aleppo pepper

¼ cup mustard oil

¼ cup vegetable oil

2 cinnamon sticks

6 cloves

20 cardamom pods

½ teaspoon fenugreek seeds

2 jalapeño peppers, finely chopped, with seeds

4 medium onions, quartered and thinly sliced

Wine Suggestions:

Serve a fresh, fruity rosé, Champagne, or a German riesling with the bouillabaisse.

Coarse sea salt

Freshly ground black pepper

8 tomatoes (about 3 pounds), peeled, seeded, and chopped

1 teaspoon light brown sugar

2 tablespoons fresh lemon juice

8 (4-ounce) pieces striped bass or monkfish fillet

2 dozen mussels, debearded and scrubbed

1. Heat the olive oil to the smoking point in a large saucepan over medium-high heat. Add the reserved shrimp shells and cook, stirring, until the shells turn pink. Pour in the fish stock, bring to a simmer, lower the heat, cover, and cook for 20 minutes. Strain the stock and discard the shells.

2. While the stock is simmering, combine the ginger, garlic, turmeric, mustard powder, saffron, ground coriander, cumin, and Aleppo pepper in a small bowl. Stir in just enough water to make a thick paste and set aside.

3. Heat the mustard oil in a 4-quart saucepan over high heat until smoking to temper its pungency. *Be careful not to breathe in the fumes while the oil heats.* Turn off the heat and add the vegetable oil to the pot. When the mustard oil is no longer smoking, add the cinnamon, cloves, and cardamom. Cook over medium heat until the spices begin to toast lightly. Stir in the fenugreek and jalapeño and cook for 30 seconds. Add the onions and cook, stirring occasionally, until their liquid evaporates and they begin to brown, 10 to 15 minutes. Season with 2 teaspoons of salt and ¼ teaspoon black pepper.

4. Create a space in the center of the onion mixture, allowing some of the oil to fill the opening. Stir the spice paste from the small bowl into the oil and cook for 1 minute, until the water has evaporated from the paste. Stir the spices into the onions, reduce the heat to medium-low and cook, stirring often, for 15 minutes. Add the tomatoes and continue

to cook for an additional 5 minutes. Pour in the reserved shrimp stock, bring to a boil, reduce the heat, cover, and simmer gently for 10 minutes. Stir in the sugar, lemon, and 2½ teaspoons of salt.

5. Sprinkle the fish fillets with 2 teaspoons of salt, add the fish to the soup, cover, and cook very gently for 3 minutes. (The soup should barely simmer.) Add the mussels and the shrimp, cover, and cook until the mussels are open and the shrimp are just cooked through, about 5 minutes more.

6. Divide the fish and seafood evenly among 8 soup bowls. Ladle the hot soup over the fish and serve.

Salt-Baked Chicken

SERVES 4

You might get some amused looks from the checkout clerk when you go to the grocery store to buy two boxes of kosher salt for this recipe, but your guests will gaze at you with appreciative amazement when they see and taste the finished product. In fact, you'll want to make sure to present the bird "en croûte" before carving it. Unlike standard roast chicken, you're not aiming for a crusty, brown skin—and in fact, this chicken is actually served without its skin. The salt-baking will turn out the moistest and tastiest chicken you can imagine, and it's a perfect foil for a decadently rich sauce of morels. The recipe can be successfully modified for a slightly smaller 3½-pound bird by using 1½ boxes of salt mixed with 6 egg whites, and cooking the chicken for 1 hour and 10 minutes.

SALT-BAKED CHICKEN

1 (4½-pound) chicken

2 (3-pound) boxes kosher salt

8 egg whites, whipped until frothy

MOREL SAUCE

1 heaping cup dried morel mushrooms (1½ to 2 ounces)

1½ cups boiling water

3 tablespoons butter

1¼ cups thinly sliced shallots

1 bay leaf

1 tablespoon chopped fresh parsley, stems reserved

2 branches fresh thyme

12 peppercorns

½ cup white wine

1 cup Chicken Stock (page 315)

2 cups heavy cream

¾ teaspoon kosher salt

¼ teaspoon freshly ground black pepper

Wine Suggestions:

This recipe shouts for French wine, and given the drama of the presentation, you may as well bring out something special. For white, go with a Meursault, St. Aubin, or Chassagne-Montrachet. Red-wise, we recommend Côte Rôtie, Hermitage, or any good wine from Burgundy's Côte de Beaune.

1. Preheat the oven to 400 degrees F.

2. Truss the chicken, tying its legs together tightly with kitchen twine. Empty the boxes of salt into a large bowl. Add the whipped egg whites and stir with a rubber scraper until all of the salt is damp.

3. In the bottom of a deep roasting pan, preferably just large enough to hold the chicken, spread a 1-inch-thick layer of the salt mixture. Set the chicken on top and heap the remaining salt over the chicken until it is completely covered. Use your hands to pack the salt tightly over the chicken, hermetically sealing the bird. Place the pan in the oven and roast the chicken for 1 hour and 25 minutes. Remove from the oven and let stand for 30 minutes.

4. While the chicken cooks, make the sauce: Place the dried morels in a bowl, pour in the boiling water and soak until the mushrooms have softened, about 10 minutes. Transfer the morels to a cutting board with a slotted spoon, split them lengthwise, and return to their liquid to soak for 10 more minutes. Lift the mushrooms out of the liquid once again, transfer to a bowl, and set aside. Strain the liquid through a coffee filter and into a bowl to remove any grit and dirt. Reserve ½ cup of the liquid and discard the rest. Squeeze the mushrooms with your hands until all the liquid has been wrung out.

5. In a 2-quart nonreactive saucepan, melt 1½ tablespoons of the butter over medium heat. Add 1 cup of the shallots, the bay leaf, parsley stems, thyme, and peppercorns. Cook until the shallots are wilted but not browned, about 2 minutes. Add the wine and the reserved mushroom liquid. Cook until the liquid is almost dry. Add the chicken stock and reduce to one-quarter of its original volume. Add the cream and boil, reducing the sauce until it coats the back of a spoon. Remove from the heat, strain into a saucepan, cover, and set aside.

6. Finely chop the remaining ¼ cup of shallots. Melt the remaining 1½

tablespoons of butter in a small skillet over medium-low heat. Add the remaining ¼ cup of shallots and the mushrooms and cook, stirring often, until tender, about 2 minutes. Scrape the mixture into the pan with the sauce, cover, and reserve.

7. Using the point of a dull knife, poke a hole in the salt toward the top of the chicken and then break away the salt in chunks until you can remove the chicken. Carefully remove the skin and any salt clinging to the chicken. Carve the chicken into serving pieces, and arrange on a serving platter.

8. Return the sauce to the stove and simmer over low heat for 2 minutes. Season with salt and pepper and stir in the chopped parsley.

9. Spoon the sauce and mushrooms over the chicken and serve immediately.

Chicken Lambrusco

SERVES 4

This recipe was inspired by a sensational dish we've enjoyed on more than one occasion at Osteria di Rubbiara, in the tiny Emilia-Romagna commune of Nonantola, between Modena and Bologna, in central Italy. The chicken spends the night marinating with vegetables and herbs in a light, fruity red wine, and is then sautéed with pancetta and the marinade vegetables. The result is a juicy, winy-tasting meat that works well with buttered noodles, a frisée salad, or even a caramelized onion frittata. This dish depends on the natural sweetness of Lambrusco wine. Believe it or not, even a simple, screw-top Lambrusco will do the trick in this recipe. You could substitute a drier light red like Beaujolais or Dolcetto d'Alba, and add a teaspoon of sugar to the marinade.

3 cups sliced onion

2 celery stalks, sliced

2 carrots, scrubbed and sliced

2 garlic cloves, sliced

2 sprigs fresh sage

1 sprig fresh basil

3 sprigs fresh parsley

2 bay leaves

1 bottle Lambrusco wine (or Beaujolais or Dolcetto d'Alba)

1 4- to 4½-pound chicken, cut into 10 pieces (thighs, drumsticks, wings, and split breast)

2 tablespoons vegetable oil

Kosher salt

Freshly ground black pepper

½ cup chopped pancetta

1 tomato, cored and chopped

1 cup brown Chicken Stock (see headnote to the recipe, page 315), or Veal Stock (page 316), or store-bought veal stock (or demi-glace)

Wine Suggestions:

The perfect accompaniment here would be a top-quality Lambrusco from Emilia-Romagna, which will be a revelation to most people unfamiliar with this wine. Fruity and lightly effervescent, it is typically served with a slight chill. The Piedmont produces a similar wine, Brachetto, which will also go well with the chicken. If you can't find a well-made Lambrusco or Brachetto, try a good *cru* Beaujolais or a fruity pinot noir.

1. Combine the onion, celery, carrots, garlic, herbs, and wine in a bowl large enough to hold all of the chicken. Add the chicken, cover, and marinate overnight in the refrigerator.

2. Remove the chicken from the marinade and pat dry with paper towels. Place a colander over a bowl, drain the vegetables, and reserve the vegetables and the marinade separately.

3. Place an 11-inch skillet over high heat, add the oil, and heat until smoking. Sprinkle the chicken with 1 teaspoon of salt and ¼ teaspoon of pepper and sauté until the skin is browned and the fat rendered, about 10 minutes. Transfer the chicken to a serving platter.

4. Pour off half of the fat from the skillet. Turn the heat to low, add the pancetta, and cook, stirring, until the fat is rendered, about 3 minutes. Add the vegetables and herbs from the marinade, turn the heat to high, and sauté until the vegetables are lightly browned, about 10 minutes. Return the chicken to the skillet along with any juices that have accumulated on the platter. Add the reserved marinade, the tomato, and the stock. Cover and simmer until the breast meat is cooked through, 10 to 15 minutes. Transfer the breast meat to a platter and cover with aluminum foil to keep warm. Continue cooking the dark meat for an additional 20 to 25 minutes. Transfer the dark meat to the platter and cover.

5. Strain the cooking liquid into a 2-quart saucepan, pressing with a ladle to extract all of the juices from the vegetables. Bring to a boil and cook until the sauce has thickened and reduced to about ¾ cup. Season with ¼ teaspoon of salt and ⅛ teaspoon of pepper. Return the chicken to the pan, and lower the temperature to a simmer to heat through. Transfer the chicken to a serving platter, pour the sauce over the chicken, and serve.

Chicken Saltimbocca

SERVES 4

This is a variation of the Roman classic, in which chicken is substituted for the more traditional veal cutlets. Our recipe also differs from the one you'd find in Rome since we coat the cutlets with a delicious cheese-flour-and-egg batter—much in the style of chicken *francese*. We serve the Chicken Saltimbocca with a generous portion of sautéed spinach, and if you're in the mood for potatoes, here's a great time to bring out the Italian Fries (page 249).

1¾ pounds boneless, skinless chicken breasts, cut and
       pounded into 12 thin cutlets
12 large fresh sage leaves
6 paper-thin slices of prosciutto, cut in half crosswise
¼ cup grated Pecorino Romano
⅓ cup all-purpose flour
3 large eggs
½ cup plus 1 tablespoon extra-virgin olive oil
Kosher salt and freshly ground black pepper
2 lemons, halved

1. Top each chicken cutlet with 1 sage leaf and cover with a half slice of prosciutto. Lightly press the prosciutto to adhere it to the chicken.

2. In a shallow mixing bowl, stir together the cheese and flour and set aside.

3. Use a fork to beat the eggs with 1 tablespoon of the olive oil in a small bowl.

4. Preheat the oven to 200 degrees F.

Wine Suggestions:
Enjoy with an Italian white from Campania or Sicily, or with an expressive red like Vino Nobile di Montepulciano, Sangiovese di Romagna, Rosso di Montalcino, or Barbera d'Alba.

5. Sprinkle the cutlets lightly on both sides with salt and pepper.

6. Heat the remaining ½ cup of olive oil in a medium or large heavy-bottomed skillet until almost smoking. Dredge 3 or 4 chicken cutlets in the flour mixture (depending on how many will fit in the pan), pressing the mixture well into the cutlets to completely coat. Dip each floured cutlet into the egg mixture, lift out with your fingers, and allow the excess egg to drip off. Immediately place in the hot pan. Sauté until golden brown on both sides, 1 to 2 minutes per side. Transfer the cooked cutlets to a plate lined with paper towels, and keep warm in the oven.

7. Place 3 cutlets on each of 4 plates and serve immediately, garnished with lemon halves.

Note: If you choose to prepare your own cutlets, here's how to do it: From each boneless, skinless chicken breast, detach the tenderloin and set aside. Use a sharp knife to split the breast in half crosswise, set aside the thinner, triangular end, and then split the thicker piece in half as if you were opening a book. You will now have 4 pieces of chicken per breast. Place each piece of chicken between 2 sheets of plastic wrap and use a meat mallet or the bottom of a small, heavy skillet to carefully pound the chicken into very thin cutlets. A good tip to facilitate pounding the cutlets evenly: sprinkle the top of each piece with a few drops of water before covering with plastic.

Pan-Roasted Chicken
with Cognac-Peppercorn Sauce

SERVES 4

The cooking method for this wonderful dish is a good example of a true French sauté. Here, the chicken and aromatic elements are cooked through before the sauce is prepared at the end. The presentation is rustic, with all the herbs and spices left in the sauce. Accompany the chicken with broccoli and Italian Fries (page 249).

1 (4 to 4½-pound) chicken, cut into 10 pieces
    (drumsticks, thighs, wings, and split breast)
1½ teaspoons kosher salt
¼ teaspoon freshly ground black pepper
2 tablespoons vegetable oil
⅓ cup thinly sliced garlic
4 sprigs fresh thyme, coarsely chopped
6 bay leaves
20 whole peppercorns
¼ cup Cognac
¼ cup white wine
1 cup brown Chicken Stock (see headnote to the
    recipe, page 315) or store-bought veal stock
    (or demi-glace)
1 tablespoon Dijon mustard
1½ tablespoons butter

1. Heat the oven to 375 degrees F.

2. Place the chicken pieces in a large bowl. Sprinkle with 1 teaspoon of salt and ¼ teaspoon of pepper and toss to season.

Wine Suggestions:
The assertive flavors would make the chicken work quite well with a spicy and juicy syrah from California, Australia, or the Rhône Valley.

3. Place an 11-inch skillet over high heat, add the oil, and heat until smoking. Add the chicken pieces and brown them on all sides, about 10 minutes. Turn the chicken so the pieces are skin side down, transfer to the oven, and bake until the breast meat is cooked through, 10 to 15 minutes. Remove the pan from the oven, transfer the breast pieces to a serving platter, and cover to keep warm. Add the garlic, thyme, bay leaves, and peppercorns to the skillet, sprinkling them around the remaining pieces of chicken. Return the skillet to the oven and continue baking until the chicken is cooked through, an additional 5 to 10 minutes.

4. Transfer the remaining pieces of chicken to the serving platter and cover. Place the skillet over medium-high heat and cook 1 to 2 minutes to lightly brown the garlic. Pour the fat from the skillet, being careful to leave in the herbs and spices.

5. Away from the open flame, pour the Cognac into the skillet. Return to the heat and reduce until almost dry. Pour in the wine and reduce until almost dry. Add the stock and any juices from the serving platter, bring to a simmer, and reduce until somewhat thickened. Whisk in the mustard and butter and season with ½ teaspoon of salt. Return the chicken to the skillet and warm over low heat. Transfer the chicken, covered with sauce, herbs, and spices, to a warm platter and serve.

Poussin al Mattone

SERVES 2

The Roman *mattone* method of using a brick to press a butterflied chicken into the pan as it cooks is a great way to end up with a bird that has beautifully crisped skin and yet remains perfectly juicy. The trick is to cook the birds with just enough heat to slowly render the fat and crisp the skin in the time it takes to cook the flesh. We use the very young chickens known as poussins, but you will also find that the technique works well with Cornish hens or small roasting chickens. While one or two foil-wrapped bricks will certainly do the weighing-down trick, we've also successfully used a heavy pot. Another unusual but very effective method for cooking 2 poussins at a time is to use a foil-wrapped 10-pound dumbbell plate! Serve the poussin with Mashed Potatoes (page 321), Swiss Chard, Leek, and Celery Tortino (page 228), or Potato–Jerusalem Artichoke Gratin (page 226).

2 (1-pound) poussins, butterflied, backbone removed
½ teaspoon kosher salt
¼ teaspoon freshly ground black pepper
2 tablespoons extra-virgin olive oil
1 lemon, halved

1. Sprinkle the poussins all over with the salt and pepper. Twist and tuck the wing tips behind the breast so that the skin side will lie flat in the pan.

2. Heat the oil in a 12-inch cast-iron or heavy-bottomed skillet over medium heat. When the oil is hot (but well before the smoking point), add the poussins, side by side and skin side down. Place the weight on top so that it is evenly distributed over the surface of the birds.

Wine Suggestions:
Pinot noir, Beaujolais, and sangiovese go beautifully with the crisped chicken.

Cook the poussins until the skin is a deep, golden brown color and very crisp, and the birds are almost cooked through, 15 to 18 minutes. (After a few minutes, remove the weight and check the skin. If it seems to be browning too fast, turn down the heat. Replace the weight and continue cooking.)

3. Remove the weight, turn the birds over, and continue cooking, with the weight, until cooked through, 2 to 3 more minutes. Serve with halved lemons.

Roast Quail

SERVES 4

For years, before semiboneless quail were readily available, few people
bothered to cook them, primarily because they were such trouble to eat.
Now they couldn't be simpler to prepare or to eat, and their succulent
meat offers a delicious change of pace. They're fun to make, and the short
cooking time makes them extremely practical for entertaining. Serve 2 quail
per person, accompanied by creamy polenta, mashed turnips, or Mashed
Potatoes (page 321). For a vegetable, try broccoli rabe, brussels sprouts, or
cabbage. For an elegant first course, serve each guest a single quail, split in
half, atop a simply dressed frisée salad.

8 boned quail, wings trimmed at the second joint
½ teaspoon salt
¼ teaspoon freshly ground black pepper
8 fresh sage leaves
8 slices slab bacon
2 tablespoons vegetable oil

1. Preheat the oven to 425 degrees F.

2. Place the quail on a work surface, breast side up.
    Combine the salt and pepper and season the quail,
    inside and out. Beginning with one quail, tuck the
    legs under the breast, and lay a sage leaf down the
    center of the breast. Wrap a slice of bacon over
    the sage leaf and around the quail so that it covers
    the legs and the ends overlap on the underside of the
    quail. Weave a toothpick through the bacon to secure
    it to the quail. Repeat the process with each of the
    remaining quail.

Wine Suggestions:
Their juicy, bacony flavor
makes the quail perfect
with a syrah-based wine,
like St. Joseph or Crozes-
Hermitage from the northern
Rhône, or shiraz from
Australia or New Zealand.

3. In an ovenproof skillet large enough to hold all the quail, heat the oil over high heat until smoking. Add the quail, breast sides down, and brown for 2 minutes. Turn the quail over and brown 3 more minutes. Transfer the skillet to the oven and roast the quail for 8 minutes. Transfer the quail to a serving platter, let them rest 5 minutes, remove the toothpicks, and serve.

Roast Turkey with Apple-Cider Gravy

SERVES 8 TO 10

Let's face it, the two goals most people have when roasting turkey are to end up with the juiciest and most flavorful bird ever. This recipe does the trick and it may single-handedly become the reason everyone insists on returning to your home for Thanksgiving! Home brining followed by slow, low-temperature roasting is a simple way to guarantee a juicy bird that bursts with flavor. The apple-cider gravy works well with our Apple and Mortadella Stuffing (page 234), but you can use any favorite family dressing you're in the mood for.

BRINE

2 gallons water

2 cups kosher salt

⅓ cup firmly packed brown sugar

1 garlic head, split

1½ tablespoons whole black peppercorns

1½ teaspoons juniper berries

3 bay leaves

1 (10- to 12-pound) turkey

1 small onion, coarsely chopped

1 celery stalk, coarsely chopped

½ apple, cored and coarsely chopped

1 small parsnip, peeled and coarsely chopped

1 small quince, cored and coarsely chopped (optional)

½ cup coarsely chopped fresh parsley with stems

¼ cup chopped fresh sage leaves

2 bay leaves

1 teaspoon whole black peppercorns

½ teaspoon juniper berries

Wine Suggestions:
Turkey is a pretty neutral foil for a wide range of wines. For white, Vouvray is terrific. We love bright, lighter reds like *cru* Beaujolais, pinot noir, or Australian Shiraz but it's hard to imagine that your favorite red wine of any stripe wouldn't go well with this bird.

¼ teaspoon celery seed

3 tablespoons butter, melted

GRAVY

2 tablespoons butter

3 tablespoons all-purpose flour

1½ cups apple cider

2 cups Chicken Stock (page 315)

¼ teaspoon kosher salt

⅛ teaspoon freshly ground pepper

1. In a pot large enough to hold the turkey, combine all of the brine ingredients and stir. Add the turkey to the pot, cover, and refrigerate for 8 to 10 hours. Remove the turkey from the pot, discard the brine, and rinse the turkey thoroughly under cold water. Pat dry.

2. Preheat the oven to 275 degrees F.

3. Combine the onion, celery, apple, parsnip, quince, herbs, and spices in a bowl and toss. Spoon into the cavity of the turkey.

4. Truss the turkey, tying its legs together tightly with kitchen twine. Place the turkey on a roasting rack set in a large roasting pan. Cover tightly with aluminum foil, place in the oven, and roast for 2½ hours.

5. Uncover the turkey and reserve the foil. Increase the oven temperature to 375 degrees F. Brush the turkey with half of the melted butter and cook for 30 minutes. Brush on the remaining butter and continue cooking for about 1 hour and 15 minutes longer, basting every 30 minutes, until a meat thermometer inserted in the thigh registers 150 degrees F. (The internal temperature will rise 10 degrees while the turkey rests).

6. Transfer the turkey to a cutting board. Pour off the fat from the roasting pan. Spoon the vegetables from the cavity of the turkey into the pan; cover the turkey loosely with the reserved foil, and let rest for 30 minutes.

7. Meanwhile, make the gravy: Add the butter to the roasting pan with the vegetables. Place the pan over medium heat, using 2 burners if necessary. Use a wooden spoon to stir and brown the vegetables lightly, 3 to 4 minutes. Add the flour and cook for 3 more minutes, stirring occasionally. Stir in the cider, bring to a boil, and cook until reduced and thickened, 2 to 3 minutes, scraping the bottom of the pan to release the turkey drippings. Transfer the gravy to a 3-quart saucepan, add the chicken stock, and bring to a boil. Reduce the heat and simmer gently, stirring occasionally, until the gravy has thickened, about 10 minutes. Pour any juices that have accumulated around the turkey into the pan and continue cooking for 1 more minute. Season with the salt and pepper. Strain the gravy into a warm sauceboat.

8. Carve the turkey and serve with the gravy.

Roast Goose

SERVES 5 TO 6

When R. W. Apple requested this recipe for a feature article he was writing for the *New York Times* just before Christmas 2000, we had no idea how much enthusiasm it would arouse among food-loving friends everywhere. There wasn't nearly enough stove space at the restaurant to keep up with the demand generated by the article, and we received literally hundreds of requests for reprints of the recipe. Roasting a goose at home is a labor of love: it can be cumbersome and takes some patience. But it's technically a cinch to pull off, and you and your guests will be absolutely

Wine Suggestions:
For white, go with a top-quality Alsatian riesling or Tokay pinot gris. If you're in the mood for red, use a reasonably tannic zinfandel, cabernet sauvignon, or Bordeaux.

delighted with the tender, succulent results. Our trick is to roast the bird "slow and low"—allowing it to self-baste as the layer of fat between the skin and meat renders, and the skin becomes golden and crisp. By all means, save as much of the rendered goose fat as you have room to store. It's the tastiest medium you'll ever use for frying fabulous potatoes (stir in some minced garlic and parsley at the last minute), and is indispensable for making any type of confit. With the goose, we serve Baked Sauerkraut (page 220) and Apple and Mortadella Stuffing (page 234). Another good option is Horseradish-Mashed Potatoes (page 253).

1 10-pound goose
1 small onion, peeled and coarsely chopped
1 stalk celery, coarsely chopped
1 small carrot, washed and coarsely chopped
1 small apple or quince, cored and coarsely chopped
1 bay leaf
8–10 sage leaves, coarsely chopped
½ teaspoon caraway seeds
10 juniper berries, lightly crushed
Freshly ground black pepper
2 teaspoons kosher salt
1 cup apple cider
2 cups chicken broth

1. Cut away the two end joints of each goose wing and set them aside along with the liver and giblets.

2. Combine the onion, celery, carrot, apple, bay leaf, sage, caraway, juniper, some black pepper, and 1½ teaspoons salt in a small bowl. Stuff the cavity of the goose with the seasoned vegetable mixture. Tie the legs together with a piece of kitchen twine. The goose can be prepared to this stage the day before and held, uncovered, in the refrigerator.

3. Preheat the oven to 250 degrees F. Place the stuffed goose breast-side down on a roasting rack in a large, heavy-bottomed roasting pan, cover the pan tightly with aluminum foil, and place in the oven. Allow the goose to cook for 4 hours.

4. Remove the roasting pan from the oven and uncover the goose, reserving the foil. Turn the oven to 350 degrees F. Lift the rack with the goose from the roasting pan, carefully pour off the fat from the pan, strain it, and reserve, refrigerated or frozen. (The fat will keep for a month or so, well covered in the refrigerator, and indefinitely in the freezer. Use it to make goose or duck confit, to fry potato slices, or to sear meat). Replace the goose, still breast-side down on the rack, in the roasting pan, return the pan to the oven, and cook, uncovered, for 1 hour.

5. Remove the pan from the oven and scatter the wings, liver, and giblets around the goose. Turn the goose breast-side up, and continue cooking for an additional hour, or until the skin is crisp and golden brown and the leg begins to come away from the body of the goose when gently tugged.

6. Remove the goose to a platter and cover lightly with the foil. Remove the rack from the pan and pour off any fat, leaving the wings, liver, and giblets in the pan. Uncover the goose, cut the twine holding the legs together, and scoop the vegetables from inside the goose and into the roasting pan. Re-cover the goose on the platter, and place the roasting pan on medium heat over one or two burners on the stove. Cook the vegetables, stirring occasionally, for two minutes. Pour in the apple cider and chicken broth and boil liquid until reduced by half. Season with the remaining salt and some additional black pepper, and strain the sauce.

7. Carve the goose and serve with the sauce.

Michael's Garlic-Lemon Steak

SERVES 4

This straightforward and delicious recipe is Michael's very favorite way to prepare steak. Perfect for summer entertaining, it's a great example of combining the highest quality ingredients you can find with a simple preparation to achieve memorable results. Steamed broccoli and Italian Fries (page 249) are good accompaniments for the steak. You'll note the recipe calls for *fleur de sel,* a delicate and sweet French sea salt that is increasingly available in gourmet shops.

4 boneless Prime or Choice strip steaks, 1 to 1¼-inches
     thick, trimmed of all fat (8 to 10 ounces each)
4 garlic cloves, peeled and split
Freshly ground black pepper
2 tablespoons finest quality extra-virgin olive oil
2 teaspoons *fleur de sel,* coarse sea salt, or kosher salt
2 lemons, halved

1. Put the steaks on a plate large enough to hold them in a single layer. Rub each side of the steaks all over with a fresh garlic half, and leave all the garlic on the plate with the steaks. Season both sides of each steak with a generous coating of freshly ground black pepper. Drizzle the oil over the steaks and turn them to coat completely with the oil. Cover the plate with plastic wrap and let the steaks marinate at room temperature for at least 1 or up to 2 hours.

2. Preheat a grill, grill pan, or barbecue until very hot.

Wine Suggestions:

Here's a good opportunity to sample a young Bordeaux from your cellar. You might also enjoy a Tuscan *vino da tavola* or a cabernet sauvignon or cabernet franc from Long Island.

3. Sprinkle the steaks on both sides with the salt and grill 3 to 4 minutes per side for medium-rare, or according to your taste. (To make a crisscross pattern on the steaks, place them on the grill so that they lie diagonally across the grates of the grill. Cook 2 minutes. Then rotate the steaks 45 degrees on the same side and cook for 2 more minutes. Turn the steaks over and repeat on the other side.) Squeeze lemon over each steak and serve hot.

Italian Beef Stew

SERVES 4

This scrumptious baked beef stew recipe uses an Italian technique that doesn't involve the painstaking steps of flouring and browning the beef in batches. The initial heat draws out the meat's juices (it will actually look like it is boiling in the pan), and then, as the juices evaporate, the meat begins to brown. The two-step cooking process allows the beef to absorb the flavor of the wine before the tomato is added and results in an incredibly tender stew. Like any stew, this one's great for company, since there's literally nothing you'll need to do for the last hour, while it's in the oven. Serve with creamy polenta, or mashed turnips or potatoes, and a heaping portion of sautéed spinach, broccoli rabe, or Swiss chard. If there are any leftovers, use them as a pasta sauce for penne, rigatoni, or pappardelle.

2 tablespoons vegetable oil

3 pounds trimmed beef chuck, cut into
    1- to 1½-inch cubes

1 cup chopped onion

1 tablespoon minced garlic

1 bay leaf

2 teaspoons coarse sea salt

¼ teaspoon freshly ground black pepper

1 tablespoon tomato paste

1 cup red wine

2 cups Basic Tomato Sauce (page 318)
    or store-bought tomato sauce

1 tablespoon sliced fresh sage leaves

2 tablespoons chopped fresh parsley

1. Preheat the oven to 350 degrees F.

2. Heat the oil to smoking over high heat in a deep, straight-sided skillet large enough to hold the meat in one layer. Add the meat and cook, stirring occasionally, until all the juices have evaporated and the meat is browned, 20 to 25 minutes. (Turn the heat down if necessary to keep the meat from burning.)

3. Reduce the heat to medium. Stir in the onion, garlic, bay leaf, salt, and pepper. Cook until the onion is soft but not brown, about 3 minutes. Stir in the tomato paste, cook for 1 additional minute, and then add the wine. Bring to a boil, cover tightly, and bake in the oven until the meat is tender and almost all of the wine has evaporated, about 1 hour.

4. Stir in the tomato sauce and the sage, return the pan to the oven, and continue baking until the meat is soft enough to cut with a spoon, about 1 hour longer. Transfer to a warm, deep platter, sprinkle with the chopped parsley, and serve piping hot.

Wine Suggestions:
Use a fruity red with some body like California sangiovese, zinfandel, or syrah. A good bottle of Chianti Classico Riserva or Vino Nobile di Montepulciano would also do the trick.

Oven-Braised Short Ribs

SERVES 4

Short ribs are one of those delicacies that are so delicious and comforting, you wonder why you forget to eat them more often. Here's a winning preparation with an unusual touch—overnight marinating in red wine begins the process of tenderizing the ribs, and long, slow braising provides a succulent finish to the meat. The darkly fragrant garam masala adds an exotic note, and the addition of a little raw wine to the cooked sauce acts as a final seasoning to brighten the taste. Serve the ribs with a green vegetable and a big bowl of Horseradish-Mashed Potatoes (page 253) or Potato–Jerusalem Artichoke Gratin (page 226).

1 large onion, sliced

2 carrots, scrubbed and sliced

2 celery stalks, sliced

1 garlic head, split in half

3 bay leaves

10 sprigs fresh thyme

2 bottles full-bodied red wine

4 to 4½ pounds beef short ribs

2 tablespoons vegetable oil

Kosher salt

Freshly ground black pepper

2 tablespoons all-purpose flour

2 cups Veal Stock (page 316) or store-bought
    veal demi-glace

1 teaspoon Worcestershire sauce

1 teaspoon garam masala (see Note on page 29)

Wine Suggestions:
This is a rich, heady dish that calls for a ripe California merlot, cabernet sauvignon, zinfandel, or syrah.

1. Combine the onion, carrots, celery, garlic, bay leaves, thyme, and all but 1 tablespoon of the wine in a large bowl. (Reserve the tablespoon of wine to finish the sauce.) Add the ribs, cover, and marinate in the refrigerator overnight.

2. Remove the ribs from the marinade and pat dry with paper towels. Place a colander over a bowl and drain the vegetables, reserving the vegetables and the marinade separately.

3. Preheat the oven to 350 degrees F.

4. Place a Dutch oven over high heat, add the oil, and bring to the smoking point. Sprinkle the ribs with 1 teaspoon of salt and ½ teaspoon pepper. Add the ribs to the pan, in batches if necessary, and brown all over. Remove the ribs from the pan, transfer to a plate, and reserve. Add the drained vegetables and sauté until browned, about 10 minutes. Add the flour and cook, stirring, 2 to 3 minutes. Add the reserved marinade to deglaze the pan. Stir well with a wooden spoon to combine the wine with the flour. Return the ribs to the pan, bone side up, return to a boil, cover, and bake in the oven until the ribs are tender, about 2 hours and 45 minutes.

5. When the ribs are cooked, carefully transfer them to a platter, cover with foil, and set aside. Strain the cooking liquid into a saucepan, pressing well on the vegetables. Discard the vegetables. Bring the liquid to a simmer over medium heat and carefully skim the fat with a ladle or a baster. Continue simmering the liquid, and reduce to about 2 cups. Add the stock and reduce once again to about 2 cups. Stir in the Worcestershire sauce, garam masala, and ½ teaspoon salt. Add the ribs and simmer gently, basting the meat often with the sauce, until the sauce has reduced and thickened enough to coat and glaze the ribs. Add the reserved tablespoon of wine a minute or so before the end of cooking.

6. Transfer the ribs to a serving platter, pour the sauce over, and serve.

Bollito di Vitello

SERVES 10 TO 12

Here's our recipe for *bollito di vitello,* which we lovingly prepare for its legion of fans every Wednesday night at dinner. Though you'll have to get started a day ahead of time, the actual process is quite straightforward and will deliver succulent, perfectly tender veal that can be cut with a spoon. Slather the veal with tangy salsa verde (see below) and accompany it with a bowl of Sweet-and-Sour Carrots (page 207). A wonderful dividend is that you will end up with plenty of savory cooking liquid, which you can reserve and use in any recipe that calls for chicken stock.

HERB RUB

3 tablespoons coarse sea salt

¼ cup coarsely chopped fresh rosemary leaves

¼ cup firmly packed fresh sage sprigs, coarsely chopped

¼ cup fresh thyme sprigs, coarsely chopped

¼ cup firmly packed parsley sprigs, coarsely chopped

¼ cup coarsely chopped garlic cloves

¼ cup white wine

⅓ cup extra-virgin olive oil

VEAL

1 bone-in (9- to 10-pound) veal shoulder, tied with butcher's twine

8 cups Chicken Stock (page 315)

2½ cups white wine

1 teaspoon kosher salt

¼ teaspoon freshly ground black pepper

SALSA VERDE

1 medium Idaho potato, peeled and cut into eighths

4 anchovy fillets in oil, drained and finely chopped

Wine Suggestions:
When it comes to pairing the veal with wine, this is a pretty versatile dish, and after hours of preparation, you'll probably want to bring out a special red from your cellar. Go for a mature Bordeaux or Burgundy, a super Tuscan, or Brunello di Montalcino.

SECOND HELPINGS FROM UNION SQUARE CAFE

¼ cup small capers, drained, or rinsed and dried if
    packed in salt
1 tablespoon minced garlic
½ cup chopped onion
2 celery stalks, peeled and finely chopped
2 tablespoons fresh lemon juice
2 tablespoons white vinegar
1 teaspoon kosher salt
¼ teaspoon freshly ground black pepper
½ cup degreased cooking liquid (see below)
¾ cup extra-virgin olive oil
½ cup coarsely chopped fresh parsley

1. The night before serving, combine all the ingredients for the herb rub
    in a bowl. Place the veal on a platter, spread the herb rub over the
    entire surface, cover with plastic wrap, and refrigerate overnight.

2. Combine the stock, wine, salt, and pepper in a large heavy pot—an
    8- to 10-quart enameled cast-iron casserole is excellent—and bring to a
    simmer. Add the meat, cover the pot, and cook at a very gentle simmer
    for 5½ to 6 hours. The meat is done when you are able to easily insert
    a spoon all the way to the bone.

3. While the veal is cooking (and up to 5 hours before serving), begin
    the salsa verde: Add the potato to the veal pot and cook until tender,
    about 30 minutes. Pass the potato through a ricer or food mill into a
    small serving bowl. Add the chopped anchovy, capers, garlic, onion,
    celery, lemon juice, vinegar, salt, and pepper and stir well to combine.
    Set aside.

4. When the veal is cooked, lift it from the pot and transfer to a large
    cutting board, using kitchen tongs or a carving fork hooked under the
    twine. Remove the twine. Allow the veal to rest while finishing the
    salsa. With a ladle, skim the fat from the cooking liquid. Strain ½ cup

of the hot liquid into the salsa verde and whisk. Drizzle the oil into the salsa in a thin stream while continuing to whisk to emulsify the sauce. Stir in the chopped parsley.

5. Carve the veal from the bone into ½-inch-thick slices and serve hot, spooned generously with the salsa verde.

Note: This is a very forgiving recipe: You can make it in advance and store for a couple of hours on the stove, off the heat, in the cooking liquid, or for a few days, refrigerated, in the cooking pot, still in the liquid. You can interrupt the cooking and restart before serving. Leftovers should be stored in the liquid. Bring to a simmer before serving. As a condiment, the salsa verde is delicious on roast chicken, roast pork, and grilled or steamed salmon, mackerel, or bluefish. In the unlikely event you have leftover salsa verde, you can reheat it in the microwave (though the parsley will lose its color).

Herb-Roasted Rack of Veal

SERVES 6 TO 8

The rack is the most luxurious cut of veal—and is commensurately expensive—but it makes an impressive presentation for special celebratory occasions. For this recipe, an elegantly trimmed, six-bone rack of veal is marinated with an aromatic rub of fresh herbs, olive oil, and garlic, then roasted to juicy perfection. We tie a length of butcher's twine around the "eye" of the roast between each of the 6 bones, which is a good technique for making the roast more compact and juicy. One chop per person yields especially generous portions, but you can certainly carve smaller slices between the bones for more delicate appetites. Accompany the veal with Cardoon Gratin (page 222) or Mashed Potatoes (page 321).

¼ cup coarsely chopped (1-inch pieces) fresh summer
     savory, thyme sprigs, or sage leaves

1 garlic clove, thinly sliced

1 tablespoon coarse sea salt

1 teaspoon cracked black peppercorns

2 tablespoons extra-virgin olive oil

1 (6-rib) rack of veal, chine removed, and denuded
     (deckle removed and fat trimmed to a thin layer),
     bones frenched, and meat tied between each rib
     (5 to 5½ pounds trimmed; see Note)

3 tablespoons olive oil

½ cup white wine

1 cup Chicken Stock (page 315) or Veal Stock
     (page 316)

1 tablespoon butter

1. In a small bowl, combine the savory, thyme, or
     sage, the garlic, salt, pepper, and extra-virgin olive
     oil. Place the veal in a baking dish and rub all over

Wine Suggestions:
Serve with an elegant, medium-bodied red such as a mature Pomerol or St. Emilion, a Burgundy from the Côte de Beaune, or a California pinot noir.

SECOND HELPINGS FROM UNION SQUARE CAFE

with the seasoned oil. Cover the baking dish with plastic wrap and refrigerate for 5 to 8 hours.

2. Preheat the oven to 350 degrees F.

3. Brush off and set aside the garlic, peppercorns, and herbs adhering to the veal. Heat 2 tablespoons of the olive oil in a 14-inch, heavy-bottomed skillet or a small roasting pan over medium heat. Add the veal and brown on both sides, about 15 minutes total.

4. Adjust the veal so that it is bone side down in the pan and roast in the oven for 20 minutes. Turn the veal bone side up and continue to roast until the meat registers 125 degrees F on a meat thermometer, 30 to 40 minutes longer. Transfer the roast veal to a serving platter, loosely cover with foil, and let rest at least 15 minutes.

5. Pour off the fat from the skillet or roasting pan. Add the remaining 1 tablespoon of oil and heat over medium-high heat until smoking. Toss in the reserved herbs, garlic, and peppercorns and cook, stirring, for about 1 minute. Pour in the wine and reduce until almost dry. Add the stock and any juices that have accumulated on the platter with the veal and reduce by about two-thirds, or until the sauce thickens slightly. Whisk in the butter until just melted, and adjust the seasoning to taste. Strain the sauce into a gravy dish and cover.

6. Remove the twine and carve the rack of veal into 6 chops. Serve the chops with the sauce.

Note: Ask your butcher for all the meat trimmings. You can freeze them for later use, either cubed in a stew, ground for juicy veal burgers, or braised with tomatoes and vegetables for a pasta ragu.

Roman-Style Braised Oxtails

SERVES 8 TO 10

The *vaccinari* were Rome's old-guard butchers, for whom this classic braised oxtail dish, *coda alla vaccinara,* is named. For us, no culinary visit to the Eternal City is complete without visiting several *trattorie* to sample signature versions of the city's classic recipe. Our hands-down favorite rendition is from La Taverna da Giovanni, where Chef Claudio shared his secret: he stirs in a small amount of unsweetened cocoa powder at the last moment to add enriching depth to the red wine and tomato sauce. It's a subtle but wonderful complement to every ingredient in the dish. Serve the oxtails with Mashed Potatoes (page 321) or polenta and broccoli rabe.

8 pounds oxtail, cut 1½ inches thick

3 quarts Chicken Stock (page 315), or 3 quarts water
seasoned with 2 tablespoons kosher salt

4 celery stalks, cut into 3 by ¼-inch sticks

¼ cup olive oil

1½ cups diced carrots

1½ cups diced celery

1½ cups diced white onion

1 bay leaf

Kosher salt

Freshly ground black pepper

½ cup raisins or currants

¼ cup pine nuts

3 cups plus 2 tablespoons red wine

2 quarts homemade or store-bought tomato sauce

2 tablespoons unsweetened cocoa powder

1. Place the oxtails in an 8- to 10-quart stockpot or Dutch oven, add the chicken stock or water, and bring to a boil. Reduce to a simmer, cover, and cook until the meat is

Wine Suggestions:
Bring out a rich, fruity red with lots of depth, such as a "super Tuscan" *vino da tavola*, Montepulciano d'Abruzzo, or Aglianico del Vulture.

SECOND HELPINGS FROM UNION SQUARE CAFE

somewhat tender, but still clings firmly to the bone, about 2 hours. About 15 minutes before the meat is done, ladle 2 cups of the broth into a small saucepan, add the celery sticks, and simmer over medium heat until the celery is tender. Set the saucepan aside.

2. Drain the oxtails in a large colander and store the cooking broth for making risotto, *tortellino in brodo,* or any dish that calls for beef stock. Transfer the oxtails to a large bowl and cover to keep warm and moist. Wash and dry the stockpot.

3. Heat the olive oil in the stockpot over high heat. Add the carrots, celery, onion, and bay leaf and cook, stirring occasionally, until the vegetables are softened but not colored, about 10 minutes.

4. Season the vegetables with the salt and freshly ground black pepper. Add the raisins and pine nuts and continue cooking an additional 3 minutes. Pour in 3 cups of the red wine, bring to a boil, and reduce by half. Add the tomato sauce and the reserved oxtails and bring the sauce to a simmer. Lower the heat to its lowest setting, cover the pot tightly, and cook until the meat is falling off the bone, about 1½ to 2 hours. Using a ladle or a baster, carefully skim and discard as much fat as possible from the surface of the oxtail sauce.

5. Place the cocoa powder in a small bowl and dissolve by whisking in the 2 remaining tablespoons of red wine. Pour the dissolved cocoa into the pot and stir gently, but thoroughly, to incorporate. Check the seasoning of the oxtails and adjust with salt and pepper to your taste.

6. Bring the saucepan with the celery sticks to a simmer. Remove the celery. Serve the oxtails in large bowls, each portion topped with sauce and a spoonful of the celery sticks.

Note: You can make the dish several days in advance and reheat gently just before serving.

Chicken-Fried Venison

SERVES 4

This is a twist on a southern staple, chicken-fried steak, in which tough
cube steak is coated in buttermilk and flour and pan-fried, just like chicken.
Since venison is so lean, we've found that it, too, benefits from marinating
in garlicky buttermilk, which both moistens and tenderizes the meat. The
buttermilk also provides a subtle, tangy seasoning and minimizes the need
for added salt. The crisped venison cutlets go well with a number of different
side dishes, and among those we'd recommend are Mustard- or Horseradish-
Mashed Potatoes (pages 251 and 253), Sautéed Cabbage (page 218), and
Cardoon Gratin (page 222).

1¼ pounds trimmed leg of venison, sliced and lightly
    pounded into ¼-inch-thick cutlets
1½ cups buttermilk
2 garlic cloves, peeled and split
¼ teaspoon freshly ground black pepper
Vegetable oil for frying
Kosher salt
1 to 2 cups all-purpose flour
1 lemon, quartered

1. Place the venison in a wide, shallow container.
    Add the buttermilk, garlic, and pepper. Coat the
    venison thoroughly by turning it several times in
    the buttermilk. Cover and marinate in the
    refrigerator for at least 2 hours or overnight.

2. Pour a ⅛-inch layer of vegetable oil into a cast-
    iron skillet and place over medium-high heat.

Wine Suggestions:
Try the venison with
a juicy California cabernet
sauvignon or zinfandel,
or with an Australian
cabernet-shiraz blend.

3. Remove the venison, one piece at a time, from the container, but do not scrape away the buttermilk clinging to the meat. Sprinkle both sides of each cutlet lightly with salt and dredge in the flour, turning the meat several times and patting the flour into the meat to make a generous coating. Working in batches, and without crowding the pan, fry the meat until the coating is crisp, 1 to 1½ minutes per side. Turn the meat carefully with a wide, flat metal spatula and drain on paper towels. Transfer to a serving platter, and serve with freshly cut lemon wedges.

Baked Lamb Chops

SERVES 4

Here's a simple recipe, perfect for entertaining. Shoulder lamb chops are layered with onions and thin potato slices, then baked slowly with a bit of white wine and chicken stock. You end up with fork-tender lamb, whose flavor marries beautifully with the other ingredients in the casserole. It's a pretty complete dish, and all you'll need to accompany it is a salad and perhaps a green vegetable like sautéed spinach, green beans, or broccoli rabe.

8 shoulder lamb chops, ½ inch thick
Kosher salt
Freshly ground black pepper
¼ cup plus 1 tablespoon olive oil
6 onions, halved and thinly sliced (about 10 cups)
1 tablespoon chopped garlic
2 tablespoons chopped fresh thyme leaves
⅛ teaspoon Aleppo pepper
½ cup white wine
1½ cups Chicken Stock (page 315)
3 large Idaho potatoes
1 tablespoon chopped fresh parsley

1. Season the lamb chops on both sides with 2 teaspoons of salt and ½ teaspoon of black pepper.

2. Heat 2 tablespoons of the olive oil in a large skillet over medium-high heat. Working in two batches, brown the lamb chops for about 2 minutes on each side. Transfer the lamb chops to a plate, and discard the fat in the skillet.

Wine Suggestions:
This goes quite well with a good Côtes du Rhône, or any of its neighbors like Gigondas, Crozes-Hermitage, or Châteauneuf-du-Pape.

3. Heat the remaining 3 tablespoons of oil in the skillet over medium-high heat. Add the onions and cook, stirring occasionally, until they are golden brown and softened, 20 to 25 minutes. Turn down the heat as necessary toward the end of cooking the onions to prevent them from burning. Add the garlic, thyme, 1 teaspoon of salt, $\frac{1}{8}$ teaspoon black pepper, and the Aleppo pepper. Cook, stirring, for an additional 2 minutes. Pour in the wine and reduce until dry. Remove the skillet from the heat and set aside.

4. Preheat the oven to 450 degrees F.

5. In a small saucepan, bring the chicken stock to a simmer and season with $\frac{3}{4}$ teaspoon of salt. Remove from the heat and reserve.

6. Peel, rinse, and slice the potatoes about $\frac{1}{16}$ inch thick. Place the potato slices in a bowl and reserve.

7. Spread about two-thirds of the cooked onions over the bottom of a baking dish large enough to hold all the chops tightly in a single layer (they may overlap slightly). Next, layer the potato slices in rows atop the onions, with both the individual potato slices and the rows overlapping slightly. Arrange the lamb chops on top of the potatoes and pour over them any juices that have accumulated on the plate. Spread the remaining onions evenly over the lamb chops and then pour the warm chicken stock over the onions. Cover the baking dish with a sheet of aluminum foil, place the dish in the oven, and immediately reduce the heat to 350 degrees F. Bake the gratin for 1 hour and 15 minutes. Remove the foil, and bake for an additional 30 minutes.

8. Remove the baking dish from the oven and allow to sit for 10 minutes. Using a pot holder, carefully tip the baking dish to one side so that any fat floating on top collects in a corner of the dish. Using a kitchen spoon or a baster, remove as much of the fat as possible. Sprinkle chopped parsley over the lamb, and serve directly from the baking dish.

Olive-Stuffed Lamb

SERVES 6

This simple recipe makes wonderful use of the harmonious Provençal combination of lamb, olives, garlic, and thyme. Ask your butcher to cut top rounds from leg of lamb. Create a pocket in each round—as you would open pita bread—and then fill the pockets with seasoned black olive paste before searing and roasting. The technique for making this quick and flavorful lamb sauce—first searing aromatic herbs in olive oil and then deglazing the pan with white wine and stock—is one you can use for any pan-roasted meat. Serve with Flageolet "Baked Beans" (page 240) or Cardoon Gratin (page 222).

2 lamb top rounds (cut from the leg),
    about 1½ pounds each
6 tablespoons olive paste (page 255)
Kosher salt and freshly ground black pepper
2 tablespoons olive oil
2 garlic cloves, sliced thinly
3 tablespoons coarsely chopped fresh thyme sprigs
1 bay leaf
½ teaspoon cracked black peppercorns
½ cup white wine
1 cup Chicken Stock (page 315)
1 tablespoon chopped fresh parsley

1. Preheat the oven to 350 degrees F.

2. To create a pocket in each of the top rounds, lay one on a work surface and cut a 1-inch-wide opening in one of the long sides. Insert the knife into the opening all the way to within ½ inch of the opposite side. Use the knife to widen the pocket on

Wine Suggestions:
This calls for a southern French red like Châteauneuf-du-Pape, St. Joseph, Gigondas, Bandol, or Cornas.

the inside of the meat, just until the lamb looks like pita bread ready to be stuffed. Repeat with the second top round. Use a spoon to fill each lamb pocket with half of the olive puree. Sprinkle the meat on both sides with salt and ground pepper.

3. Heat 1 tablespoon of the oil in a large, heavy-bottomed, ovenproof skillet over medium-high heat. Brown the filled lamb top rounds on one side for 5 to 6 minutes, and then turn them over. Transfer the skillet to the oven and roast the lamb until it is medium-rare and feels firm to the touch, 25 to 30 minutes. Remove the skillet from the oven. Transfer the lamb to a plate and cover while you make the sauce.

4. Pour off the fat from the pan. Add the remaining 1 tablespoon of oil and heat over medium-high heat until smoking. Toss in the garlic, thyme, bay leaf, and peppercorns and cook, stirring, for about 1 minute. Pour in the wine and reduce until almost dry. Add the stock and any juices that have accumulated on the plate with the lamb, and reduce by about two-thirds, or until the sauce thickens slightly. Season to taste with salt and pepper. Swirl in the parsley.

5. Cut the lamb against the grain into thin slices and fan them out on serving plates. Spoon the sauce over the lamb and serve.

Roast Rack of Lamb

SERVES 4

A properly roasted rack of lamb is such a treat, and here's a recipe that makes it easy to succeed when you're serving this elegant and festive dish at home. The trick is that the racks rest between two short roastings, allowing you to carve them for your guests while they're evenly cooked, rosy pink, and still piping hot. Serve with Olive- or Mustard-Mashed Potatoes (pages 255 and 251), Cardoon Gratin (page 222), or Scaffata (page 214).

1 cup fresh bread crumbs
1 teaspoon minced garlic
1½ teaspoons chopped fresh tarragon
2 tablespoons extra-virgin olive oil
Salt
Freshly ground black pepper
2 tablespoons vegetable oil
2 lamb racks, 8 ribs each (see Note)
1 tablespoon plus 1 teaspoon Dijon mustard

1. Preheat the oven to 425 degrees F.

2. In a bowl, combine the bread crumbs, garlic, tarragon, olive oil, ⅛ teaspoon of salt and ⅛ teaspoon of pepper, mixing with your fingers so that the bread crumbs absorb the oil. Set aside.

3. In a cast-iron skillet or ovenproof sauté pan large enough to hold both racks, heat the vegetable oil over high heat until smoking. Season the racks all over with ½ teaspoon of salt and ¼ teaspoon of pepper and sear them in the pan, meaty sides down. Cook until well

Wine Suggestions:
Rack of lamb calls for an elegant wine from the Rhône Valley like Côte Rôtie, Hermitage, or Châteauneuf-du-Pape. This would also make a good occasion to enjoy a special bottle of Bordeaux, Barolo, or California cabernet.

SECOND HELPINGS FROM UNION SQUARE CAFE

browned, about 2 minutes. Turn the racks over and cook 1 minute longer. Place the skillet in the oven. Roast 9 minutes for medium-rare or 8 minutes for rare.

4. Remove the skillet from the oven, transfer the racks to a plate, and let them rest for 15 minutes, uncovered. Use a pastry brush or a teaspoon to coat the meaty side of each rack with the mustard. Use your fingers to press the bread crumb mixture onto the mustard. Return the racks to the oven and roast for 15 more minutes to brown the crust. Slice in between each bone, and serve the chops immediately.

Note: Ask your butcher to remove the chine bone, trim the racks *completely* down to the meat, and "French" the bones by scraping away all the fat and gristle. When he's done, each rack should weigh about 1 pound.

Lamb Stew alla Romana

SERVES 4 TO 6

In Rome, home cooks enjoy using the triumvirate of white wine, anchovies, and garlic for any dish involving the slow cooking of lamb. This is a deeply flavored, soul-satisfying stew that is nicely accompanied by roast potatoes, spinach, or artichokes. As a variation, you could substitute freshly chopped mint for the parsley, or simply add it to the recipe along with the parsley.

3 pounds trimmed lamb shoulder,
     cut into 1½-inch cubes
Kosher salt
Freshly ground black pepper
3 tablespoons olive oil
6 cups thinly sliced white onions
2 tablespoons chopped garlic
1 teaspoon Aleppo pepper, or scant ½ teaspoon
     crushed red pepper flakes
3 tablespoons coarsely chopped fresh rosemary
1½ cups white wine
1 cup Lamb Stock (page 317) or chicken broth
1½ tablespoons white wine vinegar
2 tablespoons anchovy paste
2 tablespoons chopped parsley

1. Preheat the oven to 325 degrees F.

2. Spread the lamb cubes in a single layer on a baking sheet and sprinkle on both sides with 1½ teaspoons salt and ½ teaspoon freshly ground black pepper.

Wine Suggestions:
This stew calls for a robust and herbaceous red from southern Italy like Aglianico del Vulture, Colle Picchioni, or Salice Salentino. You would also do well with a zinfandel or cabernet franc from California, a Bandol from Provence, or a Rioja or Peñedes from Spain.

3. Heat the oil in a 10-inch straight-sided oven-proof pot or Dutch oven over high heat. Working in batches, brown the meat on all sides and then transfer to a platter. When the lamb has been browned, pour off all but 2 tablespoons of fat from the pot. Add the onions and cook, stirring often, until wilted and lightly browned, about 10 minutes.

4. Reduce the heat to medium. Stir in the garlic, Aleppo pepper or pepper flakes, and rosemary, and cook 3 to 4 minutes longer.

5. Add the lamb to the pot along with the accumulated juices and stir well. Pour the wine, stock, and vinegar over the lamb and bring to a boil. Cover the pot, transfer to the oven, and bake for 1½ hours.

6. Uncover the pot and stir in the anchovy paste. Return the pot to the oven and continue cooking, uncovered, until the meat is tender enough to cut with a spoon, about 30 minutes longer. The stewing liquid should be reduced enough to lightly coat the meat. If it is too thin, bring the stew to a gentle boil on top of the stove and reduce until the sauce thickens enough to cling to the meat. Taste and adjust for salt and pepper if necessary. To serve, spoon into a warmed serving bowl and sprinkle with parsley.

Spice-Rubbed Pork Tenderloin

SERVES 4

Lean and juicy pork tenderloin takes no time to cook, which makes it a
great candidate for entertaining. In this recipe, it's rubbed with a wonderful
layering of aromatic spices and enlivened with a bright sauce of apples, spices,
mushrooms, verjus, and stock. Don't be daunted by the list of ingredients.
Once they're assembled, this is a breeze to make, with memorable results.
Serve the pork with Indian-Spiced Acorn Squash (page 204) or Roasted Root
Vegetables (page 208).

2 pork tenderloins (about 1¾ pounds total),
    trimmed of fat

½ teaspoon whole cardamom pods

½ teaspoon black cumin seeds

½ teaspoon dried pomegranate seeds

½ teaspoon whole black peppercorns

1½ teaspoons coriander seeds

2 star anise

4 cloves

1 cinnamon stick, broken into pieces

⅛ teaspoon ground ginger

3 tablespoons olive oil

2 tablespoons butter

1 large onion, sliced

3½ ounces shiitake mushrooms, thinly sliced,
    stems reserved

½ tablespoon sliced fresh sage leaves, stems reserved

1 teaspoon paprika

1 tablespoon all-purpose flour

1 tablespoon cider vinegar

½ cup verjus

2 cups brown Veal Stock (page 316) or Chicken Stock
    (page 315), or store-bought veal stock (or demi-glace)

Wine Suggestions:

Pork lends itself to
either red or white wine—
depending on your preference.
For red, go with a youthful,
juicy Australian shiraz or
California zinfandel. Good
choices for white would be
a New Zealand sauvignon
blanc or a California viognier.

Kosher salt

1 Red Delicious apple

¼ cup plain whole-milk yogurt, whisked until smooth

1. Cut off about 2 inches of the thin "tail" end of each pork tenderloin, as well as any unevenness at the head of the fillets, to make 2 fairly even cylinders. Then cut each tenderloin in half crosswise. Reserve the scraps for the sauce.

2. Combine the cardamom, black cumin, dried pomegranate seeds, peppercorns, coriander, star anise, cloves, and cinnamon stick in a spice grinder and grind to a fine powder. Transfer to a small bowl and stir in the ground ginger. Set aside one-third of the ground spice mixture for the sauce, and season the pork tenderloins all over with the remaining two-thirds.

3. Heat 1 tablespoon of the olive oil with 1 tablespoon of the butter in a 3-quart saucepan over medium-high heat. Add the reserved pork scraps and cook, stirring with a wooden spoon until browned, 2 to 3 minutes. Add half of the sliced onion, the reserved shiitake and sage stems, and the paprika, and cook until the onion is softened, about 2 minutes. Reduce the heat to low, add the flour, and cook, stirring, for 2 minutes. Stir in the vinegar and the verjus. Bring to a simmer, scraping the bottom of the pan to dissolve any brown bits, and cook until reduced and very thick. Add the stock and simmer until the sauce has thickened and reduced to 1 cup, about 15 minutes. Set aside.

4. Preheat the oven to 425 degrees F.

5. Heat the remaining 2 tablespoons of oil in an ovenproof, 11-inch skillet until hot but not smoking (so as not to burn the spices). Sprinkle the pork with 1 teaspoon of salt, place it in the skillet, and cook, turning occasionally, until browned all over. Place the pan in the oven and roast for 8 minutes for medium-rare, 10 minutes for medium.

6. Meanwhile, peel, core, and cut the apple into ½-inch dice.

7. When the pork is cooked, transfer it to a plate, cover loosely with aluminum foil, and let rest while you finish the sauce. Discard the fat from the pan. Melt the remaining 1 tablespoon of butter in the pan over medium-high heat. Add the reserved spice mixture and cook, stirring, for 30 seconds. Toss in the remaining sliced onion and the sliced shiitakes, and cook, stirring, for 3 minutes. Add the diced apple and 1¼ teaspoons of salt. Strain the reserved sauce into the pan through a fine-mesh strainer, pressing with a ladle to extract all of the juices. Pour in any pork juices that have accumulated on the plate and bring to a simmer. Whisk in the yogurt and sliced sage, and taste for seasoning. Remove the sauce from the heat.

8. Cut the pork on a slight angle into ½-inch slices and arrange on a serving platter. Spoon the sauce over the pork, and serve.

Sage-Fried Rabbit

SERVES 4

This is an incredibly delicious way to enjoy rabbit, blending Tuscan flavors with American Low-Country frying. It's a simple recipe that also works well with chicken to yield juicy, succulent morsels of meat. At Union Square Cafe, we serve it with a squeeze of lemon and accompany it with our creamy polenta and broccoli rabe. It's equally good with mashed potatoes and asparagus or any green vegetable. Most rabbit is sold whole, but any good butcher will be able to bone it and cut it into portion-size pieces for you.

1 rabbit (about 3 pounds), boned and cut into
    2- to 3-inch pieces (see Note)

2 cups buttermilk

4 peeled garlic cloves, smashed

¾ cup all-purpose flour

¾ cup coarse cornmeal

2 tablespoons minced fresh sage leaves

2 teaspoons kosher salt

¼ teaspoon freshly ground black pepper

¾ cup olive oil

2 lemons, halved

1. Combine the rabbit, buttermilk, and garlic in a bowl. Cover and marinate overnight, or for at least 4 hours, in the refrigerator.

2. Combine the flour, cornmeal, and sage in a large bowl.

3. Remove the rabbit from the marinade and season with the salt and pepper.

4. Heat the oil in a 10½-inch cast-iron skillet until shimmering. Dredge the rabbit pieces in the cornmeal mixture to coat evenly. Put as many pieces in the pan as will comfortably fit in one layer, and cook until crisp and golden, 5 to 6 minutes.

5. Transfer the rabbit to a platter lined with paper towels. Cook the rest of the rabbit in the same way. Serve immediately with lemon halves.

Note: Use a sharp paring knife to remove the rabbit meat from the bone—neatness doesn't count.

Wine Suggestions:
This is great with any fruity wine with good acidity. Excellent choices would be a good rosé wine from California or Italy (*rosato*), an Australian shiraz, or an Oregon pinot noir.

Calf's Liver with Bacon and Sage

Serves 4

Here's a winning recipe that combines both French and Italian flavors to great effect. Soaking the liver in milk for an hour tenderizes it. Crisp bacon, sweet onions, and sage are the key ingredients in this creamy sauce, which also works nicely with veal chops or veal scaloppine.

4 (4-ounce) slices calf's liver
Milk for soaking
½ cup all-purpose flour
Kosher salt
Freshly ground black pepper
2 tablespoons olive oil
4 ounces bacon, cut into ¼-inch-thick strips
2 cups sliced onion
2 tablespoons drained capers
2 teaspoon sliced fresh sage
¼ cup white wine
1 cup brown veal stock or store-bought veal demi-glace
¼ cup heavy cream
2 tablespoons Dijon mustard

1. Place the liver in a bowl and add enough milk to cover. Refrigerate for 1 hour.

2. Preheat the oven to 200 degrees F.

3. Pour the flour onto a dinner plate. Sprinkle the liver slices with salt and pepper and dredge in the flour. Shake off the excess.

Wine Suggestions:

A rich, buttery chardonnay would suit this dish if you're in the mood for white, or, alternatively, go for a heady, smoky red like Châteauneuf-du-Pape, Australian shiraz, or Rioja.

4. In a large skillet, heat the oil over medium-high heat. Sauté the liver until golden brown, about 2 minutes on each side for medium-rare. Transfer the cooked liver to a serving platter, cover loosely, and keep warm in the oven while you make the sauce.

5. Discard the oil from the skillet and place over medium-high heat. Add the bacon and cook 2 minutes. Add the onion and cook until the slices are lightly browned and tender but still have body, about 5 minutes. Stir in the capers and sage. Pour in the wine and reduce until almost dry. Add the stock and reduce by two-thirds. Add the cream, mustard, ½ teaspoon of salt, and ¼ teaspoon of pepper. Bring the sauce to a boil and reduce until thick enough to coat the back of a spoon. Spoon the sauce over the liver and serve immediately.

Trippa alla Trasteverina

SERVES 8

Tripe is one of those specialty dishes that we'll occasionally offer on our menu, knowing full well that the majority of our guests won't even dream of trying it. For the cognoscenti who enjoy it, though, our goal is to cook the best version they've ever had. This outstanding recipe is adapted from Rome's colorful Trastevere neighborhood, in which the tripe is cooked long and slow along with white wine, tomatoes, pecorino cheese, and pancetta, and is refreshed with a sprinkling of fresh mint. Save this recipe for real tripe lovers, and cook it with the confidence that they'll be enormously impressed. We serve the tripe in bowls as a main course or appetizer, accompanied by toasted bread rubbed with garlic and drizzled with good olive oil.

TRIPE

4 pounds honeycomb tripe

1 onion, sliced

2 carrots, scrubbed and sliced

3 celery stalks, sliced

1 head garlic, split

1 bay leaf

5 sprigs fresh parsley

1 tablespoon kosher salt

10 whole black peppercorns

3 quarts water

4 cups white wine

TOMATO SAUCE

4 (28-ounce) cans whole, peeled tomatoes in juice,
     drained, about half of the juice reserved

¼ cup extra-virgin olive oil

2 tablespoons chopped pancetta

1 cup chopped onion

Wine Suggestions:
Accompany the tripe
with chilled Frascati
or Chianti Classico.

1 cup peeled and chopped carrot

1 cup chopped celery

1 teaspoon chopped garlic

1½ pound fresh tomatoes, peeled, seeded, and diced

2 tablespoons sliced fresh basil leaves

½ tablespoon coarse sea salt

½ teaspoon freshly ground pepper

½ cup grated Pecorino Romano

1 heaping tablespoon sliced fresh mint leaves

1. Soak the tripe for at least 3 hours in cold water, changing the water at least once per hour. Drain the tripe, trim it of all fat and cartilage, and cut it into 3 by 5-inch pieces.

2. Transfer the tripe to an 8-quart pot, cover with cold water, and bring to a boil. Drain and rinse the tripe and rinse out the pot. Return the tripe to the pot and add the onion, carrots, celery, herbs, salt, peppercorns, water, and wine. Return to a boil, reduce the heat until the tripe is barely simmering, and cook, covered, for 5 hours.

3. Meanwhile, make the tomato sauce: Puree the canned tomatoes with their reserved juice in a food processor and strain through a fine-mesh strainer to remove the seeds. Reserve.

4. Heat the oil and pancetta in a 3-quart saucepan over medium heat until the fat is rendered, about 5 minutes. Add the onion, carrot, and celery and cook slowly, stirring occasionally, until soft, but not colored, about 10 minutes. Add the garlic and cook for 1 minute.

5. Add the fresh tomato, basil, salt, and pepper, and cook until the tomatoes are juicy, about 5 minutes. Add the reserved tomato puree, bring to a boil, reduce the heat, and simmer gently for 1½ hours. Remove from the heat and reserve.

6. When the tripe is cooked, remove from the heat and allow to cool in its liquid until it can be handled. Drain the tripe, cut it into thin strips, and add to the pan with the tomato sauce. Simmer very gently for 1½ hours. Just before serving, stir in the pecorino and the mint.

Note: This dish can be made in steps in advance. You can stop after step 2. Refrigerate in the broth for up to 3 days. The tomato sauce can also be made in advance and refrigerated for up to 3 days.

Eggplant-Spinach Rollatine

SERVES 4

For this all-vegetable, dairy-free version of an Italian standard, we've replaced the traditional eggplant stuffing of ricotta and mozzarella cheese with a succulent, smooth blend of white beans, spinach, and onions. The eggplant rollatine are topped with tomato sauce and baked until piping hot. Serve 3 rollatine per person as a main course, accompanied by a big green salad, or 1 to 2 as an appetizer portion.

1 large eggplant (about 1¾ pounds), unpeeled,
ends trimmed, cut lengthwise into ¼-inch slices
(about 12 to 14 slices)

Kosher salt

2½ tablespoons olive oil

1 medium onion, coarsely chopped

1 pound spinach, stemmed, well washed, and dried

1½ cups cooked cannellini or Great Northern beans
      (2 tablespoons cooking liquid reserved), or
      1 (15½-ounce) can cannellini or Great Northern
      beans, drained (2 tablespoons liquid reserved)

Freshly ground black pepper

Wine Suggestions:
Eggplant has a lot of natural tannins, which are well balanced by a red wine with ample tannins itself. Try a youthful Chianti Classico Riserva, Vino Nobile di Montepulciano, or Valpolicella Classico.

1 cup all-purpose flour

¾ to 1 cup vegetable oil, for frying

1½ cups Basic Tomato Sauce (page 318) or good-quality
store-bought tomato sauce, at room temperature

1. Layer the eggplant slices in a large colander and sprinkle each layer
    with kosher salt, using a total of 1 tablespoon of salt. Cover the
    eggplant with plastic wrap and place a heavy bowl on top. Allow the
    eggplant to drain for about 2 hours in the sink.

2. Heat 1 tablespoon of the olive oil in a small skillet over medium-high
    heat. Add the chopped onion and cook, stirring occasionally, until the
    onion is soft and lightly browned, about 15 minutes. Remove the pan
    from the heat and set aside.

3. Bring 6 quarts of water to a boil over high heat and add 2 tablespoons
    of salt. Have ready a bowl of ice water. Blanch the spinach in the boiling
    water until it is completely wilted. Drain in a colander, then refresh the
    spinach in the ice water. Drain once again, pressing the spinach against
    the sides of the colander to squeeze out more of the water. Pulse in a
    food processor until the spinach is chopped, but not pureed. Transfer
    the chopped spinach to a 2-quart saucepan and reserve.

4. Combine the cooked beans, the 2 tablespoons of reserved bean liquid,
    and the cooked onions in the bowl of the food processor and process
    until smooth.

5. Add the bean and onion puree to the chopped spinach in the saucepan,
    along with 1 tablespoon of the olive oil. Season with 1½ teaspoons of
    kosher salt and ⅛ teaspoon of pepper and cook over low heat, stirring
    occasionally, until the filling is heated through.

6. Remove the pressed eggplant slices from the colander and pat dry on
    paper towels. Pour the flour onto a large plate.

7. Heat ¾ cup of the vegetable oil in a heavy-bottomed, 10½- to 11-inch

skillet over medium-high heat. Working in batches, dredge the eggplant slices in the flour, and sauté, turning once, until the slices are golden brown and softened, 2½ to 3 minutes total. (If the eggplant browns too quickly, turn down the heat.) Drain and cool the eggplant on paper towels. Use the additional ¼ cup oil, if necessary, to sauté the final few batches of eggplant.

8. Preheat the oven to 350 degrees F.

9. Prepare the rollatine: Oil a 2½ quart baking dish with the remaining ½ tablespoon of olive oil. Lay a slice of eggplant on the work surface. Spread 2 to 3 tablespoons of the filling mixture evenly atop the eggplant slice. (The amount of filling will depend on the size of the slice, but you'll want a generous amount.) Beginning with the narrow end, roll up the entire eggplant slice around the filling. Place the rolled, stuffed eggplant slice, seam side down, in a gratin dish. Repeat to fill and roll all of the slices.

10. Pour the tomato sauce over the rollatine to cover completely. Bake, uncovered, until the rollatine are hot, 20 to 25 minutes. Serve hot, in the gratin dish.

When you have a date to dine,
always be sure to be on time.
For your lonely one and only
may not resist an ad hoc tryst.
So if you arrive with a
contrived excuse,
don't be surprised.
That you've cooked your own goose.

A DAY IN THE LIFE OF A LEEK

ROASTED ASPARAGUS

———

GLAZED CIPOLLINI

———

INDIAN-SPICED ACORN SQUASH

———

ZUCCHINI PUREE WITH MARJORAM

———

SWEET-AND-SOUR CARROTS

———

ROASTED ROOT VEGETABLES

———

CARROT-MUSHROOM SFORMATO

———

ROASTED CAULIFLOWER
WITH TOMATO AND GREEN OLIVES

———

SCAFFATA

———

SPICED CREAMED SPINACH

———

SAUTÉED CABBAGE

———

BRUSSELS SPROUTS WITH BACON
AND OREGANO

———

BAKED SAUERKRAUT

———

CARDOON GRATIN

———

JERUSALEM ARTICHOKE PANCAKES

———

POTATO–JERUSALEM ARTICHOKE GRATIN

———

SWISS CHARD, LEEK, AND CELERY TORTINO

———

Roasted Asparagus

SERVES 4

As a technique, roasting is every bit as simple to do as boiling, steaming, or grilling, and flavor-wise, it's a revelation. A quick shake in a pan with some olive oil, salt, and pepper and about 10 minutes in a hot oven, and you're all set. The asparagus take on a wonderfully nutty flavor, and when they're done cooking, they'll give off a lovely asparagus-and-olive-oil jus. Serve it over the asparagus themselves, or let it come to room temperature and whisk with some red wine or balsamic vinegar for an asparagus vinaigrette—a subtle dressing for a salad of Bibb lettuce or frisée. Another option is to throw a split clove or two of garlic in the roasting pan. Shake the asparagus halfway through the roasting process to incorporate the garlic flavor. The roasted asparagus make a versatile accompaniment for lamb chops, steak, salmon, or chicken. It also makes a good appetizer.

2 pounds medium asparagus, washed,
    tough ends snapped off, stalks peeled
¼ cup extra-virgin olive oil
1 teaspoon coarse sea salt
¼ teaspoon freshly ground black pepper
2 teaspoons aged balsamic vinegar
½ cup grated Parmigiano-Reggiano

1. Preheat the oven to 450 degrees F.

2. Place the asparagus in a roasting pan and add the oil, salt, and pepper. Shake the pan to coat the asparagus with oil. Place in the oven and roast until the asparagus are softened, but retain a little crunch, about 10 to 12 minutes.

3. Arrange the asparagus on a serving platter and sprinkle with the vinegar. Top with the grated cheese and serve.

Glazed Cipollini

SERVES 4

The sweet baby onions known as cipollini, once only available in Italy, are turning up in fine American markets. Soaking the nearly flat onions in ice water for an hour before peeling them with a paring knife makes the otherwise onerous process a breeze. Glaze the onions with the classic sweet-sour combination of honey and wine and serve them as a side dish for grilled steak, veal chops, turkey, or roast beef.

2 tablespoons butter
1 pound peeled cipollini onions
½ teaspoon kosher salt
⅛ teaspoon freshly ground black pepper
2 cups red wine
2 tablespoons honey
1 bay leaf

1. Heat the butter in a 3-quart saucepan or straight-sided skillet over medium heat until it turns a nutty-brown color.

2. Add the onions and cook, stirring, until golden brown, about 8 minutes. Sprinkle with the salt and pepper.

3. Add the wine, honey, and bay leaf. Bring to a boil, reduce the heat, and simmer gently, uncovered, until the onions are tender, 20 to 25 minutes. Raise the heat and boil the wine until it has reduced and glazed the onions. Stir often as the wine reduces to coat the onions with the glaze; adjust the heat as necessary to keep the glaze from sticking to the pan. Transfer to a bowl and serve immediately.

Indian-Spiced Acorn Squash

Michael learned this delicious recipe from his friend Usha Cunningham, who
served it to him one evening as part of a home-cooked Indian feast. Indian
spices are a wonderful way to transform acorn squash into a comforting side
dish that's great with salmon or slowly braised meats like short ribs, oxtail,
and osso buco. It's also delicious with something as simple as broiled lamb
chops or pork chops. Not to be confused with the spice mix known as curry
powder, fresh curry leaves (available in Indian specialty stores) are an herb
that lends a subtle nuttiness. They are best used within several days of
purchasing, before they lose their bright green color. Acorn squash works well
in this recipe because of its firm texture, but butternut squash, though softer,
adds additional sweetness, which makes it a perfectly good substitute.

¼ cup vegetable oil

4 dried Thai chilies

30 curry leaves (see Note)

4 cups sliced white onion

2 large acorn squash (4 to 4½ pounds total), peeled and
    cut into large dice (about 10 cups)

Kosher salt

¼ teaspoon freshly ground black pepper

1 tablespoon light brown sugar

1 packed cup cilantro leaves

1. Heat the oil in a 9-inch pot over medium heat until almost smoking.
    Add the chilies and cook, stirring, for 30 seconds. Add the curry leaves
    to the pan and cook, stirring, until they have spluttered and darkened,
    about 15 seconds. Add the onion slices and cook until soft, but not
    browned, 5 to 7 minutes. Stir in the squash, 1 tablespoon of salt, and

the black pepper. Turn the heat to medium-low, cover, and cook, stirring every now and then, until the squash has cooked to a chunky puree, 50 to 60 minutes.

2. Remove and discard the Thai chilies. Stir in the brown sugar and cilantro leaves, and the remaining ½ teaspoon of salt, or to taste. Spoon into a bowl and serve hot.

Note: If you are unable to find fresh curry leaves, 2 teaspoons of yellow or brown mustard seeds would be a suitable substitute. Add the mustard seeds to the pot in step 1, lower the heat, and cover the pan to pop the seeds. They will sputter and darken. Return the heat to medium and proceed with the remainder of the recipe as written.

Zucchini Puree with Marjoram

SERVES 4

Fresh marjoram and zucchini are a terrific combination, and here they costar to make a subtle but eminently satisfying side dish that captures the elusive flavor of zucchini. This recipe makes a great accompaniment for grilled chicken or fish. If you're looking for something unusual to serve for brunch, spoon the puree onto warm plates and top with poached or fried eggs. Serve with toasted garlic bread.

2 tablespoons extra-virgin olive oil
3 garlic cloves, sliced
1½ pounds zucchini, washed, quartered lengthwise, and
  thinly sliced
1 teaspoon chopped fresh marjoram
1 cup seeded and diced tomato
1 cube or 1 teaspoon chicken bouillon base
½ teaspoon kosher salt
⅛ teaspoon freshly ground black pepper

1. Combine the oil and garlic in a 12-inch, straight-sided skillet and place over low heat. Cook until the garlic is softened but not browned, 2 to 3 minutes. Raise the heat to high; add the zucchini, marjoram, tomato, chicken base, salt, and pepper. Cook, stirring occasionally, until the zucchini is *al dente,* 4 to 5 minutes.

2. Transfer to a food processor and pulse until the mixture is smooth, but not finely pureed. Return the zucchini to the pan and warm through, stirring constantly, over medium heat. Adjust the seasoning to your taste. Serve hot.

Sweet-and-Sour Carrots

SERVES 6

Sweet and sour notes marry beautifully with floral, fresh herb flavors for a simple and delightful dish to accompany Bollito di Vitello (page 168), Oven-Braised Short Ribs (page 166), or Lamb Stew alla Romana (page 184).

2 large sprigs fresh mint

2 small sprigs fresh rosemary

1 stem fresh basil with leaves

1 sprig fresh sage

2 sprigs fresh thyme

1 bay leaf

1 pound carrots, peeled and thinly sliced on the bias (2¾ cups)

1 garlic clove, peeled and split

⅓ cup sugar

⅓ cup white vinegar

½ cup white wine

1 teaspoon coarse sea salt

⅛ teaspoon freshly ground black pepper

1 tablespoon butter

1. Tie together the fresh herb sprigs with kitchen twine.

2. Combine the herb bundle and all of the remaining ingredients, except the butter, in a large saucepan. Add water to barely cover the carrots. Bring to a boil, reduce the heat, and simmer until the carrots are very tender, 30 to 40 minutes. Uncover the saucepan, return the liquid to a boil, and reduce to about ¾ cup. Swirl in the butter. Spoon the carrots and their liquid into a warm serving bowl and serve.

Roasted Root Vegetables

SERVES 4

This homey recipe makes great use of the late-season harvest, and yields a colorful, hot bowl of jewel-like root vegetables, gently glazed with honey. It's a versatile side dish that works equally well with braises and roasts, whether meat, fowl, or fish. The beets are roasted separately and added to the dish only in the final step to prevent them from coloring the other vegetables.

8 ounces beets
2½ tablespoons vegetable oil
8 ounces carrots, peeled and cut on a bias into
    ¾- to 1-inch pieces (1⅓ cups)
8 ounces parsnips, peeled and cut on a bias into
    ¾- to 1-inch pieces (1½ cups)
8 ounces turnips or rutabaga, peeled and cut into
    chunks (1⅓ cups)
2 small white onions, cut into 1- to 1¼-inch wedges
3 tablespoons honey
1 tablespoon plus 1 teaspoon chopped fresh sage
½ teaspoon kosher salt
½ teaspoon freshly ground pepper
1 tablespoon chopped fresh parsley

1. Preheat the oven to 400 degrees F.

2. Trim the beet greens, leaving a ½- to 1-inch stem attached to the beets. Rinse the beets, and wrap them in aluminum foil. Place the wrapped beets on a rack in the oven and roast for 1 hour and 10 minutes.

3. Pour the oil into a 13 by 9-inch metal baking dish, and heat over medium-high heat until smoking. Add all of the remaining vegetables and toss in the oil. Place the roasting pan in the oven and roast for

10 minutes. Add the honey and 1 tablespoon of the sage to the pan and continue roasting, shaking the pan every 10 or 15 minutes, until the vegetables are tender, about 60 to 70 minutes. When the beets are done, unwrap them, cut into ¾-inch chunks, and toss them in with the other vegetables just before serving. Season with the remaining 1 teaspoon of sage, the salt, pepper, and parsley. Transfer to a large bowl and serve.

Carrot-Mushroom Sformato

SERVES 4 TO 6

Sformato—literally, "misformed" in Italian—is the name given to a soufflélike, savory pudding that can be made with any number of ingredients, primarily vegetables. Here, the *sformato* is a colorful vehicle for pure carrot and mushroom flavors, and can work equally well as an appetizer, side dish, or even a light vegetarian main course, accompanied by a fresh tomato sauce and a salad. At the restaurant, we've served the *sformato* alongside chicken, brisket of beef, lamb, and veal.

3½ tablespoons cold butter, plus ½ tablespoon at room
    temperature

1 cup chopped onion

Kosher salt

2 tablespoons all-purpose flour

1 cup milk

¼ cup plus 1 tablespoon finely grated Parmigiano-
    Reggiano

1 pound carrots, peeled, split, and sliced about ⅛ inch
    thick (2¾ cups)

½ teaspoon sugar

1 cup water

1 tablespoon vegetable oil

8 ounces white mushrooms, cut into ¼-inch dice

⅛ teaspoon freshly ground black pepper

2 large eggs, lightly beaten

2 tablespoons chopped fresh basil

2 tablespoons chopped fresh parsley

1. Thoroughly brush the bottom and sides of a
6-inch round soufflé mold with the ½ tablespoon
of room-temperature butter; refrigerate.

Wine Suggestions:
If you're serving
the *sformato* as an
appetizer or main
course, pair it with
Piedmont's floral
white arneis or with
Vouvray from France's
Loire Valley.

2. Make a béchamel sauce: Over medium-low heat, melt 2 tablespoons of the cold butter in a 2-quart, heavy-bottomed saucepan. Add the onion and ½ teaspoon of salt and cook until the onion is wilted and translucent, 4 to 5 minutes. Add the flour and cook, stirring, 3 minutes. Add ⅓ cup of the milk and stir until smooth. Stir in the remaining milk, bring to a simmer, and cook, stirring, until the sauce has become quite thick, about 3 minutes. Stir in ¼ cup of the cheese, transfer the sauce to a large bowl, and let cool completely.

3. Combine the carrots, 1 tablespoon of the cold butter, the sugar, water, and ¾ teaspoon of salt in a 2-quart saucepan. Bring to a boil, reduce the heat, and simmer gently, covered, until the carrots are very tender, 25 to 30 minutes. Uncover and continue cooking until the water has almost evaporated and the carrots are glazed. Transfer to the bowl of a food processor and pulse to chop coarsely, but do not puree. (Alternatively, chop the carrots by hand with a large knife.) Let cool.

4. Preheat the oven to 350 degrees F.

5. Heat the oil to almost smoking in a large skillet over high heat. Add the mushrooms and the remaining ½ tablespoon of butter and cook until the mushroom liquid has evaporated, 3 to 4 minutes. Season with ½ teaspoon of salt and the pepper and remove from the heat.

6. Stir the eggs into the cooled béchamel. Stir in the carrots, mushrooms and herbs, mixing well. Scrape the mixture into the prepared soufflé mold, smooth the surface, and sprinkle the remaining tablespoon of cheese over the top. Place the mold into a roasting pan. Add boiling water to come about halfway up the side of the mold to make a *bain-marie*. Place the pan into the oven and bake for 50 minutes. Then increase the oven heat to 400 degrees F and bake 20 more minutes to brown the top. Let stand 10 minutes, cut into wedges, and serve.

Roasted Cauliflower with Tomato and Green Olives

SERVES 4 TO 6

This dish uses the winning Sicilian combination of briny green olives, onions, tomatoes, and cauliflower to make a stunning dish that can be enjoyed hot as a vegetable accompaniment for fish or fowl, or at room temperature as part of an antipasto platter. We first served this at a Union Square Cafe Wine and Food Dinner celebrating the flavors of Italy. Our guests loved it that night and demanded we include its recipe in the cookbook. As with almost any vegetable, roasting the cauliflower is a good way to concentrate its flavor. If you have a convection oven, the cauliflower will brown more evenly than in a standard oven and will also cook in about 5 minutes less time.

1 head cauliflower, stem trimmed,
    cut into 2-inch florets
¼ cup olive oil
Kosher salt
Freshly ground black pepper
2 cups quartered and thinly sliced onion
1 teaspoon chopped garlic
1 teaspoon coarsely chopped fresh oregano
½ cup pitted and sliced green olives
¼ teaspoon Aleppo pepper
1 cup seeded and diced tomatoes
1 tablespoon chopped fresh parsley

1. Preheat the oven to 450 degrees F.

2. Toss the cauliflower in a bowl with 2 tablespoons of the olive oil, ½ teaspoon of salt, and ⅛ teaspoon of black pepper. Spread out in

a single layer on a cookie sheet and roast until the cauliflower is just tender and lightly browned, about 20 minutes.

3. Meanwhile, heat the remaining 2 tablespoons of oil in a large skillet over medium-high heat. Add the onion and cook until it is lightly browned but still has crunch, about 4 minutes. Stir in the garlic, oregano, olives, ¾ teaspoon of salt, ¼ teaspoon black pepper, and the Aleppo pepper; cook a few seconds until the garlic is fragrant but not brown. Stir in the tomato and parsley, cook for 30 seconds, and remove from the heat.

4. When the cauliflower has finished roasting, return the tomato-onion mixture to high heat, toss in the cauliflower, and sauté quickly to combine and heat through. Serve hot or at room temperature.

Scaffata

SERVES 4

This melange of fresh shell beans, artichokes, lettuce, and mint is adapted from the traditional Pugliese dish *scaffata,* whose name literally translates as "shelled." Variations of *scaffata* are served throughout Italy in the springtime, where they're enjoyed as an all-vegetable main course, or as an accompaniment for roast lamb or chicken. In all of the versions we've enjoyed, the vegetables are well cooked like a stew, where the sum is greater than the parts.

1 lemon, split
12 baby artichokes
Kosher salt
2 pounds fresh fava beans, shelled
1 cup shelled fresh peas
2 tablespoons extra-virgin olive oil
¾ cup thinly sliced spring onions or scallions (white and green parts) cut diagonally into ¾ inch lengths
⅛ teaspoon freshly ground black pepper
¼ cup dry white vermouth (preferably Cinzano)
¾ cup Chicken Stock (page 315), Vegetable Stock (page 318), or water
2 packed cups sliced Boston or Bibb lettuce leaves (leaves cut into thirds and then crosswise into wide strips)
¼ teaspoon dried red pepper flakes
¼ cup sliced fresh mint

1. Prepare the artichokes: Squeeze the lemon into a bowl of cold water large enough to hold the artichokes. Cut off only the very tip of each artichoke stem. Peel the outer layer of the remaining stem with a paring knife or vegetable peeler. Pull off the outer, tougher leaves of the

artichoke to expose the innermost core of tender yellow leaves. Slice off the tips of the yellow leaves, and cut the artichokes in half lengthwise. With a paring knife, remove and discard the small choke. Lay each artichoke half, cut side down, on the cutting board, and then slice the artichoke halves vertically as thinly as possible. To prevent discoloration, place the slices in the lemon water as soon as they are cut.

2. Prepare a bowl of ice water. In a large saucepan, bring 2 quarts of water to a boil with 1 tablespoon salt. Add the fava beans to the boiling water and cook until tender, but not mushy, 3 to 4 minutes. Remove the saucepan from the heat, and using a slotted spoon, transfer the cooked beans to the bowl of ice water to refresh them. When the fava beans have cooled, drain, peel, and reserve them.

3. Return the water in the saucepan to a boil, and add the shelled peas. Cook until the peas just begin to get tender, about 3 to 4 minutes; then drain the peas in a colander and refresh them in the ice water. When chilled, drain the peas from the ice water and reserve.

4. Drain the sliced artichokes well and blot them dry with paper towels. Heat the olive oil in a large skillet set over medium heat; add the artichoke slices to the pan and cook, stirring occasionally, for 2 minutes. Add the onions, season with 1 teaspoon of salt and the black pepper and cook until the artichokes begin to become tender, 1 to 2 more minutes. Pour in the vermouth and cook until almost dry. Stir in the peas and fava beans and cook for 1 minute. Pour in the stock or water and bring to a simmer. Cover and cook, stirring occasionally, until the vegetables are very tender, 8 to 10 minutes. (The beans and peas will not remain bright green.) Fold in the lettuce, pepper flakes, and mint and stir just until the lettuce wilts. The *scaffata* should be moist but not soupy, and the vegetables should all be quite tender. Taste for seasoning and adjust accordingly. Transfer to a bowl and serve.

Spiced Creamed Spinach

SERVES 4

In this popular recipe, Indian spices lend an exotic note to an American comfort-food classic. At the restaurant, we serve the creamed spinach as part of an Indian-spiced vegetable array, including chickpeas and eggplant; it also makes a fabulous accompaniment for lamb chops, roast chicken, salmon, and shrimp.

2 pounds fresh spinach
2 tablespoons plus 1½ teaspoons kosher salt
2 tablespoons butter
¼ cup finely chopped onion
1 tablespoon finely chopped gingerroot
½ jalapeño, seeded and chopped
¾ cup crème fraîche or heavy cream
⅛ teaspoon freshly ground black pepper
½ teaspoon garam masala (see Note, page 29)

1. Remove the stems from the spinach leaves. Discard any leaves that are discolored or tough. Soak the spinach in a large bowl of cold water, stirring to dislodge sand and grit. Change the water at least 2 or 3 times to ensure that the spinach is absolutely clean. With each change of water, lift the spinach out of the bowl with your hands, rather than draining the water through a colander: That way, you won't pour the sandy water back onto the spinach. Dry the spinach thoroughly in a salad spinner or on paper towels.

2. To blanch all the spinach at once, bring 2 gallons of water to a boil in a 3- to 4-gallon pot with 2 tablespoons salt. (You can also blanch the spinach in smaller batches.) Add the spinach and cook, stirring occasionally, until the water just returns to a boil. Drain in a colander, refresh under cold running water, then press the spinach against the sides of the colander to press out most of the water. Pulse in a food processor until finely chopped, but not pureed; reserve.

3. Melt the butter in a large skillet over medium heat. Add the onion, ginger, and jalapeño and cook, without coloring, stirring occasionally, until tender, about 5 minutes.

4. Add the crème fraîche or heavy cream and bring to a boil. Add the spinach and ¼ cup water and stir until the spinach is heated through. Season with the 1½ teaspoons salt, the pepper, and garam masala and serve.

Sautéed Cabbage

SERVES 4

Though it's hard to imagine what *wouldn't* taste good with this versatile cabbage dish, we can recommend serving it with practically any recipe for poultry, pork chops, calf's liver, shrimp, or monkfish. A complementary side dish is Mustard-Mashed Potatoes (page 251).

Kosher salt

2 medium heads Savoy cabbage, coarse outer leaves, core, and ribs removed, cut into 1-inch dice (10 cups)

4 ounces bacon, sliced crosswise into 1-inch pieces (¾ cup)

3 cups thinly sliced white onions

2 tablespoons chopped fresh sage

1 tablespoon all-purpose flour

2 cups Chicken Stock (page 315)

¼ teaspoon freshly ground black pepper

1. Bring 2 quarts of water to a boil and add 1 tablespoon salt. Add the cabbage and blanch for 1 minute. Drain the cabbage in a colander, refresh under cold running water until cool, and reserve.

2. Put the bacon in a large skillet and cook over medium heat until the fat is rendered, 4 to 5 minutes. Pour off all but 1 tablespoon of the fat. Add the onion and sage and cook, stirring, until the onion is wilted but not browned, about 10 minutes. Add the blanched cabbage and cook for 2 more minutes. Stir in the flour and cook, stirring, 3 minutes. Pour in the stock, bring to a boil, reduce the heat, and cook until thickened, 2 to 3 more minutes. Season with ½ teaspoon salt and the pepper and serve.

Brussels Sprouts with Bacon and Oregano

SERVES 4

In our early days, garnishing a main course with brussels sprouts was a sure way to "torpedo" its sales: no one liked them, it seemed. In recent years we've noted that this cruciferous vegetable is finally winning its way into the hearts of diners, actually lending additional support and interest to a dish. Bacon adds a heady smokiness to the sprouts, and we suggest serving them alongside venison, lamb shanks, rabbit, or duck.

6 ounces sliced bacon, cut crosswise into
    1-inch-wide pieces
1 pound brussels sprouts, washed and trimmed;
    larger sprouts quartered, smaller sprouts halved
1½ tablespoons chopped fresh oregano
¾ teaspoon kosher salt
1½ teaspoons fresh lemon juice
⅛ teaspoon Aleppo or freshly ground black pepper

1. Preheat the oven to 425 degrees F.

2. Cook the bacon in a large ovenproof sauté pan over medium heat until the fat is rendered, 6 to 7 minutes. Toss in the brussels sprouts and stir to coat. Add the oregano and salt and roast in the oven, stirring every now and then during the last half of the cooking, until the sprouts are tender, about 25 minutes.

3. Remove from the oven, stir in the lemon juice and pepper, transfer to a warm platter, and serve.

Baked Sauerkraut

SERVES 4

Sauerkraut, or pickled cabbage, is an underrated and underappreciated garnish for cold-weather dishes like roasted birds, braised meats, and grilled sausages. It's also the star ingredient of the classic Alsatian dish, choucroute. At Union Square Cafe, we take the stuff seriously and have found that the trick is to begin with a good-quality sauerkraut (packed in plastic is preferable to canned) and then lovingly bake it with homemade chicken stock, a judicious amount of juniper berries, and dry white wine (riesling and chenin blanc are ideal). Compared to the sharp, acidic bite of store-bought sauerkraut right out of the bag, slow-baked sauerkraut delivers mellow, complex, and satisfying flavor.

4 ounces thickly sliced slab bacon,
     cut into ½-inch pieces
½ cup coarsely chopped onion
½ cup peeled, coarsely chopped carrots
½ cup coarsely chopped celery
2 pounds best-quality sauerkraut,
     rinsed well and drained
15 juniper berries
2 bay leaves
1½ teaspoons coarse sea salt
¼ teaspoon freshly ground black pepper
1½ cups dry white wine
½ cup Chicken Stock (page 315)
Parchment paper

1. Preheat the oven to 350 degrees F.

2. Crisp the bacon over medium-high heat in a 3-quart ovenproof saucepan, 5 to 7 minutes.

3. Add the onion, carrots, and celery to the saucepan and cook, stirring, for 3 minutes. Add the sauerkraut, juniper berries, bay leaves, salt, and pepper; stir to thoroughly combine all of the ingredients.

4. Pour in the wine and chicken stock and bring to a boil. Lay a round of parchment paper over the sauerkraut, cover the pan with its lid, and bake for 1 hour and 15 minutes. Remove the lid (but leave the parchment paper) and bake 20 minutes longer. Serve hot.

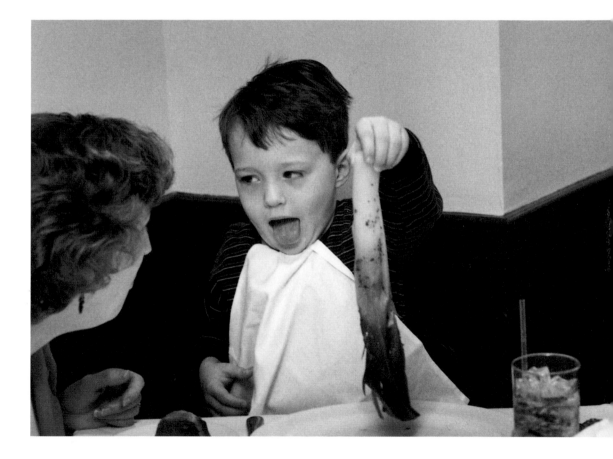

Cardoon Gratin

SERVES 4 TO 6

Though they're highly esteemed in Italy, cardoons remain an unfamiliar but happy taste discovery for our guests. A member of the thistle family, a cardoon appears to be overgrown celery and has a pleasantly subtle, artichokelike taste. It's easiest to peel the fibrous stalks using a European nonswivel-style peeler or a paring knife. To make this a vegetarian dish, replace the chicken stock with vegetable stock. As with artichoke hearts or salsify, covering the simmering cardoons with bread slices is a simple trick to keep them from discoloring while blanching, without adding the more traditional flour or lemon to the water. The gratin is a versatile and soothing side dish that works well with poultry, veal, and lamb.

1 lemon, halved

1 large head cardoons (5 to 6 stalks)

1 tablespoon salt

5 to 6 slices white bread

2 tablespoons olive oil

2 large onions (1½ to 1¾ pounds total weight),
     quartered and thinly sliced lengthwise

⅛ teaspoon freshly ground black pepper

2 tablespoons plus 1 teaspoon butter

½ cup plus 1 tablespoon grated Pecorino Romano

½ to ¾ cup Chicken Stock (page 315), well seasoned
     with salt and pepper

¼ cup panko (Japanese bread crumbs), or homemade
     coarse bread crumbs

1. Squeeze the juice from the lemon into a large bowl filled with water; then add the lemon halves to the bowl as well. Cut and separate the cardoon stalks from the root. Trim the ends and tops of the stalks, and cut away any leaves from the edges. Peel the stalks thoroughly to remove

the strings and all of the grayish-green skin. Cut the stalks in half lengthwise and then crosswise into 3-inch pieces. Place the cut pieces into the bowl of lemon water to prevent discoloration while you're working. (You should have about 10 cups.)

2. Drain the cardoons and discard the lemon. Transfer the cardoons to a large pot. Add water to cover, and 2 teaspoons of the salt. Lay the bread slices on top to completely cover. Bring to a simmer and cook until the cardoons are very tender, about 1½ hours. Remove the bread slices with a slotted spoon and drain the cardoons.

3. While the cardoons are cooking, heat the oil in a large skillet over medium-high heat. Add the onions and cook until limp and golden, 8 to 10 minutes. Stir in the remaining 1 teaspoon of salt and the pepper.

4. Heat the oven to 375 degrees F. Lightly butter a 2½-quart gratin dish with 1 teaspoon of the butter. Layer one-third of the onions over the bottom of the gratin dish. Arrange one-third of the cardoons in a single layer, in neat rows, over the onions. Sprinkle the cardoons with 2½ tablespoons of the cheese. Repeat the process to make two additional layers. Warm the stock to a simmer in a small saucepan and pour ½ cup over the gratin. Sprinkle the top with the panko and the remaining ¼ cup of cheese; dot with the remaining 2 tablespoons butter. Cover with aluminum foil and bake 1 hour. Remove the foil and continue baking until the cardoons are meltingly tender, about 30 more minutes. If the gratin appears dry during the cooking, add the remaining ¼ cup stock.

5. Warm the stock to a simmer in a small saucepan and pour ½ cup over the gratin. Sprinkle the top with the panko and the remaining ¼ cup of cheese; dot with the remaining 2 tablespoons of butter. Cover with aluminum foil and bake for 1 hour. Remove the foil and continue baking until the cardoons are meltingly tender, about 30 more minutes. If the gratin appears dry during the cooking, add the remaining ¼ cup of stock.

6. Preheat the broiler. Place the gratin under the broiler and cook until the top is evenly browned. Let stand for 15 minutes before serving.

Jerusalem Artichoke Pancakes

SERVES 4

Neither from Jerusalem, nor from the artichoke family, these misshapen knobs
are actually the roots of a type of sunflower. Their name derives from a
mispronunciation of *girasole*—Italian for sunflower—and the resemblance
of their nutty flavor to the meat of the artichoke. Despite their forbidding
appearance, there are so many different ways to enjoy Jerusalem artichokes:
baked with olive oil and salt, sliced and fried into chips, or as the base of a
soup. At the restaurant, we have even shaved them thinly over risotto, where
they serve as a delicious and economical stand-in for white truffles. Here, they
are shredded to make a wonderful riff on potato latkes. Enjoy them garnished
with sour cream and applesauce or Apple-Pear Chutney (page 256). They're
also a terrific accompaniment for roast poultry and braised meats. Once
you've shredded the Jerusalem artichokes, work quickly so they won't darken
and become watery.

1 small onion
1½ pounds Jerusalem artichokes, scrubbed
1 large egg, lightly beaten
½ cup all-purpose flour
1 tablespoon pure maple syrup
1 tablespoon walnut or hazelnut oil (optional)
1½ teaspoons kosher salt
⅛ teaspoon freshly ground black pepper
Pinch of cayenne
⅛ teaspoon freshly grated nutmeg
¼ cup vegetable oil, or more as needed
1 tablespoon butter

1. Using the shredder attachment, grate the onion in a food processor or through the largest holes of a hand grater, and transfer to a large bowl. Do the same with the Jerusalem artichokes.

2. Add the egg to the bowl and stir with a wooden spoon or spatula until well blended. Add the flour and stir in lightly; do not overwork. Add the maple syrup and the nut oil, if using, and season with the salt, black pepper, cayenne, and nutmeg. Form into 8 or 9 equal pancakes, about 3 inches in diameter and ½ inch thick. Place each pancake on a cookie sheet lined with wax paper.

3. Heat the vegetable oil and butter in a large heavy-bottomed skillet or on a griddle over medium heat. Working in batches, cook the pancakes until golden brown, about 5 to 7 minutes per side. You may need to adjust the heat as you work to avoid browning the outside of the pancakes too much before the inside cooks through. If the pan or griddle gets dry, add up to 1 more tablespoon of oil. Place the cooked pancakes on a plate lined with paper towels to drain, and cover loosely with foil to keep warm until ready to serve.

Potato–Jerusalem Artichoke Gratin

SERVES 4 TO 6

Try this dish. We promise it will become a family favorite. Jerusalem artichokes contribute a nutty counterpoint to the rich combination of potatoes, Gruyère, and cream.

1 garlic clove, peeled and split in half
1 teaspoon butter
3⅓ cups heavy cream
Rounded ⅛ teaspoon freshly grated nutmeg
2¼ teaspoons kosher salt
Rounded ⅛ teaspoon freshly ground white pepper
⅛ teaspoon cayenne
1¾ pounds Idaho potatoes
8 ounces Jerusalem artichokes, scrubbed
2½ cups grated Gruyère cheese (8 ounces)

1. Preheat the oven to 350 degrees F.

2. Rub a 10-cup gratin dish with both halves of the cut garlic clove, then lightly butter the dish.

3. Combine the cream, nutmeg, salt, pepper, and cayenne in a large bowl.

4. Peel the potatoes and slice them paper-thin on a mandoline or on the blade of a hand grater. As you work, place the potato slices in the bowl with the cream and seasonings.

5. Using the mandoline, slice the Jerusalem artichokes paper-thin, carefully pat dry on paper towels, and add to the cream. Add the cheese and stir gently to combine.

6. Pour the vegetable-cheese mixture into the prepared gratin dish, making sure the vegetable slices are flat and level. Place the gratin dish inside a roasting pan and fill the pan three-quarters of the way up the sides of the dish with hot water to make a *bain-marie*. Carefully place the roasting pan in the center of the oven and bake, uncovered, for 2½ hours, or until the gratin has completely set and is golden on top. If the top browns too quickly during cooking, cover with aluminum foil. Let stand 15 minutes before serving.

I hate leeks!

Swiss Chard, Leek, and Celery Tortino

SERVES 6 AS A MAIN COURSE, 10 AS A SIDE DISH

Home cooks in northern Italy make excellent use of the *tortino*—a sort of crustless quiche—as a vehicle for utilizing in-season vegetables. When it's late autumn or winter in New York and all we can find at the greenmarket are hardy greens and root vegetables, our thoughts also turn to *tortino*. In this version, we've lightened the texture a bit with the addition of fluffy fresh ricotta cheese. Serve it as a main course, preceded by a salad or soup, or as a winning side dish for veal chops, roast chicken, or lamb.

2 medium bunches green Swiss chard
¼ cup extra-virgin olive oil, plus ½ tablespoon
    for oiling the dish
Kosher salt
Freshly ground black pepper
5 cups washed, drained, and sliced (⅛ inch thick) leeks
    (white and light green parts only)
3 cups peeled and thinly sliced celery
8 large eggs
2 cups heavy cream
1½ cups ricotta cheese
1 cup finely grated Parmigiano-Reggiano
1 teaspoon Aleppo pepper

1. Remove the stems from the chard leaves and reserve. Discard any leaves that are discolored or tough. Wash the leaves in a large bowl of cold water, changing the water several times until the leaves are free of all grit. Then lift the leaves out of the bowl, and drain well in a colander. Chop coarsely.

2. Trim and discard the ends from the reserved chard stems. Rinse the stems in a bowl of cold water, drain, and slice them crosswise, ¼ inch thick.

3. Heat 1 tablespoon of the oil in a very large skillet over medium heat. Add the chopped chard leaves and cook, stirring often, until tender, 10 to 12 minutes. Stir in ¼ teaspoon of salt and a pinch of black pepper, drain in a colander, and transfer to a large bowl.

4. Heat 3 tablespoons of the oil in the skillet over medium heat. Add the sliced chard stems, leeks, and celery. Cover and cook until tender, stirring occasionally, about 10 to 12 minutes. Season with ¾ teaspoon of salt and ¼ teaspoon of pepper and stir. Transfer the vegetables to the colander to drain and add to the bowl with the cooked chard leaves. Let the vegetables cool completely.

5. Preheat the oven to 350 degrees F. Oil a 13 by 9-inch baking dish with the remaining ½ tablespoon of olive oil.

6. Combine the eggs, cream, ricotta, ½ cup of the grated Parmigiano, 1¼ teaspoons of salt, ¼ teaspoon black pepper, and the Aleppo pepper in a large bowl; whisk until combined.

7. Stir the cooled vegetables into the egg-and-cheese mixture and combine well. Pour into the prepared baking dish and spread evenly with a spatula. Cover with aluminum foil, making sure that the foil doesn't touch the top of the *tortino*. Make a *bain-marie:* place the baking dish inside a large roasting pan, and fill the pan with enough hot water to come three-quarters of the way up the sides of the baking dish. Carefully place the *bain-marie* in the center of the oven and bake for 40 minutes. Uncover and continue baking until the *tortino* is set, about 30 more minutes. Remove the *tortino* from the oven and from the *bain-marie*.

8. Preheat the broiler. Sprinkle the remaining ½ cup Parmigiano over the top of the *tortino* and broil until golden brown. Cut into square serving pieces and serve hot.

DUNCAN'S DELIGHTFUL ADVENTURES

SIDE DISHES AND CONDIMENTS

Apple and Mortadella Stuffing

———

Basmati Rice Pilaf

———

Lentil-Bulgur Pilaf

———

Flageolet "Baked Beans"

———

Butternut Squash-Poppy Seed Spaetzle

———

Polenta with White Beans and Chard

———

Maple-Roasted Sweet Potatoes

———

Baked Potatoes with Roasted Onion
and Sour Cream

———

Italian Fries

———

Mustard-Mashed Potatoes

———

Bottarga-Mashed Potatoes

———

Horseradish-Mashed Potatoes

———

Olive-Mashed Potatoes

———

Apple-Pear Chutney

———

Plum Chutney

———

Green Tomato Chutney

———

Quince Chutney

———

Apple and Mortadella Stuffing

SERVES 8 TO 10

Since the genuine article only recently became available in the United States, most American cooks have missed out on mortadella—one of Italy's greatest culinary gifts and secret ingredients. Mortadella is a processed sausage that may look like bologna, but it's about as close to that product as Prosciutto di Parma is to packaged sliced ham from the grocery store. While it's marvelous on its own with bread, fresh mozzarella, and a drizzle of good olive oil, mortadella adds an exciting depth of garlicky, meaty flavor when used as a cooking ingredient in sauces, soups, braises, and roasts. Here, along with green olives, it plays a starring role in a stove-top stuffing you could use as a succulent accompaniment for roast turkey, duck, chicken, or roast loin of pork. We like the stuffing moist and somewhat loose, but if you prefer it a bit drier, simply continue cooking the stuffing, uncovered, stirring occasionally, until you achieve the desired texture.

⅓ cup raisins

4½ cups apple cider

1½ tablespoons butter

1 medium onion, diced (about 1 cup)

3 celery stalks, split lengthwise and cut into
    ¼-inch slices

3 tablespoons pine nuts

8 ounces mortadella, cut into ¼-inch dice

1 cup pitted and coarsely chopped green olives

2 apples, peeled, cored, and diced

6 fresh sage leaves, chopped

6 cups day-old sourdough bread (crusts removed),
    cut into 1-inch cubes

½ teaspoon kosher salt

¼ teaspoon freshly ground black pepper

1. To plump the raisins, combine them with the apple cider in a small saucepan and bring to a boil over medium heat. Immediately remove from the heat and set aside.

2. In a large, nonreactive saucepan or Dutch oven, melt the butter over medium heat. Add the onion, celery, and pine nuts. Cook, stirring occasionally, without coloring, 6 to 8 minutes.

3. Add the mortadella, olives, apples, and sage and cook 5 more minutes.

4. Strain the raisins, reserving the cider, and add the raisins to the saucepan. Stir in the bread cubes, season with the salt and pepper, and add the reserved cider. Bring to a boil, lower the heat, and simmer, covered, for 15 minutes. Stir thoroughly, cover, and continue cooking for an additional 15 minutes. The stuffing will be very moist. Serve hot. The stuffing can be kept hot and held for up to 1 hour in a *bain-marie*.

Basmati Rice Pilaf

SERVES 4

Basmati is a long-grained rice prized in Indian cookery for its fragrance and nutty flavor. Once exclusively an Asian import, good-quality basmati is now grown in Texas as well. In this recipe, the rice is enhanced with freshly toasted spices, sautéed onions, and mushrooms to make a fabulous pilaf. At the restaurant, we've served it alongside our Spiced Creamed Spinach (page 216) and as an accompaniment for lamb, salmon, and chicken. Black cumin is a smoky spice, prized in northern Indian cooking, that is available in most Middle Eastern or Indian specialty stores.

1½ cups basmati rice
3 tablespoons butter
1 cinnamon stick
4 cardamom pods
2 cloves
5 peppercorns
1 bay leaf
¾ teaspoon black cumin or cumin
1½ cups chopped onion
4 cups thinly sliced cremini mushrooms
2 teaspoons kosher salt
⅛ teaspoon freshly ground black pepper

1. Preheat the oven to 400 degrees F.

2. In a large bowl, cover the rice with cold water and stir with your fingers until the water becomes cloudy. Carefully pour off the water, reserving the rice. Repeat 2 to 3 times, until the water is almost clear. Cover with fresh, cold water and soak for 10 minutes.

3. Bring 2 cups of water to a boil and set aside.

4. Heat the butter over medium-high heat in a 3-quart straight-sided saucepan until it begins to turn nut-brown. Add the spices and cook until fragrant, 30 to 60 seconds. Add the onion and cook until it begins to brown, 4 to 5 minutes. Add the mushrooms and cook until softened, 2 to 3 minutes.

5. Drain the rice, add it to the pan, and cook, stirring, for 1 minute to coat the rice with the butter. Season with the salt and pepper, and pour in the reserved hot water. Bring to a boil and cook for 1 minute. Cover with a tight-fitting lid or aluminum foil, place in the oven, and bake for 10 minutes. Remove from the oven and let stand, still covered, for 5 minutes. Uncover the rice, fluff with a fork, and serve hot.

Lentil-Bulgur Pilaf

SERVES 4

This is a Middle Eastern side dish with an Indian accent, which our guests love with grilled lamb paillard. We'd use it as an accompaniment for leg of lamb, lamb chops, or shish kebabs, and the pilaf is also wonderful with chicken, salmon, or shrimp. We've even enjoyed a big bowl of the pilaf all on its own, topped with a dollop of fresh, plain yogurt or raita. Bulgur wheat (or cracked wheat) is a wonderful grain that is available in Middle Eastern grocery stores and in many health-food stores. It's ground in varying degrees of coarseness, and we find that the medium size works best with the lentils. To toast spices like cumin or coriander seeds, place them in a small, heavy-bottomed skillet over medium heat and shake them over the flame until they darken slightly and begin to give off wisps of smoke. Transfer to a plate to cool and then grind.

1 cup medium bulgur wheat
2 cups water
½ teaspoon garam masala (see Note on page 29)
Pinch of cayenne
Kosher salt
⅓ cup green lentils, picked over and rinsed
1¼ cups Chicken Stock (page 315)
2 tablespoons olive oil
1½ cups chopped red onion
1 jalapeño pepper, stemmed, seeded, and chopped
2 garlic cloves, finely chopped
1 teaspoon cumin seed, toasted and ground
1¼ teaspoons coriander seeds, toasted and ground
¼ teaspoon Aleppo pepper
1 cup seeded and diced fresh or canned tomato
1 tablespoon sliced fresh mint leaves
¼ teaspoon freshly ground black pepper

1. Pour the bulgur into a large mixing bowl. Bring the water to a boil with ¼ teaspoon of the garam masala, the cayenne, and ½ teaspoon of salt. Pour the boiling water over the wheat, stir once, and cover the bowl tightly. Let stand until the bulgur wheat is plumped and tender, 30 to 40 minutes.

2. Combine the lentils in a small saucepan with the stock. Bring to a boil, reduce the heat, and simmer, covered, for 15 minutes. Add ¼ teaspoon of salt and continue cooking until tender, 15 to 20 more minutes. Drain and transfer to a bowl.

3. Heat the oil in a 2-quart saucepan over medium heat. Stir in the onion and cook until lightly browned, about 5 minutes. Add the jalapeño, garlic, cumin, coriander, Aleppo pepper, and the remaining ¼ teaspoon garam masala, and cook for 30 seconds. Then add the tomatoes and cook until juicy, 2 to 3 minutes. Transfer to the bowl with the lentils.

4. Drain and discard any excess liquid from the bulgur and add the wheat to the bowl with the lentil mixture. Stir in the mint, ¾ teaspoon of salt, and the black pepper, and combine. Adjust the seasoning to your taste. Serve the pilaf at room temperature.

Flageolet "Baked Beans"

SERVES 4

This is a Gallic riff on American baked beans. Fresh herbs and a touch of cream lend a satisfying note of elegance, making the green shell beans a fabulous accompaniment for lamb, roast pork loin, fresh or smoked ham, or brook trout.

1 cup dried flageolets
1 large sprig fresh rosemary
2 sprigs fresh sage
2 large sprigs fresh thyme
Kosher salt
4 ounces sliced bacon, cut crosswise
    into ¼- to ½-inch strips
½ cup heavy cream
1 large tomato, peeled, seeded, and diced (about 1 cup)
¼ teaspoon freshly ground black pepper

1. Soak the flageolets for 6 hours, or overnight, in enough cold water to cover. Drain.

2. Using a piece of kitchen twine, tie the herbs into a bundle. Combine the flageolets and the herb bundle in a 2-quart saucepan with enough water to cover generously. Bring to a simmer, cover, and cook until the beans are almost tender, about 1 hour. Add 2 teaspoons of salt and continue cooking until the beans are completely tender, about 30 more minutes. You can test for doneness by gently squeezing a bean between your fingers—it should give without resistance.

3. Drain the beans, reserving their cooking liquid. Discard the herb bundle, and wipe out the saucepan.

4. In the same saucepan, cook the bacon over medium heat until the fat is rendered and the bacon is brown but not crisp, 5 to 7 minutes. Pour in the cream and ¼ cup of the bean cooking liquid, bring to a simmer, and scrape the bottom of the pan to loosen any browned bits of bacon. Add the beans, tomato, ½ teaspoon of salt and the pepper and simmer gently until the cream thickens, 3 to 4 minutes. Add more of the bean cooking liquid if at any time the sauce seems too thick. Transfer to a bowl and serve hot.

Butternut Squash–Poppy Seed Spaetzle

SERVES 4

In the Northeast, butternut squash is so plentiful that it's smart to have lots of delicious ways to use it. We've found that spaetzle are a great vehicle for the squash. These squiggly, Swiss-style dumplings are simple to prepare, even if you don't have a spaetzle press. Simply substitute a colander with ¼-inch holes, and use a rubber spatula to press the batter through. In this recipe, poppy seeds provide a nice crunch, and a smidgen of maple syrup adds richness and depth. The spaetzle are great with chicken, venison, osso buco, or pork.

1½ pounds butternut squash
3½ tablespoons butter
1 teaspoon maple syrup
Kosher salt
Freshly ground black pepper
Pinch of freshly grated nutmeg
½ cup milk
1 large egg
1½ cups all-purpose flour
1 teaspoon poppy seeds

1. Preheat the oven to 400 degrees F.

2. Split the squash lengthwise, and scoop out and discard the seeds. Place the squash halves, cut side down, on a cookie sheet or roasting pan. Add just enough water to come ⅛ inch up the sides of the squash, and bake until the flesh can be easily pierced with a paring knife, about 1 hour. If the water evaporates during cooking, add a little more hot water. Let the squash stand until cool enough to handle. Using a large

spoon, scoop the flesh from the skin and drop into a bowl. Discard the skin.

3. Melt 1 tablespoon of the butter in a large saucepan over medium heat and cook until it turns light brown. Add the squash and maple syrup and cook, stirring often, until the mixture thickens to the consistency of porridge and measures about 1 cup, 15 to 20 minutes. Transfer to a large bowl and let cool. Using a wooden spoon, stir in 1½ teaspoons of salt, a pinch of pepper, nutmeg, milk, egg, and flour. Beat the mixture with the spoon or mix with your hand until the batter becomes shiny and very elastic, 3 to 4 minutes.

4. Bring 2 quarts of water to a boil with 1½ teaspoons of salt. Place a spaetzle press or a colander with ¼-inch holes over the boiling water. Working in 3 or 4 batches, use a rubber spatula to force the batter through the holes of the colander and into the boiling water. Cook until all of the spaetzle float to the surface, transfer them to another colander with a slotted spoon, and refresh under cold running water for a moment or two to prevent sticking. Continue the process until you've used all the batter.

5. To serve, melt the remaining 2½ tablespoons of butter in a 12-inch sauté pan or nonstick pan over medium-high heat. Add the poppy seeds and cook, stirring every now and then, until the butter turns light brown. Add the spaetzle and cook, stirring gently, until they become light golden brown and slightly puffed. Serve immediately.

Polenta with White Beans and Chard

SERVES 4

Known as *polenta integrale,* coarse-grained cornmeal flecked with buckwheat
makes a wonderfully wholesome dish, which we serve as a hearty change of
pace from our popular Creamy Polenta. Continuous stirring is the key to
smooth polenta. Chock-full of beans and vegetables, this polenta would make
a satisfying, all-vegetable main course for two. Or serve it, as we do, as an
accompaniment for roast quail, chicken, or turkey. *Polenta integrale* is
available in many Italian specialty stores, but if you can't find it, substitute
regular polenta.

1½ cups cooked cannellini or Great Northern beans
    (3 cups cooking liquid reserved), or canned cannellini
    or Great Northern beans, drained (liquid reserved)
1 cup polenta integrale or plain polenta
¼ cup extra-virgin olive oil, plus more for drizzling
1 medium carrot, peeled and chopped (about ½ cup)
1 leek (white and light green parts only), washed,
    drained, and chopped (about ½ cup)
1 celery stalk, peeled and chopped (about ½ cup)
1 small clove garlic, minced
1 bunch stemmed, washed, and coarsely chopped
    Swiss chard leaves (about 4 firmly packed cups)
Kosher salt
Freshly ground black pepper

1.   In a 3-quart saucepan, combine 3 cups of water with the 3 cups of
    liquid from the cooked or canned beans plus enough additional water
    to equal 6 cups total, and place over medium-high heat.

2.   Holding the cup of polenta in one hand and a firm whisk in the other,
    slowly pour the polenta into the bean liquid with a sprinkling motion,
    whisking constantly. Bring the liquid to a boil, whisking every few

minutes to avoid lumps. Turn the heat down to low so that the liquid is barely simmering and cook, whisking well every 5 to 10 minutes, until the polenta has lost its raw taste and has the consistency of mashed potatoes, about 50 minutes.

3.   When the polenta is almost cooked, heat the olive oil in an 11-inch skillet over medium heat. Add the carrot, leek, and celery and cook, stirring occasionally, for 5 minutes. Add the garlic and stir well for about 30 seconds. Add the beans, chard, and ½ cup water, increase the heat to medium-high, and cook, stirring every now and then, until the chard wilts and most of the water has evaporated, 3 to 4 minutes. Season with ¾ teaspoon of salt and ⅛ teaspoon of pepper and set aside.

4.   When the polenta is cooked, stir in the vegetable mixture and combine thoroughly. Season with 2 teaspoons of salt and ⅛ teaspoon of pepper. Spoon into a warm serving bowl, drizzle with olive oil, and serve.

Maple-Roasted Sweet Potatoes

SERVES 4

From the time he was a boy, when his grandmother accompanied every Thanksgiving turkey with sweet-potato-and-marshmallow pie, Danny has been a staunch sweet-potato hater. As a result, he's lost out on enjoying dish after dish of Michael's crowd-pleasing recipes that feature the orange tubers. This version marked the first time Danny *ever* enjoyed the stuff. It could be the gentle cayenne heat, or the nuttiness lent by roasting the potatoes with cinnamon and pecans. Let these sweet potatoes become part of your holiday dinner, or enjoy them during the rest of the cold months with pork chops, ham, roast chicken, or duck.

2 tablespoons butter

2 tablespoons brown sugar

2 pounds sweet potatoes, peeled, split lengthwise, and
    sliced crosswise, ¼ to ⅓ inch thick

⅛ teaspoon ground cinnamon

⅛ teaspoon dried red pepper flakes

1 tablespoon good-quality maple syrup

¼ cup chopped pecans

½ teaspoon kosher salt

2 tablespoons chopped fresh parsley

1. Preheat the oven to 400 degrees F.

2. Put the butter in a 13 by 9-inch metal baking dish, place in the oven, and heat until the butter is melted. Remove the pan from the oven, sprinkle with the brown sugar, and add the sweet potatoes. Sprinkle with the cinnamon and red pepper flakes, and stir to coat the potatoes. Roast, shaking the pan every now and then, until the potatoes are tender and browned, 45 to 50 minutes. Remove from the oven.

3. Gently stir in the maple syrup, pecans, and salt. Return the pan to the oven and roast until the potatoes are glazed and beginning to fall apart, an additional 10 to 15 minutes. Spoon into a serving bowl, sprinkle with the parsley, and serve.

Baked Potatoes with Roasted Onion and Sour Cream

Serves 4

Here's a simple variation on traditional baked potatoes, in which olive oil–rubbed spuds are pan-roasted along with a sweet white onion over a bed of sea salt. Rather than topping the crispy-skinned baked potatoes with butter, we fill them with an immensely satisfying combination of the chopped roasted onion and sour cream. Serve them with grilled steak, lamb chops—or just about anything at all you would want to eat with baked potatoes.

1½ cups coarse sea salt
1½ tablespoons olive oil
1 medium white onion, unpeeled
4 Idaho potatoes, about 8 ounces each, scrubbed
4 to 6 tablespoons sour cream

1. Preheat the oven to 400 degrees F. Place the salt in an even layer over the bottom of a 12-inch cast-iron skillet.

2. Pour the olive oil into a medium bowl and dip the onion into the oil to coat all over. Place the onion on the salt in the center of the skillet. Roast in the oven for 10 minutes.

3. Coat the potatoes with the oil remaining in the bowl and set them around the onion in the skillet. Return the skillet to the oven and continue roasting until the onion is tender and the potatoes are cooked through, about 1 hour and 10 minutes. Using tongs or a kitchen spoon, transfer the onion to a cutting board. Measure ¼ teaspoon of coarse salt from the skillet and set aside. Turn off the oven and return the skillet with the potatoes to the oven, leaving the door ajar, while you prepare the onion.

4. Peel and coarsely chop the onion. Transfer to a small bowl and season with the reserved salt.

5. Place the potatoes on a serving platter. Split and squeeze open each potato. Spoon one-quarter of the salted onion into each potato. Top with the sour cream and serve hot.

Italian Fries

SERVES 4

In Italy, many *trattorie* serve roasted meats with a side platter of parsleyed fried potato cubes—golden brown on the outside, and still soft and piping hot within. The potatoes are fried twice; the preliminary cooking, or blanching, is done at a lower temperature than the final frying, which browns and crisps them. As much as we've loved them in Italy, we've made one simple addition that puts them over the top. Just after frying, we toss the potatoes with smashed whole garlic cloves—an easy and quick way to provide fresh garlic flavor without overdoing it. The Italian Fries are great with just about any roast, including chicken, pork, lamb, and beef.

6 cups vegetable oil
4 Idaho potatoes, about 12 ounces each, scrubbed
2 garlic cloves, peeled and smashed with the side of a
     large knife
1 tablespoon chopped fresh parsley
½ teaspoon kosher salt
⅛ teaspoon freshly ground black pepper

1. Pour the oil into a 6-quart, heavy-bottomed saucepan, 8 to 10 inches in diameter. Heat over medium-high heat until the oil registers 275 degrees F on a deep-fat thermometer.

2. Meanwhile, prepare the potatoes: Trim off both ends and 4 sides of each potato, so that you have cut off most of the skin and squared off the potato. Remove the remaining skin with a vegetable peeler, then cut the potatoes into ½- to ¾-inch cubes. Using a slotted spoon, add the potatoes to the hot oil in 2 batches and blanch until they are almost cooked through and beginning to brown, about 5 minutes. (The temperature of the oil may dip to 250 degrees F, but don't let it rise above 275 degrees F.) Remove the potatoes to a large plate lined with paper towels and let stand at room temperature until you are ready to serve, up to 3 hours in advance of serving.

3. When you are ready to serve, heat the oil until it registers 375 degrees F on a deep-fat thermometer.

4. Fry the blanched potatoes in 2 batches until they are crisp and golden brown, about 1 minute. Remove the Italian Fries from the oil with a slotted spoon and drain on the plate, lined with fresh paper towels. When all of the fries are cooked, toss them in a large serving bowl with the garlic, parsley, salt, and pepper. Serve hot.

Mustard-Mashed Potatoes

Any devotee of USC knows we love using our mashed potatoes as a vehicle for other flavors, and here's one that's both delicious on its own and an amazingly versatile and complementary garnish as well. We serve these bright and pungent spuds with Calf's Liver with Bacon and Sage (page 190), but they're equally delicious with chicken, rabbit, pork chops, and salmon.

4 cups Mashed Potatoes (page 321)
2 tablespoons dry mustard
1 tablespoon warm water
1 tablespoon honey
¼ teaspoon salt
⅛ teaspoon freshly ground black pepper
⅛ teaspoon ground turmeric

1. Prepare the mashed potatoes; remove from the heat, cover, and set aside.

2. Stir together the mustard, water, honey, salt, pepper, and turmeric in a small bowl. Fold the mustard mixture into the warm mashed potatoes and stir over low heat until piping hot.

Bottarga-Mashed Potatoes

SERVES 4

We first encountered bottarga—the sun-dried roe of tuna or red mullet—
in Sardinia, where it is enjoyed shaved thinly, on its own, with a glass of
sherrylike vernaccia. Like the Sardinians, we enjoy crumbling a bit of bottarga
into a simple olive oil and garlic sauce for spaghettini. One night, during a busy
dinner service at USC, Michael was tasting a batch of mashed potatoes and
Danny was tasting the bottarga mixture we had prepared for the spaghettini.
Danny asked for an accompanying spoon of mashed potatoes. They tasted great
together. You can store bottarga for weeks, well wrapped and refrigerated. The
mashed potatoes are a terrific garnish for tuna, lobster, shrimp, or salmon.

4 cups Mashed Potatoes (page 321)

SEASONED BOTTARGA MIXTURE
2 tablespoons extra-virgin olive oil
1 tablespoon minced garlic
2 tablespoons chopped Oven-Dried Tomatoes
    (page 319), or 1 teaspoon tomato paste
1 teaspoon chopped fresh oregano
1 tablespoon chopped fresh parsley
¼ cup skinned, thinly sliced, then minced bottarga
    (dried tuna or mullet roe)

1. Prepare the mashed potatoes; remove from the heat, cover, and set aside.

2. Make the bottarga mixture: Combine the oil and the garlic in a small
   skillet and warm for 1 minute, without browning, over low heat. Add the
   chopped tomatoes, oregano, parsley, and bottarga. Stir to combine and
   remove from the heat.

3. Add the bottarga mixture to the warm mashed potatoes. Stir over low
   heat and serve piping hot.

Horseradish-Mashed Potatoes

SERVES 4

As with any flavored mashed potato recipe, the added ingredient suggests the main course. We serve our horseradish-mashed potatoes with Oven-Braised Short Ribs (page 166), and find that they're also fabulous with brisket, salmon, and roast pork tenderloin. Fresh horseradish is so much better than bottled for clean, sweet flavor and pungency. Unfortunately, horseradish from a jar is not a good substitute, since the vinegar in which it's packed tends to curdle the milk.

2 pounds Idaho potatoes, peeled and quartered

2¼ teaspoons kosher salt

8 tablespoons (1 stick) butter

½ cup heavy cream

½ cup milk

¼ cup plus 2 tablespoons finely grated fresh
   horseradish

⅛ teaspoon cayenne

⅛ teaspoon freshly ground white pepper

1. Place the potatoes in a 2-quart saucepan with 1 teaspoon of the salt and cold water to cover. Bring to a boil, lower the heat, and simmer, covered, until completely tender, about 30 minutes. Test the potatoes by piercing them with a paring knife—there should be no resistance. Place in a colander and allow to drain for several minutes.

2. While the potatoes are cooking, combine the butter, heavy cream, milk, horseradish, and cayenne in another saucepan and heat gently until the butter has melted. Remove from the heat, cover, and allow to steep for at least 10 minutes. Strain the mixture into a bowl, pressing well on the solids to extract the most flavor. Return the strained mixture to the saucepan, and cover to keep warm.

3. Working over the saucepan used to cook the potatoes, pass the potatoes through a food mill or a potato ricer. If you have any difficulty, add a little of the warm horseradish-milk mixture to the potatoes.

4. Before serving, place the potatoes over a low flame and begin adding the warm horseradish-milk mixture, whipping the potatoes with a wooden spoon or spatula. When all the liquid is absorbed, season with the remaining 1¼ teaspoons of salt and the white pepper. Serve piping hot.

Olive-Mashed Potatoes

SERVES 4

When we introduced this riff on the mashed potato theme, some of our guests thought we had finally gone too far—until they tasted it! These potatoes are perfect with lamb, and they'll enliven chicken, turkey, rabbit, and most any fish, as well. To pit the olives, place them on a cutting board, cover with wax paper, and give them a gentle pounding with a meat mallet. The pits will be easy to remove. Save any leftover olive paste in a jar, covered with a thin layer of olive oil, and refrigerated. You can stir the paste into *spaghetti all'aglio e olio,* mix it with fresh goat cheese, use as a topping for grilled salmon, or use as a sandwich spread with mortadella, arugula, and mozzarella.

4 cups Mashed Potatoes (page 321)
1 cup pitted Gaeta or Kalamata olives
2 packed teaspoons coarsely chopped fresh rosemary
1 teaspoon fresh thyme leaves
3 juniper berries
1¼ teaspoons anchovy paste
2 tablespoons extra-virgin olive oil
2 tablespoons chopped fresh parsley

1. Prepare the mashed potatoes; remove from the heat, cover, and set aside.

2. Combine the olives, rosemary, thyme, juniper berries, anchovy paste, and olive oil in the bowl of a mini–food processor or blender and process or chop to a chunky paste. Do not puree. (Alternatively, combine the olives, herbs, and juniper berries on a cutting board and chop to a paste; stir in the anchovy paste and olive oil.)

3. Stir ¼ cup plus 2 tablespoons of the olive paste and the parsley into the warm mashed potatoes over low heat and cook, stirring, until piping hot.

Apple-Pear Chutney

MAKES ABOUT 5 CUPS

This mouthwatering chutney is a versatile condiment that works well with duck, pork, liver, or even shellfish like lobster or shrimp. At the restaurant we use it as an accompaniment for an Indian-spiced terrine of foie gras. Tightly covered and refrigerated, the chutney will keep nicely for up to 2 weeks.

2½ tablespoons coriander seeds

14 green cardamom pods

1 teaspoon ground turmeric

2 tablespoons vegetable oil

1½ tablespoons yellow or brown mustard seeds

2 cups minced onion

2 cups minced celery

1 teaspoon minced gingerroot

1½ cups sugar

1 teaspoon kosher salt

1 cup cider vinegar

1 cup pineapple juice

2 Bosc or Bartlett pears, peeled, cored,
    and cut into ½-inch dice

2 Rome Beauty apples, peeled, cored,
    and cut into ½-inch dice

Grated zest of 1 lemon

Grated zest of 1 orange

2 medium jalapeño peppers, seeded and minced,
    plus seeds of 1 pepper

¼ teaspoon freshly ground black pepper

1. Combine the coriander and cardamom in a spice grinder and grind to a very fine powder. Transfer to a small bowl, add the turmeric, and stir in 2 tablespoons water to make a paste.

2. Heat the oil in an 11-inch, straight-sided skillet or pot over medium heat until very hot, but not smoking. Reduce the heat to low, add the mustard seeds, and cover the pan. Shake the skillet until the seeds have popped and darkened in color. Uncover the skillet, add the spice paste, and increase the heat to medium. Cook, stirring constantly, until the water has evaporated, about 2 minutes. (If the spices begin to stick, add a drop of water and continue cooking.)

3. Add the onion, celery, and ginger to the skillet and cook, stirring often, until the vegetables are softened but not browned, 3 to 4 minutes. Add the sugar and the salt and stir to melt the sugar. Pour in the vinegar and the pineapple juice and bring to a boil. Stir every now and then, until the liquid reduces to a syrupy consistency, 12 to 15 minutes.

4. Stir in the pears and apples, reduce the heat to low, and simmer, covered, until the fruit is very tender, about 25 minutes. (If the mixture gets dry during cooking, add a little water.) Stir in the zests, the jalapeño peppers and seeds, and the black pepper and cook for 5 additional minutes. Taste and adjust the seasoning, if necessary. Transfer to a bowl, allow to cool, and serve at room temperature. The chutney will keep, refrigerated, for up to 1 week.

Plum Chutney

MAKES ABOUT 4 CUPS

Here's another Indian-inspired condiment we like to make to take advantage
of one of summer's abundant pleasures—plums. Like most chutneys, it's a
terrific accompaniment for spicy dishes, but also provides some relief from the
richness of dishes like duck, lamb, pork, and foie gras. For a change of pace,
try grilling baby back ribs rubbed with a mixture of the spices in this recipe,
and then serve the Plum Chutney instead of barbecue sauce.

1 tablespoon butter
1½ tablespoons chopped gingerroot
1 jalapeño pepper, seeded and chopped
Zest of 1 small orange, julienned
¼ teaspoon ground dried pomegranate seeds
¼ teaspoon ground cloves
¼ teaspoon ground cinnamon
¼ teaspoon ground coriander
¼ teaspoon ground turmeric
½ cup verjus
3 tablespoons cider vinegar
⅔ cup honey
2 pounds black plums, pitted and cut into eighths

1. Heat the butter in a 3-quart saucepan over medium heat. Add the
    ginger, jalapeño, orange zest, ground pomegranate seeds, cloves,
    cinnamon, coriander, and turmeric and cook, stirring, for 1 minute.

2. Add the verjus, vinegar, and honey. Bring to a boil, lower the heat to
    medium, and simmer until the mixture reduces to a syrupy consistency,
    8 to 10 minutes. Watch carefully as the syrup thickens: it should remain
    light colored and not caramelized.

3. Add the plums and cook over medium heat until they are soft, but still hold their shape, about 8 minutes. Use a slotted spoon to transfer the plums to a bowl. Continue cooking the syrup until it is quite thick, about 4 minutes. Pour the liquid over the plums, mix well, and refrigerate the chutney. Serve chilled or at room temperature.

Green Tomato Chutney

MAKES ABOUT 5 CUPS

Just looking at this sweet-sour chutney will make your mouth water. It's a great way to use early tomatoes, as well as the late-season ones that just never ripened. As a condiment, it wakes up neutral meats like pork or chicken, and stands tall next to spicy dishes as well. At the restaurant we serve the Green Tomato Chutney with our Chili and Sage–Rubbed Salmon (page 119).

2 pounds green tomatoes, stemmed, cored,
    and peeled with a vegetable peeler
2 tablespoons olive oil
2 teaspoons mustard seeds
24 curry leaves (see Note)
1 tablespoon coriander seeds, finely ground
½ cup chopped onion
½ cup finely chopped celery
1 tablespoon peeled and chopped gingerroot
Kosher salt
Freshly ground black pepper
¼ cup honey
¼ cup fresh lime juice
½ cup verjus
1 small jalapeño pepper, stemmed and minced,
    with seeds
1 green (unripe) mango, peeled and diced

1. Quarter the peeled tomatoes and cut out the pulp; slide your thumb along the inside of the flesh to remove any seeds and pulp that cling. Puree the pulp and strain through a sieve; set aside. Cut the tomato flesh into dice.

2. Heat the oil in a 3-quart saucepan over high heat until very hot, shimmering but not smoking. Remove the pan from the heat, add the mustard seeds, and cover the pan. Shake the pan, still off the heat, until the seeds have darkened and popped. Return the pan to the heat and add the curry leaves. Cook until the leaves have darkened and wilted. Add the coriander and stir a few seconds until fragrant. Add the onion, celery, ginger, 1¼ teaspoons salt, and ¼ teaspoon pepper. Cook, stirring, about 1 minute. Pour in the honey, lime juice, and verjus, and bring to a boil. Add the pureed tomato pulp and the tomato dice, and return to a boil. Reduce the heat, and simmer, uncovered, until the tomatoes are tender but not mushy, 10 to 15 minutes. (The mixture should be somewhat soupy; cover the pan if the liquid is boiling away too quickly)

3. Add the jalapeño and mango and cook, stirring occasionally, just until the mango softens, about 5 minutes. Serve warm as a sauce or at room temperature as a condiment. The chutney will keep for 5 days, refrigerated.

Note: Curry leaves are available at Middle Eastern and Indian markets.

Quince Chutney

MAKES ABOUT 3 CUPS

The elusive flavor and faint pink color of quince—unlike its second cousin the apple—emerge only after gentle cooking. This chutney provides a tart and expressive counterpoint to dishes that are rich and spicy, and perks up foods that are neutral in flavor. We'd recommend having a bowl on hand as a condiment for your Thanksgiving turkey, or for something as simple as sautéed chicken livers or scrambled eggs and sausage. It would also be wonderful with leg of lamb, venison, or short ribs. At the restaurant we enclose the spices in a cheesecloth bundle, to be removed before serving, but if you don't mind encountering a few whole spices, you needn't bother with the cheesecloth.

1 lemon, halved
1½ to 1¾ pounds quince (2 large)
1 small cinnamon stick
1 star anise
2 juniper berries
7 whole black peppercorns
2 cloves
1½ cups white wine
½ cup sugar
⅛ teaspoon kosher salt

1. Squeeze the lemon into a bowl filled with 4 cups of water; and then add the lemon halves to the bowl as well.

2. Peel and core the quince, cut them into ½-inch chunks, and place in the bowl of lemon water to prevent discoloration.

3. Make a spice bundle: In a small piece of clean cheesecloth, place the cinnamon stick, star anise, juniper berries, peppercorns, and cloves. Close the bundle by tying it with a piece of kitchen twine.

4. Drain the quince in a colander, reserving 1 cup of the lemon water, and transfer the fruit to a 4-quart saucepan. Add the reserved lemon water, the wine, sugar, salt, and the spice bundle. Bring to a boil, reduce the heat, cover, and simmer gently until the quince is very soft, about 30 minutes. Uncover the pan and continue cooking until the fruit turns a pinkish color and is the consistency of a juicy applesauce, an additional 1 to 1¼ hours, depending on the fruit. As the liquid reduces and becomes syrupy, stir every now and then to keep the fruit from sticking to the bottom of the pot, mashing with the spoon to help break the fruit down. The chutney should cook slowly enough so that the fruit stays covered with liquid during the entire cooking time; it should never be dry. If the liquid seems to be evaporating too quickly, reduce the heat and add a little more water.

5. Remove the spice bundle and let the chutney cool to room temperature before serving. The chutney will keep, refrigerated, for up to 1 week.

CAN I RUN A TAB ?

Chocolate Dulce de Leche Crêpes

SERVES 6 TO 8

Victoria Burghi, Union Square Cafe's pastry chef, first learned the recipe for *dulce de leche*–filled crêpes at the side of her grandmother Victoria in Montevideo, Uruguay. For her winning job audition, Victoria gave her grandmother's crêpes a fresh twist by adding cocoa powder to the batter and serving them topped with her homemade chocolate sauce and *dulce de leche* ice cream. You can use the Häagen-Dazs version (which is *almost* as good as Victoria's) or substitute vanilla or chocolate ice cream.

DULCE DE LECHE
2 (14-ounce) cans sweetened condensed milk

CHOCOLATE CRÊPES
2 cups milk

4 tablespoons butter, melted

6 tablespoons sugar

½ cup all purpose flour

½ cup cake flour

Pinch of salt

3 tablespoons cocoa powder (preferably
    Dutch-processed)

4 large eggs

CHOCOLATE SAUCE
6 ounces bittersweet chocolate, finely chopped

1 cup heavy cream

1. For *dulce de leche,* place unopened cans of sweetened condensed milk in a large pot, and fill with water to cover the cans by at least 2 inches. Bring to a boil and cook, uncovered, *always maintaining the water level above the can.* Add hot water to the pot frequently, and keep it at

a steady boil. After 3 hours, pour off the water, remove the cans from the pot, and let cool for 30 minutes before opening. Transfer the dark, thick *dulce de leche* to a clean container. Store in the refrigerator, well covered, for up to 2 weeks.

2. To make the batter, put all of the crêpe ingredients into a blender or food processor in the order listed. Blend on high for about 30 seconds, scrape down the sides of the jar, and then continue blending for another 30 seconds. Pour the batter through a fine strainer and let rest for 30 minutes at room temperature.

3. To cook the crêpes, place a nonstick, 8-inch crêpe pan (or a nonstick, 10-inch skillet with a 7- to 8-inch flat bottom) over high heat for 1 minute. Reduce the heat to moderate. Ladle in about 3 tablespoons of batter and swirl the pan rapidly to thinly coat the entire bottom and just a bit of the sides of the pan. Fill any dry spots with additional drops of batter. Cook for about 30 seconds and run the tip of a small spatula all around the edge of the crêpe, separating it from the pan. Lift the edge with the spatula or your fingers, quickly flip the crêpe over, and cook on the second side for another 20 to 30 seconds.

4. Invert the pan over a large plate or platter and, with a quick shake, drop the finished crêpe out of the pan. Cook another in the same way, and unmold the crêpe right on top of the first one. Repeat with the rest of the batter, piling up the crêpes as they are done, until you have about 20. The unfilled crêpes can be wrapped and refrigerated for up to 2 days.

5. To make the sauce, place the chopped chocolate in a heatproof mixing bowl. Bring the cream to a boil over moderate heat, and immediately pour it over the chocolate. Set aside and let sit for a few minutes. Then whisk until the sauce is completely smooth. Keep warm in the top of a double boiler set over hot water until ready to use.

6. To assemble and serve, have the *dulce de leche* at room temperature or warmer—reheat in the microwave or in a double boiler, if necessary. Using a small spatula, spread one side of each crêpe with 2 tablespoons of *dulce de leche*. Fold the crêpe into quarters, and repeat with the others. For each serving, arrange 3 filled and folded crêpes on a dessert plate, points toward the center, and drizzle them with circles of warm chocolate sauce in a spiral pattern.

Note: Most condensed milk labels advise against cooking caramel in an unopened can. For safety's sake, make certain to always maintain the water level at least 2 inches above the can while cooking.

Caramel Baked Apples

SERVES 8

Just saying "baked apples" brings a smile to the face of most dessert lovers, and this decadent version—a cross between baked and caramel apples—is certainly the best we've ever had. We use Cortland or Empire apples, but you'll also get good results with Rome Beauty, Jonagold, or Golden Delicious. Serve the apples ladled with warm caramel sauce, or adorn them further, as we do, with a scoop of homemade Malted Vanilla Ice Cream (page 313) or a dollop of Country Cream (page 312). You can bake the apples a day in advance and refrigerate them. To serve, reheat the apples in a 350-degree oven for 8 to 10 minutes and warm the caramel sauce in a double boiler or microwave.

1⅛ cups sugar
½ cup water
2 cups heavy cream
8 medium baking apples (6 to 8 ounces each),
    such as Cortland or Empire

1. Stir together the sugar and water in a deep, heavy-bottomed 2- to 3-quart pot. Set over high heat and let the sugar cook at a rapid boil for 8 to 10 minutes, without stirring or shaking. When the syrup starts to caramelize, swirl the pan to spread the color. The moment it reaches a dark caramel shade, remove the pan from the heat. Using oven mitts or a towel to protect your hands, pour in the cream, stirring constantly with a long wire whisk as the caramel bubbles up. When the cream is incorporated and the bubbling has subsided, reheat the sauce just to the boil, still whisking. Remove from the heat and allow to cool.

2. Preheat the oven to 350 degrees F..

3. Peel and core the apples. Slice just enough from the top and bottom of each apple so that it can balance on either end. Arrange the trimmed apples in a roasting pan, deep baking dish, or casserole large enough to allow about 1 inch of space between them. The sides should be higher than the fruit. Pour the sauce all over the apples and seal the dish with foil or a tightly fitting ovenproof cover.

4. Bake for 20 minutes; then remove from the oven and uncover the dish. Using tongs or two large spoons, gently turn each apple upside-down, reseal the pan, and bake for another 20 minutes. Turn the apples over a second time, cover, and bake for an additional 10 minutes. Test for doneness by pressing the sides and piercing with the point of a paring knife. The apples should be tender all the way through, but not mushy. If necessary, bake for another few minutes.

5. When the apples are done, use a slotted spoon to stand each apple upright in a warm serving bowl. Strain the apple-caramel sauce into a saucepan and simmer over medium heat until the juices evaporate and the sauce returns to its original consistency. Pour or spoon an equal amount of the sauce over each apple and serve immediately.

Strawberry-Rhubarb Pandowdy

SERVES 10 TO 12

Beyond being a fabulous word that conjures up the best in classic American desserts, pandowdies are darned good—and easy to make. Actually, a pandowdy is similar to a cobbler, with one small, but important distinction: in the middle of baking, the crust is cut into pieces and then smooshed down into the fruit filling. While this pandowdy uses the tried-and-true coupling of strawberries and rhubarb, you can certainly make it with other fruits when they're in season. Plums, peaches, apricots, apples, and pears work particularly well. Serve it piping hot, accompanied by a dollop of Country Cream (page 312) or a scoop of vanilla ice cream.

PIE CRUST

1 scant cup all-purpose flour

1 scant cup cake flour

1 tablespoon sugar

¼ teaspoon salt

8 tablespoons (1 stick) cold butter, cut into ½-inch cubes

2 tablespoons vegetable shortening, such as Crisco, cut into ½-inch cubes and frozen

½ cup ice water, plus more if needed

FRUIT FILLING

6 cups trimmed, rinsed, and coarsely chopped (1½-inch pieces) rhubarb

3 cups rinsed and stemmed strawberries, split if very large

½ cup maple syrup

3 tablespoons butter, in small pieces

2 tablespoons milk

2 tablespoon sugar

1. Make the dough for the crust: Place the flours, sugar, salt, and chilled butter in the bowl of a standing electric mixer fitted with the paddle attachment. Mix on the lowest speed for 30 seconds to 1 minute, until most of the butter is blended with the flours, but there are a few larger lumps of butter still visible. Add the frozen pieces of shortening and mix slowly for another 30 seconds to 1 minute, until the dough is crumbly, and some small lumps of butter and shortening remain.

2. Still mixing on low speed, pour in the ice water and blend for a few seconds, until the dough just comes together. Transfer the dough to a sheet of plastic wrap and press into a smooth disk; wrap tightly and refrigerate for at least 1 hour, or up to 2 days.

3. Preheat the oven to 425 degrees F.

4. Prepare the filling: In a mixing bowl, gently toss the rhubarb pieces and strawberries with the maple syrup; then spread an even layer of the fruit into a 9- by 13-inch Pyrex baking dish or a cake pan. Dot the top with the bits of butter.

5. On a floured work surface, roll the chilled dough into a rectangle about ⅛ inch thick and the same size as the pan. To transfer the dough, roll it up on a rolling pin, then unroll it over the fruit. Trim any excess dough, brush the crust with milk, and sprinkle evenly with the sugar. Pierce 12 small steam vents in the dough with the tip of a paring knife.

6. Bake for 40 minutes, or until the crust has started to turn golden brown. Remove the pan from the oven and slice the crust lengthwise into 4 equal strips; then slice crosswise to divide the crust into 16 small rectangles. With an offset spatula (such as a pancake turner), push the pieces of crust down into the bubbling fruit juices. Bake for another 30 minutes or so, until the crust becomes a deep golden brown and the fruit is thickened.

7. Serve the pandowdy warm, spooned into dessert dishes, with the browned crust showing.

Plum Clafoutis

SERVES 8 TO 10

A popular bistro dessert whose roots are in France's Limousin *département*, clafoutis is a wonderful baked custard tart. It's also a terrific vehicle for fresh fruit—most commonly cherries—that have been macerated in *eau-de-vie*. In this version, we use fresh prune-plums, the small, oblong, deep-purple ones that arrive toward the end of summer. Baking the batter in two separate stages is a good trick to keep the fruit from settling to the bottom of the *clafoutis*.

1 pound small Italian plums (prune-plums), almost ripe,
    but still firm
3 tablespoons Mirabelle (plum *eau-de-vie*) or Amaretto
Vegetable oil spray
6 tablespoons butter
1 vanilla bean

CLAFOUTIS BATTER
4 eggs
1 cup sour cream
½ cup sugar
½ cup all-purpose flour
¼ cup cornstarch
1 cup milk
1 tablespoon freshly grated lemon zest

1. Quarter the plums and discard the pits. Toss the cut plums in a bowl with the Mirabelle or Amaretto, and macerate at room temperature for 30 minutes.

2. Arrange a rack in the lower third of the oven and another rack in the upper third, and preheat the oven to 375 degrees F. Lightly coat the inside of a 9-inch round cake pan (at least 2 inches deep) with vegetable oil spray and set aside.

3. Place the butter in a small, heavy-bottomed saucepan. Slit the vanilla bean lengthwise and scrape the seeds into the saucepan; toss the bean pod in, as well. Place the butter over moderate heat. When it starts to bubble, lower the heat and cook, without stirring, for 5 to 7 minutes. When the butter is a deep, nut-brown color, strain it into a small bowl. Discard the vanilla pod and let the brown butter cool until just warm.

4. Make the batter: Place the eggs, sour cream, sugar, flour, cornstarch, warm vanilla butter, and milk into the jar of a blender. Hold the lid tightly, and process on high speed until smooth, scraping the sides of the jar as necessary to blend all the dry ingredients. (If the batter ingredients fill the jar of your blender to more than two-thirds full, avoid an overflow by blending all the ingredients *except* the milk, which you can then whisk in by hand in a large mixing bowl.) Strain the batter into a large measuring cup or pitcher, and stir in the lemon zest.

5. Pour 1½ cups of batter into the prepared cake pan. Set it on the bottom rack of the oven and bake about for 8 minutes, until the batter is just set, but not at all colored. Remove the pan from the oven.

6. Spread the macerated plum wedges atop the set layer of batter, then pour over the remaining batter, covering the fruit. Place on the upper oven rack and bake for 50 minutes to 1 hour, or until the *clafoutis* is lightly puffed and nicely browned on top. Allow the *clafoutis* to cool in the pan, on a wire rack, for 1 hour.

7. To unmold, run a knife around the sides of the pan to loosen the *clafoutis,* place a cake cardboard or a flat plate on top and invert. Shake gently, if necessary, to help the *clafoutis* drop out; then invert once again onto a serving plate. Serve the *clafoutis* warm, or at room temperature, sliced into wedges.

Poached Peach Shortcakes

SERVES 8

Once you master the process of making shortcake, there's no reason to limit the accessories to strawberries and whipped cream. We've found that poached peaches and a whipped blend of almond extract, heavy cream, and crème fraîche work beautifully. So they'll stand up to the poaching and remain whole and "sliceable," use peaches that are just slightly underripe—not quite as soft as you'd want if you were eating them out of hand.

POACHED PEACHES

2½ pounds large, nearly ripe freestone peaches
    (about 5 peaches)
2 cups water
1 bottle (750 ml) white wine
¾ cup sugar
1 vanilla bean

BROWN SUGAR SHORTCAKES

2¾ cups all-purpose flour
2 tablespoons baking powder
3 tablespoons dark brown sugar
1 teaspoon kosher salt
4 tablespoons cold butter, cut into ½-inch pieces
3 eggs
½ cup heavy cream, plus 2 tablespoons for brushing
3 tablespoons sugar

ALMOND DOUBLE CREAM

1⅓ cups heavy cream, well chilled
⅓ cup cold crème fraîche or sour cream
2 tablespoons sugar
½ teaspoon almond extract

1. Poach the peaches: Split the peaches lengthwise. Reserve the pits and the peach halves separately.

2. Pour the water, wine, and sugar into a 4-quart pot. Split the vanilla bean lengthwise, scrape the seeds into the liquid, and add the bean pod and the reserved peach pits. Bring to a boil over high heat, stirring occasionally, and gently drop in the peach halves. Lower the heat to maintain a steady simmer.

3. Simmer until the fruit halves are tender, but still retain their shape, 5 to 10 minutes, depending on the ripeness of the peaches. Test for doneness by piercing the peaches with the tip of a paring knife. With a slotted spoon, carefully place the cooked peaches on a large plate or platter in one layer. When the peaches are cool enough to handle, peel away their skins. Cut the peeled halves lengthwise into ¼-inch-thick slices and place the slices in a large, nonreactive bowl. Cover with plastic wrap and set aside.

4. Return the poaching liquid to a medium boil and cook, uncovered, until reduced to 2 cups, 20 minutes or more. When the liquid has reduced, strain it through a sieve onto the peach slices in the bowl. Cover the bowl and refrigerate. The recipe can be prepared to this point up to several days in advance.

5. Preheat the oven to 425 degrees F. Line a baking sheet with parchment paper.

6. Make the shortcakes: Place the flour, baking powder, brown sugar, and salt in the bowl of a standing electric mixer fitted with the paddle attachment, and mix briefly at low speed. Add the butter pieces and mix on medium-low speed for about 2 minutes, until the butter is broken up and the mix is crumbly.

7. In a small bowl, beat the eggs just to break them up, stir in the ½ cup of heavy cream, and pour the liquid into the mixer bowl all at once. Mix on low speed for about 20 seconds, just until the dough comes together—it will be soft and sticky.

8. Scrape the dough onto a well-floured surface and knead it briefly and gently into a smooth mass. Pat the dough flat, roll it to an even thickness of ¾ inch, and cut out circles with a 3-inch round pastry or biscuit cutter, dipping the cutter in flour to prevent sticking. Arrange the shortcakes 2 inches apart on the parchment-lined baking or cookie sheet. Gather up the dough scraps, roll them out gently and cut more rounds, using up all the dough. Let the shortcakes rest at room temperature for 15 minutes.

9. Just before baking, brush the shortcake tops with the cream, and sprinkle each one with an equal amount of the sugar. Bake for about 12
10. minutes, or until the shortcakes are puffed, lightly browned, and glazed with sugar on the top. Remove from the oven and allow to cool.

In a mixing bowl set over a larger bowl filled with ice, whip together the chilled heavy cream, crème fraîche, sugar, and almond extract to
11. form stiff, smooth peaks.

For each serving, ladle ¼ cup of the chilled poaching syrup into a small soup bowl. Slice a shortcake in half crosswise and set the bottom piece in the syrup. Cover with a layer of peach slices, a mound of Almond Double Cream (about ⅓ cup), and then the sugar-glazed shortcake top.

Lemon–Poppy Seed Angel Food Cake with Fresh Raspberries

SERVES 6

This is the recipe Victoria Burghi most enjoys cooking at home on her day off. It's an excellent example of how to take a straightforward, home-style cake batter and elevate it a few notches in both flavor and elegance, simply by adding a couple of unexpected ingredients and cooking it in individual mini-cake pans. Like any good angel food cake, this one is delicate, fluffy, and nearly fat-free. It's perfectly delicious on its own, but may be just a little bit better with a wonderful Raspberry-Lemon Glaze, or with a scoop of vanilla ice cream, or raspberry or lemon sorbet. By the way, the individual cakes are made in a mini–angel food cake pan, comprised of six nonstick molds in one unit. The pans are inexpensive and widely available at kitchenware stores.

ANGEL FOOD CAKES

6 egg whites at room temperature
¾ teaspoon cream of tartar
¾ cup sugar
2 tablespoons grated lemon zest
2 teaspoons fresh lemon juice
1 teaspoon vanilla extract
½ cup cake flour
2 tablespoons poppy seeds
1 pint fresh raspberries
Raspberry-Lemon Glaze (optional; recipe follows)

1. Preheat the oven to 350 degrees F.

2. In the bowl of an electric mixer fitted with the whip attachment, beat the egg whites and the cream of tartar at high speed until frothy and just forming soft mounds, about 1 minute. Pour in the sugar in a slow,

steady stream, continuing to whip on high speed, until stiff peaks form. Stop the machine, add the lemon zest, lemon juice, and vanilla; then resume whipping on high speed for 2 minutes.

3. Remove the bowl from the mixer, sprinkle all of the flour and poppy seeds over the top of the whipped egg whites, and gently fold them in with a large rubber spatula until the batter is well blended.

4. Fill a pastry bag with the batter and pipe a thick ring into each of the angel food cake molds, filling each by one-third. If you don't have a pastry bag, you can fill the molds with a spoon. Arrange 6 to 8 of the nicest raspberries into each ring of batter (save the soft or broken berries for the glaze), and then pipe or spoon another layer of batter over the berries to fill each mold.

5. Place the pan in the oven immediately and bake for 15 to 20 minutes, until the cakes are set and just starting to pull away from the sides of the molds. Let the cakes cool in the pan.

6. Unmold by carefully running the blade of a paring knife around the outside of each cake and around the central tubes, separating the cake from the sides. Holding the pan nearly upside down, use the knife to pry and loosen each cake, one at a time, and let it fall into your hand. Place each cake on a dessert plate.

7. To serve, pour about ½ cup of the optional Raspberry-Lemon Glaze over the top of each cake, letting it drip down the sides and center.

RASPBERRY-LEMON GLAZE

MAKES ABOUT 2½ CUPS

1 pint fresh raspberries
¾ cup fresh lemon juice (about 6 lemons)
1 (14-ounce) can sweetened condensed milk
6 egg yolks

1. In a 2-quart, heavy-bottomed nonreactive saucepan set over medium heat, stir the raspberries and lemon juice together and bring to a boil. Lower the heat and simmer for 5 minutes.

2. Remove the pan from the heat and whisk in the condensed milk. Pour the mixture into a blender, puree until smooth, and then pour the puree back into the saucepan.

3. Fill a large mixing bowl halfway with ice and place a second mixing bowl over the ice. Have at hand a fine-mesh strainer.

4. Whisk the egg yolks into the saucepan with the raspberry-lemon puree and place the pan over low heat. Cook the glaze carefully, whisking constantly to avoid curdling the eggs. When the mixture has thickened a bit and the first few small bubbles appear in the center of the pan, immediately strain into the chilled mixing bowl. Whisk for a minute or two to cool, and refrigerate until needed. (If the eggs have accidentally curdled, immediately pour the glaze into a blender and process to return the smooth texture.)

Blueberry–Lemon Meringue Pie

SERVES 8

Here's a wonderful twist on a classic lemon meringue pie, taking full advantage of the sweet-tart affinity between blueberries and lemon. As good as the pie is on its own, a spoonful of the simple Blueberry-Buttermilk Sauce served on the side adds a delicious sweet-and-sour component. Though cultivated blueberries are available pretty much year-round, if you're lucky enough to get a late-summer stash of the tiny wild ones that just burst with true blueberry flavor, grab them and make sure to try them out in this recipe.

BLUEBERRY-BUTTERMILK SAUCE
1 cup blueberries, rinsed, stemmed, and drained
⅓ cup plus 2 tablespoons sugar
1 cup buttermilk

PIE DOUGH

12 tablespoons (1½ sticks) butter, softened

¼ cup sugar

2 egg yolks

½ cup plus 1 tablespoon fine yellow cornmeal

1¼ cups cake flour

Pinch of salt

Vegetable oil spray

PIE FILLING

⅔ cup freshly squeezed lemon juice

3 tablespoons all-purpose flour

1 tablespoon grated lemon zest

5⅓ tablespoons butter, melted

⅔ cup sugar

4 eggs

MERINGUE TOPPING

4 egg whites

1 cup sugar

3 cups blueberries, rinsed, stemmed, and drained

1. Make the Blueberry-Buttermilk Sauce: Place the blueberries and sugar in a small saucepan set over medium heat, and bring to a boil, stirring frequently with a wooden spoon. When the berries begin to burst and release their juices, reduce the heat and simmer for about 3 minutes, stirring often.

2. Scrape the cooked blueberries and all the juices into a blender jar; add the buttermilk, and puree until smooth. Strain through a fine-mesh sieve and refrigerate until chilled, or for up to 2 days.

3. Prepare the pie dough: In the bowl of a standing electric mixer fitted with the paddle attachment, cream the butter and sugar on medium speed until thoroughly blended, about 1 or 2 minutes. Add the egg yolks and mix briefly to incorporate, scraping down the sides of the

bowl. Stop the mixer, add the cornmeal, flour, and salt, and resume mixing on low speed just until the dough comes together. Scrape the dough onto a large piece of plastic wrap, press it into a flat disk, wrap tightly, and refrigerate for at least 2 hours, or as long as 24 hours.

4. Lightly coat the inside of a 10-inch pie pan with vegetable oil spray. Place the chilled dough on a well-floured work surface and roll to a thickness of ⅛ inch. Rotate often while rolling to assure that the dough is not sticking to the surface, and flour the surface and rolling pin as needed. Drape the dough over the lightly floured rolling pin, unroll it over the pie pan, and press it into the pan. Place the pie pan in the freezer and chill thoroughly, about 30 minutes.

5. Preheat the oven to 375 degrees F. Line the pie shell with aluminum foil and fill with dried beans or pastry weights.

6. Bake until the pastry is set and the top edges of the crust are light brown, about 25 minutes. Remove the pie shell from the oven and reduce the oven temperature to 350 degrees F. Let the shell cool for 30 minutes and then carefully lift out the foil and beans.

7. While the pie is cooling, make the filling: Place all the ingredients in a blender jar and blend at high speed for about 1 minute. Let the foam settle, then pour the filling into the pie shell. Return the pie to the oven for 12 minutes or so, until the filling is set, but not browned at all. Let cool while you prepare the meringue.

8. With a hand whisk, stir together the egg whites and the sugar in the bowl of a standing electric mixer. Place the bowl directly over a low burner—or over simmering water—and whisk constantly as the sugar dissolves and the egg whites warm. When the whites feel quite warm to the touch, set the bowl on the mixer fitted with the whip attachment, and beat at high speed until a stiff meringue forms and has cooled to room temperature.

9. Preheat the broiler. Arrange the fresh blueberries atop the lemon filling. Scoop the meringue into a pastry bag fitted with a star tip, and pipe it in a thick layer of swirling peaks, completely covering the berries. Lightly toast the meringue by browning for a few moments under the broiler, watching the pie quite carefully.

10. To serve, cut the pie into wedges and serve on dessert plates with chilled Blueberry-Buttermilk Sauce spooned alongside.

Banana "Cup" Cakes

SERVES 8

Intense banana flavor and a touch of whimsy make this a showstopper. For a real treat, try it topped with our Coffee Cream. The banana cake on its own makes a terrific breakfast or brunch item, served with a seasonal fresh fruit compote. Part of the fun of this dessert is that it is baked in 6- to 8-ounce ovenproof ceramic coffee cups. You could also substitute custard cups or soufflé molds of the same size.

BANANA CAKE

Vegetable oil spray

1½ cups cake flour

¾ teaspoon baking soda

¼ teaspoon baking powder

Pinch of salt

2 medium bananas, very ripe and soft

¼ cup sour cream

1 tablespoon vanilla extract

8 tablespoons (1 stick) butter, softened

¾ cup sugar

2 large eggs

CUSTARD

2½ cups milk

1¼ cups heavy cream

½ cup sugar

1 vanilla bean

2 eggs

4 egg yolks

3 large bananas, ripe but still firm

Coffee Cream (page 311)

1. Preheat the oven to 350 degrees F. Lightly coat a small sheet pan or large jelly-roll pan, approximately 12 by 18 inches, with vegetable oil spray. Line the bottom of the pan with parchment and spray the paper lightly.

2. Sift together the flour, baking soda, baking powder, and salt. Set aside.

3. In a small bowl, mash the peeled soft bananas with a fork or wire whisk, and whisk in the sour cream and vanilla extract. Set aside.

4. Using a standing electric mixer fitted with the paddle attachment, cream the butter and sugar on medium speed until light and fluffy, 3 to 4 minutes. Beat in the eggs one at a time, mixing well and scraping down the bowl after each addition. Reduce the speed to low and add the dry ingredients in 3 parts, alternating with the banana mixture in 2 parts, beginning and ending with the dry mixture. Mix each addition briefly, just to incorporate. Finally, scrape and stir the batter by hand with a rubber spatula for a few moments to blend well.

5. Spread the batter in the prepared sheet pan in a thin, smooth layer. Run your thumb along the inside of the rim all around the sheet, clearing away the batter and leaving a narrow gap next to the rim— the batter will expand into this gap as it bakes. Bake for 30 minutes, or until the top is golden brown and springs back to the touch. Cool the cake in the pan for about 15 minutes. Reduce the oven temperature to 300 degrees F.

6. To unmold, lay a piece of parchment or wax paper on top of the cake, and then a large cutting board or a flat cookie sheet. Flip everything over so the cake drops out onto the board, then peel the baked parchment off the cake bottom. With a long ruler and a sharp knife, slice ¾-inch strips, lengthwise and crosswise, creating ¾-inch cubes of soft cake. Line the original baking sheet with a fresh piece of parchment, spread out the cubes, and toast them in the oven for about 20 minutes, turning occasionally with a metal spatula. The cubes should

all be fairly dry and golden colored, yet not totally crisp or dark. Allow them to cool completely. (If you like, you can store the banana cake for up to a week in an airtight container at room temperature).

7. Make the custard: Stir together the milk, cream, and ¼ cup of the sugar in a 3-quart saucepan. Slit the vanilla bean lengthwise, scrape all the seeds into the pan, and then add the pod pieces as well. Bring the mixture to a boil, stirring occasionally; turn off the heat and steep for 1 hour.

8. Arrange a rack on the middle shelf, and preheat the oven to 350 degrees F.

9. In a large mixing bowl, whisk until smooth the eggs, yolks, remaining ¼ cup of sugar, and 1 cup of the warm milk mixture. Steadily whisk in the rest of the milk mixture. Strain the custard base through a sieve, discarding the vanilla bean pieces.

10. Arrange 8 coffee cups in a roasting pan large enough to hold them all. Distribute about ⅓ cup of baked cake cubes into each cup; then ladle ¼ cup of the custard base over the cubes. Let soak for about 10 minutes while you slice the bananas into ¼-inch-thick rounds. Arrange 6 to 8 banana slices over the moist cubes in each cup, press down gently, then pile on another ⅓ cup of dry cubes, to come a bit above the rim of the coffee cup. Pour over another ¼ cup of the custard base, let soak for a couple of minutes, and then divide the remaining custard equally among the cups.

11. Set the roasting pan on the oven rack and pour in enough hot water to reach halfway up the sides of the cups. Cover and seal the roasting pan with aluminum foil. Bake for 1 hour; then test for doneness by gently pressing the cubes in one of the cups. If wet custard appears around the cubes, reseal and continue baking. When the custard is set, uncover

the pan and carefully remove it from the oven. Serve the banana "cup" cakes immediately, topped with a generous mound of whipped Coffee Cream and presented on a matching saucer. Alternatively, you can allow the cups to cool completely and store them in the refrigerator, covered, for 1 or 2 days. If you do, reheat them for 5 minutes in a 350 degree F oven, or for 1 minute or so in a microwave.

Almond Cake

SERVES 8

This is a wonderfully moist almond cake whose tangy frosting can be used for many other applications as well. Try it with your favorite carrot cake or banana bread recipe, or between layers of a vanilla or chocolate birthday cake. As an optional garnish, spoon a generous portion of Fresh Summer Berries (see page 298) alongside each slice of cake.

ALMOND CAKE

Vegetable oil spray

2½ cups (about 10 ounces) sliced almonds

1¼ cups all-purpose flour

1¼ teaspoons baking powder

¼ teaspoon baking soda

Pinch of salt

¾ cup buttermilk

1½ teaspoons almond extract

10 tablespoons butter, softened

1 cup sugar

2 tablespoons grated orange zest

2 eggs

3 ounces extra-bittersweet chocolate,
    chopped into ¼-inch bits (about ½ cup)

CREAM CHEESE–WHITE CHOCOLATE FROSTING

6 ounces cream cheese

4 ounces good-quality white chocolate,
    melted and slightly warm (use a microwave
    oven or a double boiler)

5 tablespoons butter, softened

2 teaspoons fresh lemon juice

1. Arrange a rack on the middle shelf and preheat the oven to 350 degrees F. Cut a circle of parchment paper to fit the bottom of an 8-inch round cake pan with 3-inch sides. Lightly coat the insides of the pan with vegetable oil spray. Line the bottom of the pan with a parchment circle and spray it lightly.

2. In a clean electric coffee grinder or food processor, grind 1 cup of the sliced almonds with ¼ cup of the flour to a fine powder, working in batches if your grinder is small. Set aside.

3. Sift the remaining 1 cup of flour, the baking powder, baking soda, and salt into a mixing bowl. Whisk in the reserved almond powder. Set aside.

4. In another bowl, stir together the buttermilk and almond extract.

5. In the bowl of a standing electric mixer fitted with the paddle attachment, cream the butter and sugar on medium-low speed for about 3 minutes, until smooth and very light, occasionally scraping down the bowl with a rubber spatula. Beat in the orange zest, and then the eggs, one at a time, creaming 2 to 3 minutes after each addition and scraping the bowl in between.

6. Beating on low speed, add one-third of the almond flour, mixing briefly just to incorporate. Next add half of the buttermilk and mix briefly. Continue in this manner, adding another third of the almond flour, the second half of the buttermilk, and the final third of the flour. Scrape the bowl frequently while mixing. Finally, fold the chocolate pieces into the batter by hand with a rubber spatula, until evenly distributed.

7. Scrape the batter into the cake pan and level the top. Set the pan in the oven and bake for 50 minutes to 1 hour. *Do not open the oven door during the first 30 minutes of baking.* The cake is done when the top springs back to the touch and a toothpick inserted into the center comes out clean. Transfer the cake pan to a wire rack and cool for about 20 minutes. To unmold, run a knife around the sides to loosen

the cake. Place a flat plate atop the cake pan and invert the cake onto the plate. Peel away the parchment paper and once again invert the cake, this time onto a rack, so the cake is right side up; let it cool completely.

8. Spread the remaining 1½ cups of sliced almonds in a single layer on a parchment-covered cookie sheet and toast them for about 8 minutes, stirring once or twice, until lightly golden. Let the almonds cool, and reserve.

9. Make the frosting: Using an electric mixer fitted with the paddle attachment, beat the cream cheese at medium speed until smooth and fluffy, about 5 minutes. With the mixer running, pour in the melted chocolate and beat until well incorporated. Scrape down the bowl and begin beating in the soft butter, 1 tablespoon at a time, scraping down occasionally. Beat in the lemon juice; then increase the speed to high and cream the mixture until it is very light.

10. Transfer the cake to a cardboard cake round or platter and brush away any loose crumbs. Using a metal icing spatula, spread about half the frosting atop the cake in a smooth layer. Scoop up more frosting with the spatula and coat the sides. Press in handfuls of toasted almonds to coat the frosted sides, then sprinkle the remaining almonds all over the cake top. The frosted cake can remain at room temperature for 1 hour. Refrigerate the cake for longer storage, but return it to room temperature for about 30 minutes before serving to soften the frosting.

11. To serve, cut the cake into wedges with a serrated knife, rinsing the blade in hot water and wiping it dry before each cut.

Fig and Walnut Crostata

SERVES 6 TO 8

This is a wonderful, rustic recipe that's a kissing cousin to an American cobbler—with a layer of fresh figs baked under a blanket of walnut crumble. At the restaurant, we bake the dessert in individual round ramekins (3½ inches in diameter and 1 inch deep), but the recipe will work equally well in almost any shape of ovenproof mold, as long as all the figs fit in one layer. You can garnish the *crostata* with vanilla ice cream or USC's Country Cream (page 312), which is fabulous here if you freeze it for a couple of hours and then scoop it like ice cream.

Vegetable oil spray

1¼ pounds fresh Black Mission figs (about 18 to
    20 small figs), stems trimmed, halved lengthwise

1 cup walnut pieces

½ cup all-purpose flour

8 tablespoons (1 stick) butter, softened

½ cup sugar

2 eggs

Pinch of salt

Confectioners' sugar

1. Preheat the oven to 350 degrees F. Lightly coat a 12-inch, straight-sided tart pan with vegetable oil spray.

2. Arrange the fig halves in the tart pan, cut side down, packed closely together in one layer. If the figs are quite plump, press the fruit down gently to leave a small amount of space on top for the walnut topping. Place the tart pan on a baking sheet.

3. For the topping, place the walnuts and flour in a food processor and grind to a fine but slightly gritty powder, 30 seconds to 1 minute.

4. With an electric mixer fitted with the paddle attachment, cream the butter and sugar together on medium-high speed, scraping the bowl occasionally, until light and fluffy. Add the eggs, one at a time, and beat well. Reduce the speed to low and add the walnut-flour mixture and the salt. Mix briefly, just until the dry ingredients are incorporated. Using a rubber spatula, scrape down the bowl and fold the batter for a few moments to blend thoroughly.

5. Scoop the batter into a pastry bag fitted with a ½-inch round tip. Beginning at the inside edge of the pan, pipe a spiral layer about ½ inch thick to completely cover the figs. The piped batter should only reach a bit above the rim of the tart pan, since it will rise and possibly spill over the sides as it bakes.

6. Place the baking sheet in the oven and bake the *crostata* for 30 to 35 minutes, until the walnut topping is a deep golden brown, and the fruit juices are almost bubbling through the top. Serve warm, dusted with confectioners' sugar.

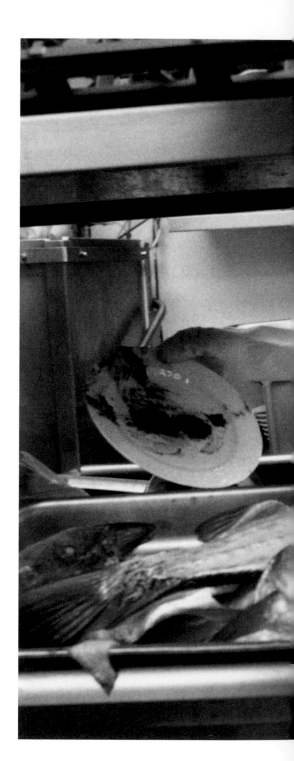

Honey Semifreddo

SERVES 8

Semifreddo is a wonderful frozen confection whose consistency is somewhere between custard and ice cream. In this recipe, honey and sour cream play starring roles, lending sweetness and tangy richness, as well as extra body, to the semifreddo. Though it's certainly wonderful on its own, we like to garnish each portion of Honey Semifreddo with a big spoonful of fresh berries, macerated simply with sugar. For ease of serving, you can unmold the semifreddo up to several hours in advance and return it to the freezer, loosely covered with plastic wrap, until ready to slice and serve. We like a mixed variety of fresh berries, which you can vary according to what's in season. Use the macerated berries as a topping for pound cake or your favorite ice cream.

HONEY SEMIFREDDO

1 cup heavy cream, chilled

⅓ cup sour cream

5 egg yolks

⅓ cup clover honey

2 tablespoons water

Vegetable oil spray

Sugar for lining molds

FRESH SUMMER BERRIES

1 cup raspberries

1 cup blueberries, rinsed and drained

1 cup strawberries, rinsed and drained

¼ cup sugar

1. In a large mixing bowl, whisk together the heavy cream and sour cream by hand or with an electric mixer until they form medium peaks that appear soft but hold their shape well. Cover the bowl with plastic wrap and refrigerate.

2. Using a standing electric mixer fitted with the whisk attachment, whip the egg yolks on high speed for 10 minutes or so, until they are thick, pale yellow, and have doubled in volume. When the yolks are fully whipped, turn off the mixer.

3. Stir together the honey and water in a small, deep saucepan and set the pan with the honey water over high heat. Bring to a boil (it will only take a few seconds) and let the syrup bubble up high for 30 seconds. Immediately remove the pan from the heat.

4. Return the mixer to high speed, and carefully pour in the hot syrup in a steady stream. Whip for 1 minute, and then scrape down any syrup that may have splattered on the sides of the bowl. Resume rapid whipping for 5 minutes or more, until the yolk mixture is thick and cool to the touch.

5. Meanwhile, lightly coat a 5-cup pound cake pan, terrine, or soufflé mold with vegetable oil spray. Sprinkle about 2 tablespoons of sugar into the mold, tilt it all around to coat the oiled surfaces, and pour out the excess sugar.

6. When the honey-yolk mixture is cool, spoon all of it on top of the reserved chilled whipped cream, and gently fold the two together with a large rubber spatula until thoroughly blended. Fill the sugar-coated mold with the semifreddo base and level the top with a spatula. Freeze for at least 4 hours. Once frozen, wrap the semifreddo well in plastic and store in the freezer for up to 1 week.

7. About 30 minutes before serving the semifreddo, toss the berries with the sugar in a large bowl and let stand at room temperature.

8. To unmold and serve the semifreddo, dip the bottom of the mold in hot water for 2 or 3 seconds, run the blade of a small spatula or knife around the inside edge of the mold, and then invert the mold onto a platter. Using a serrated knife dipped in warm water, cut 8 equal slices of semifreddo, dipping the knife in the water between each slice. Arrange each of the slices on a chilled dessert plate, spoon a portion of the summer berries on top, and serve immediately.

Chocolate Pudding Flan

SERVES 12

This intensely chocolatey dessert sets up nicely in a flan mold, but its consistency is soft and delicate. The delicious cocoa and semisweet chocolate flavors are heightened by just a pinch of salt. Chocolate Pudding Flan is completely satisfying served in its own caramel sauce, but you may want to present it, as we do, accompanied by both Coconut-Rum Sauce (page 310) and whipped cream. The molds for the flan can be ceramic or glass custard cups or soufflé molds, but you can also simply use disposable 5-ounce foil cups (3 inches in diameter, 1½ inches high), sold as foil "cupcake cups" in supermarkets.

CARAMEL
1 cup sugar
¼ cup water

CHOCOLATE CUSTARD
3 cups milk
½ cup sugar
¼ cup premium-quality cocoa (alkalized or
    Dutch-processed)
Pinch of salt
13 ounces semisweet chocolate, 10 ounces coarsely
    chopped, and 3 ounces grated
4 eggs
3 yolks

1. Arrange the molds in a baking or roasting pan, which will serve as a water bath.

2. To make the caramel, stir together the sugar and water in a small, heavy-bottomed saucepan. Set the pan over high heat and, without stirring or shaking, let the sugar cook at a rapid boil for 5 minutes or

so. As the syrup begins to darken, carefully swirl the pan to spread the color uniformly. When it turns deep amber, remove the pan from the heat and quickly pour 1 tablespoon of the caramel into each mold, completely coating the bottom. Set aside and let the caramel harden.

3. Pour the milk into a 3-quart saucepan; whisk in ¼ cup of the sugar, the cocoa, and the salt. Bring to a full boil over high heat, whisking frequently to prevent scorching; remove from the heat and immediately add the chopped chocolate. Whisk steadily until the pieces have completely melted and the mixture is smooth. Transfer the chocolate base to a mixing bowl and set aside until lukewarm, about 30 minutes (or, to cool more rapidly, set the bowl into a larger container of ice water and stir).

4. Arrange a rack in the center of the oven and preheat to 350 degrees F.

5. In a small bowl, briefly whisk together the eggs, yolks, and the remaining ¼ cup of sugar; then whisk in 1 cup of the chocolate base and continue whisking until smooth. Pour this chocolate-and-egg mixture back into the chocolate base. Whisk well to blend, and then strain the custard through a fine sieve into a large pitcher or measuring cup.

6. Pour ½ cup of custard into each mold. Set the roasting pan on the oven rack and pour in hot water to come halfway up the sides of the molds. Cover and seal the pan with aluminum foil.

7. Bake the flans for about 40 minutes, just until they are set on top but still jiggle when gently shaken. Carefully remove the baking pan from the oven, let the flans cool in the water for 30 minutes, and then refrigerate the molds for at least 2 hours. You can keep them in the refrigerator, well covered, for up to 3 days.

8. To serve, dip the bottom of a mold into a bowl of warm water for a few moments, then run the blade of a small knife around the inside edge. Cover the flan with a dessert plate, invert, and shake sharply to release. Lift off the mold and serve the flan, along with its caramel syrup. Repeat with each mold. Sprinkle an equal amount of grated chocolate over each flan and serve.

Butterscotch Pudding with Brown Sugar Sauce

SERVES 8 TO 10

Butterscotch is one of those heartwarming flavors that everyone seems to love in almost any guise. Though the butterscotch flavor here is far from elusive, the texture of the pudding itself is especially delicate. The trick is to handle it gently and cook it briefly after adding the cornstarch mixture. Although the pudding is a soulful and rustic dessert, you can certainly dress it up by serving it, as we do, in tall, chilled parfait glasses or red wine goblets. Swirl some of the brown sugar sauce in a spiral around the inside of the glass, and then chill the glasses for 15 minutes. Carefully spoon in the pudding without disturbing the swirls of sauce, and finish with a dollop of whipped cream flavored with sugar and vanilla.

BUTTERSCOTCH PUDDING

2½ cups milk

1 (12-ounce) can evaporated milk

1 packed cup dark brown sugar

⅓ cup cornstarch

8 egg yolks

4 tablespoons butter cut into pieces

3 tablespoons Scotch whiskey

BROWN SUGAR SAUCE

1 packed cup dark brown sugar

¼ cup water

1 cup heavy cream

1. In a heavy-bottomed, 3-quart saucepan, stir together 2 cups of the milk, the evaporated milk, and ½ cup of the brown sugar. Set over medium-high heat and bring to a full boil, stirring occasionally. Remove the pan from the heat and reserve.

2. In a medium bowl, combine the cornstarch and remaining ½ cup brown sugar, stirring to break up any lumps. Stir in the egg yolks and the remaining ½ cup of milk, whisking until smooth and well blended. Pour into the pan of hot milk and whisk vigorously to blend.

3. Place the pan over medium heat and, whisking constantly, bring the mixture to a boil. As soon as a few large bubbles burst through the thick pudding, turn off the heat. Whisk in the butter and then the whiskey and continue whisking until thoroughly incorporated.

4. Pour the pudding through a fine strainer into a heatproof glass serving dish or bowl. Press a piece of plastic wrap onto the surface, to prevent a skin from forming, and refrigerate the pudding for 2 to 3 hours, until completely cool and set.

5. While the pudding chills, make the sauce: Stir the brown sugar and water together in a heavy 2-quart pan; bring to a boil over high heat. Reduce the heat to medium and cook the syrup for 2 to 3 minutes at a vigorous boil, until it has thickened slightly and starts to caramelize on the sides of the pan. Remove from the heat. Whisk in the heavy cream; then return to a boil, whisking. Continue to cook for 5 minutes at a steady boil, lowering the heat slightly if the sauce bubbles too high in the pan. Remove from the heat and let cool to room temperature. Set aside.

6. To serve, spoon the pudding into chilled dessert bowls or parfait glasses, swirl a bit of the brown sugar sauce onto each pudding.

Alfajores

MAKES ABOUT 15 FILLED SANDWICH COOKIES

Alfajores are soft, *dulce de leche*–stuffed sandwich cookies; they are a generous gift to us from the Latin American countries where they are so popular. The addition of cornstarch as a primary ingredient in the dough gives the cookies a soft, almost chewy, texture, which is why they are best enjoyed the day they are made. The *alfajores* are a delicious snack on their own, and also work beautifully as an accompaniment for vanilla ice cream topped with sliced peaches, or alongside Caramel Baked Apples (page 271).

COOKIE DOUGH

½ cup all-purpose flour

1¼ cups cornstarch

1 tablespoon baking powder

6 tablespoons butter, softened

½ cup sugar

1 tablespoon grated lemon zest

1 large egg

1 large egg yolk

Vegetable oil spray

FILLING

1 cup *dulce de leche* at room temperature (see page 268), made with 1 can sweetened condensed milk

½ cup (approximately) unsweetened, shredded coconut

1. Sift together the flour, cornstarch, and baking powder; set aside.

2. In the bowl of a standing electric mixer fitted with the paddle attachment, cream together the butter, sugar, and lemon zest on medium speed until smooth, 1 to 2 minutes. Beat in the egg, and then the egg yolk, scraping down the sides of the bowl as necessary. (The mixture will look somewhat curdled.)

3. Add the sifted ingredients all at once to the ingredients in the mixing bowl. On low speed, beat just until the dough comes together. Scrape out the sticky dough onto plastic wrap, press into a disk, wrap tightly, and refrigerate for at least 2 hours, or overnight.

4. Preheat the oven to 325 degrees F. Lightly coat a large cookie sheet or jelly-roll pan with vegetable oil spray, line with parchment, and then lightly spray the paper. Set aside.

5. Place the chilled dough on a well-floured surface and roll out with a floured rolling pin to an even ¼-inch thickness. Using a sharp 2-inch round cookie cutter, cut as many circles as possible, occasionally dipping the cutter in flour to prevent sticking. Arrange the circles 1 inch apart on the cookie sheet. Gather the remaining scraps of dough, roll them out, cut more circles, and add them to the cookie sheet. If the dough becomes overly soft and sticky, chill it briefly until it is workable. Refrigerate the filled cookie sheet for 15 minutes.

6. Bake the cookies for about 10 minutes, until they have just set and are slightly puffed, but not at all colored. Cool for 1 or 2 minutes, and then loosen the cookies with a spatula.

7. To form the *alfajores,* pipe or spoon about 1 tablespoon of soft *dulce de leche* onto the bottom (flat side) of a cookie. Make a sandwich by placing another cookie on top. Press the cookies together gently to spread the filling to the edges. Roll the sticky rim in the grated coconut, and repeat with the remaining cookies.

Chocolate Chip–Oatmeal Cookies

MAKES ABOUT 2 DOZEN COOKIES

At the risk of going head-to-head with your favorite family recipe for chocolate chip cookies, we're pleased to share our version—a much-loved and steady component of the Union Square Cafe cookie plate, which is enjoyed by nearly half the tables in the restaurant each evening. These chunky chocolate-chip-and-oatmeal cookies are dotted with semisweet chocolate "buttons"—thin disks about ¾ inch in diameter. Alternatively, you can chop a semisweet bar into chunks, or simply use good old chocolate chips. These cookies are not meant to be dark brown, and it's important not to overbake them. Also, while they'll certainly be delicious the next day, they're best the first day, when they retain a soft, almost pliable texture.

8 tablespoons (1 stick) butter, softened, plus more for
    the cookie sheets
½ cup sugar
½ cup dark brown sugar
1 large egg
½ teaspoon vanilla extract
1 cup all-purpose flour
1¼ cups rolled oats
¼ teaspoon salt
½ teaspoon baking powder
½ teaspoon baking soda
6 ounces semisweet chocolate, chopped; or "buttons";
    or chocolate chips (see Note)

1. Set a rack in the middle of the oven, and preheat the oven to 400 degrees F. Lightly butter two large cookie sheets, about 12 by 18 inches, or, alternatively, line them with parchment paper.

2. In the bowl of a standing electric mixer fitted with the paddle attachment, cream the butter and the two sugars together on medium speed, scraping down the sides of the bowl as needed, until smooth and fluffy. Beat in the egg and the vanilla extract to blend thoroughly.

3. Add to the bowl all the remaining ingredients except the chocolate. Mix on low speed for a few seconds, just to incorporate. Fold in the chocolate pieces by hand, with a rubber spatula, scraping the bowl and blending the dough evenly.

4. With a small (1-ounce) ice-cream scoop or a tablespoon measure, scoop out mounds of dough, about 2 tablespoons each. Dip the scoop in water to prevent the dough from sticking. Leave 3 inches between each mound of dough, and not more than 1 dozen cookies on each sheet.

5. Press down on each mound with wet fingers, flattening it into a 2-inch disk. Bake one sheet at a time for 9 minutes, until the cookies have spread and puffed slightly, but have not browned. Let the soft cookies cool on the sheet for about 10 minutes; then loosen with a spatula. When completely cool, store the cookies in an airtight container at room temperature.

Note: Chocolate "buttons" can sometimes be found at specialty food stores. They may also be mail-ordered through the King Arthur Flour *Baker's Catalogue*, which offers Mercken's Yucatán chocolate in ¾-inch buttons.

Peanut Butter Cookies

MAKES ABOUT 2 DOZEN LARGE COOKIES

When Danny makes his midday appearance in the USC kitchen, it's rare that he doesn't make a beeline for the pastry rack and reach directly for one of these beguilingly good peanut butter cookies. Unlike our Chocolate Chip–Oatmeal Cookies (page 306), these are meant to be golden brown and crisp. They're made with smooth peanut butter, and, best of all, a generous addition of fresh peanuts, which gives each bite even more texture and flavor. Make sure not to crowd the mounds of unbaked cookie dough on the cookie sheets, since they'll spread out while baking.

6 tablespoons butter, softened, plus more for the
    cookie sheets
½ cup corn oil
⅓ cup smooth peanut butter
½ cup packed dark brown sugar
1 egg
2 teaspoons vanilla extract
1¾ cups all-purpose flour
1 cup confectioners' sugar
¼ teaspoon salt
1 teaspoon baking soda
1 cup dry-roasted unsalted peanuts, coarsely chopped

1. Preheat the oven to 375 degrees F. Lightly butter 2 large cookie sheets, about 12 by 18 inches, or line them with parchment paper.

2. In the bowl of a standing electric mixer fitted with the paddle attachment, mix the oil, butter, peanut butter, and brown sugar on medium speed for 2 or 3 minutes, until well blended. Add the egg and vanilla, increase the speed, and beat for another 2 or 3 minutes, until the mixture becomes smooth and creamy. Set aside.

3. Sift together the flour, powdered sugar, salt, and baking soda, breaking up any lumps. Add this dry mix and the peanuts to the mixer bowl all at once, and incorporate on low speed, mixing for only about 20 seconds. Finish blending the cookie dough by hand with a large rubber spatula for a few moments to make sure the nuts are well distributed.

4. Using a small (1-ounce) ice-cream scoop or a measuring tablespoon—dipped in water to prevent sticking—scoop out the batter to form even mounds, each about 2 tablespoons. Space the mounds 3 inches or more apart on the parchment, with no more than 1 dozen per cookie sheet. With moistened fingers, flatten each mound into a 2-inch disk.

5. Bake the cookies, one sheet at a time, for 20 to 22 minutes, until they are deep golden brown. If you choose to bake two trays at a time, rotate the trays, back to front and top and bottom, halfway through the baking time, and bake longer, if necessary. Let cool on the cookie sheet until crisp. Store in an airtight container.

Coconut-Rum Sauce

MAKES ABOUT 2 CUPS

Here's a versatile sauce whose flavors work well with both chocolate and banana desserts. We use it as a garnish for Chocolate Pudding Flan (page 310), and it would also work well as a topping for vanilla, rum-raisin, or banana ice cream.

2 teaspoons cornstarch
½ cup sugar
⅓ cup Myers's rum (dark Jamaican)
1 (13½-ounce) can coconut milk

1. In a small bowl, mix the cornstarch with ¼ cup of the sugar; then whisk in the rum until completely smooth.

2. Heat the coconut milk and the remaining ¼ cup of sugar in a 2-quart saucepan over medium-high heat, stirring frequently, until it reaches a full, rolling boil. Reduce the heat to medium, whisk in the rum-cornstarch mixture, and return the coconut milk to a rapid boil. Let it cook for about 30 seconds (it will bubble up and thicken); then remove from the heat. Allow the sauce to cool, and then refrigerate. Serve chilled. It will keep for up to 1 week.

Coffee Cream

MAKES ABOUT 3 CUPS

This is a useful garnish to enliven desserts where an intense coffee flavor would provide a complementary note. We spoon it over Banana "Cup" Cakes (page 288), and it's also wonderful with Almond Cake (page 292), or almost any brownie or chocolate cake recipe.

⅔ cup good-quality whole dark-roast coffee beans
3½ tablespoons sugar
Pinch of baking soda
2 cups heavy cream

1. Start the coffee cream at least 6 hours—but preferably 24 hours—before serving. Place the coffee beans in a plastic bag and crush into coarse bits with a rolling pin or a heavy pan. Stir together the crushed beans, sugar, baking soda, and cream in a nonreactive saucepan and bring to a boil. Remove from the heat and transfer to a bowl. Allow the cream to cool, and store, tightly covered, in the refrigerator.

2. When ready to serve, strain the mixture through a wire-mesh sieve into a large metal bowl, rubbing the crushed coffee to release all the cream. Set the bowl with the cream over a larger bowl filled with ice. Whip the cream with a flexible wire balloon whip or an electric mixer until it will hold smooth, stiff peaks. Serve immediately.

Country Cream

MAKES ABOUT 2 CUPS

"Country Cream" is our name for a topping we use with lots of desserts as a tangy and slightly richer alternative to crème fraîche or whipped cream. To create a wonderfully simple summer dessert, ladle a heaping dollop of Country Cream onto a big bowl of fresh berries, sprinkled generously with brown sugar. Try it with Strawberry-Rhubarb Pandowdy (page 274), Poached Peach Shortcakes (page 278), or your favorite apple pie.

½ cup sour cream
½ cup mascarpone
½ cup plain, whole-milk yogurt
¼ cup sugar
2 teaspoons vanilla extract

Place all the ingredients in a deep mixing bowl and set the bowl over a larger bowl filled with ice. Whisk together all the ingredients until the mixture will hold soft, smooth peaks, and is the consistency of whipped heavy cream. Serve immediately or refrigerate, covered, for up to 3 to 4 days. Frozen, the cream is delicious scooped like ice cream and served as a topping.

Malted Vanilla Ice Cream

MAKES ABOUT 3 CUPS

We use Malted Vanilla Ice Cream as a garnish for our Caramel Baked Apples (page 271). It's also perfectly delicious on its own, or topped with hot fudge sauce.

1 cup heavy cream
1 cup milk
⅓ cup sugar
½ cup packed malted-milk powder
1 vanilla bean
4 egg yolks

1. In a heavy-bottomed, 2-quart saucepan, whisk together the cream, milk, half the sugar, and half the malted-milk powder. Slit the vanilla bean lengthwise, scrape the tiny seeds into the pan, and then toss in the bean pods as well. Bring to a boil over moderate heat, stirring occasionally. Remove from the heat and allow to steep for 1 hour.

2. Prepare an ice bath by filling a large bowl with ice and setting a smaller bowl on top.

3. Whisk the egg yolks in a small bowl with the remaining sugar and malted-milk powder. Return the cream mixture to a boil, and remove from the heat. Temper the yolks by slowly ladling ½ cup of the hot liquid into the bowl with the yolks, whisking constantly. Still whisking, pour the warm yolk mixture back into the hot cream, and then stir with a wooden spoon for a few moments to thicken the custard.

4. Strain the custard through a fine-mesh strainer into the bowl set over ice, and stir occasionally until chilled. Freeze in an ice-cream maker, following the manufacturer's directions.

THERE ARE NINE (10 OR 11) MISTAKES IN THIS PHOTOGRAPH.
CAN YOU FIND THEM?

(See opposite page for the answers.)

PANTRY

DID YOU FIND THEM?

11. Unlike most Union Square Café diners, this one does not appear to be happy.
10. The diner is reading the *New York Times* upside down.
9. There is a flower in the drinking water.
8. A meat cleaver replaces a knife.
7. The table has three salt shakers.
6. Cherries are on the table in lieu of olives.
5. The diner is eating soup with a fork.
4. The diner's tie is in the soup.
3. There is an uncooked duck on the table.
2. There are pieces of birthday cake in the bread basket.
1. The wine glass has a straw in it.

Chicken Stock

MAKES 3 QUARTS

A clear, flavorful chicken stock is indispensable for sauces, soups, and most risotto recipes. The key to a clear, brilliant stock is to skim as much fat and foam as possible from the surface, and to cook the stock at a barely perceptible simmer. For a brown chicken stock, a darker, more richly flavored stock that can be substituted for veal stock, roast the chicken bones with the vegetables and 1 tablespoon of tomato paste in a 350-degree oven for 30 minutes, or until browned. Add the water, herbs, and spices and proceed with the recipe below. In addition to getting chicken bones from your butcher, use leftover carcasses from roast chicken.

5 pounds chicken bones, rinsed well in cold water

4 quarts water

1 large onion, coarsely chopped (2½ cups)

3 medium carrots, scrubbed and quartered (2½ cups)

3 celery ribs, quartered

1 medium parsnip, peeled and coarsely chopped (1½ cups)

1 bay leaf

1 teaspoon fresh thyme

10 whole black peppercorns

¼ cup fresh parsley sprigs

1. Combine all the ingredients in an 8-quart stockpot. Over medium heat, bring slowly to a boil. Skim the foam that rises to the surface with a ladle.

2. Reduce the heat and simmer very slowly, uncovered, for 4 to 5 hours. Skim the surface with a ladle every 30 minutes to remove any accumulated fat or impurities.

3. Strain the stock into a clean pot or metal bowl and set it over a large bowl filled with ice. Refrigerate for 1 or 2 days, or freeze for several months. Remove any hardened fat from refrigerated stock before reheating.

Fish Stock

MAKES 3½ CUPS

For a brilliant and flavorful fish stock, rinse the bones and heads well to remove any blood or impurities. If you are using fish heads, be sure to have the gills removed. A word of caution: never cook the stock beyond a barely perceptible simmer, to prevent it from becoming murky and unappealing.

1 tablespoon olive oil

1 cup sliced onions

1 cup well-rinsed sliced leeks
    (white and light green parts only)

½ cup chopped celery

1 fresh thyme sprig

3 fresh parsley sprigs

1 small bay leaf

1 teaspoon whole black peppercorns

1 pound fish bones from white-fleshed
    fish (such as flounder, sole, bass,
    or snapper), cleaned and chopped

½ cup white wine

4 cups cold water

1. Heat the olive oil over medium heat in a 3-quart stockpot or saucepan. Add the vegetables, herbs, and peppercorns and cook over medium heat, stirring frequently, until softened, about 10 minutes.

2. Raise the heat to high, add the fish bones, and stir well for 3 to 4 minutes. Add the white wine and reduce by boiling for an additional 3 to 4 minutes.

3. Add the cold water, lower the heat to medium, and slowly bring the stock to a boil. Skim the surface with a ladle to remove any foam that rises. Lower the heat some more and simmer very slowly for 45 minutes.

4. Strain the stock through a fine-mesh or cheesecloth-lined strainer and chill over ice. Refrigerate for up to 4 days, or freeze for future use.

Veal Stock

MAKES 3 QUARTS

Often considered the backbone of classic French cuisine, well-made veal stock is essential to the success of several slow-cooked dishes that we make at the restaurant. As with any stock, freeze what you don't need, for future use. Veal stock is also available from many fine butchers and grocery stores.

7 pounds veal bones, preferably knuckle
    and shank

5 quarts water plus 1 cup

2 cups scrubbed and coarsely chopped
    carrots

3 cups quartered, unpeeled medium onions

2 cups coarsely chopped celery

2 cups well-rinsed sliced leeks

1 head garlic, halved

2 tablespoons olive oil

3 tablespoons tomato paste

½ teaspoon whole black peppercorns

1 teaspoon dried thyme

1 bay leaf

6 fresh parsley sprigs

1. Preheat the oven to 450 degrees F.

2. Rinse the veal bones well in cold water. Place the bones in an 8-quart stockpot and cover with the 5 quarts of water. Bring to a boil over medium heat. With a small ladle, skim the surface to remove the foam and impurities. Reduce the heat to low, and simmer very slowly.

3. Place the vegetables in a roasting pan and toss with the oil and the tomato paste to coat. Roast for 45 minutes to 1 hour, until the vegetables are well browned.

4. Transfer the roasted vegetables to the stockpot and add the peppercorns, thyme, bay leaf, and parsley. Pour the remaining 1 cup of water into the roasting pan and place it on the stove over high heat. Deglaze the pan by stirring to dissolve and incorporate any browned bits into the water. Pour the water into the stock. Cook over low heat at a barely perceptible simmer, uncovered, for 12 to 16 hours. Skim occasionally to remove any fat or foam that rises to the surface.

5. Strain the stock into a clean pot or metal bowl and chill over a larger bowl filled with ice. Remove any fat that rises to the top. Refrigerate for 1 to 2 days, or freeze for later use.

Lamb Stock

MAKES 2 QUARTS

Making your own lamb stock might seem a bit excessive, but it's really quite simple. Just ask your butcher for some bones when you buy the meat for your lamb recipe. It's the secret ingredient that lends depth and richness to every braised lamb dish we make. You'll notice that this recipe calls for using chicken stock as a base. You need not prepare two stocks from scratch to succeed here. Canned chicken broth will deliver highly successful results!

5 pounds lamb bones (preferably leg and/or neck)

2 cups scrubbed and coarsely chopped carrots

1 large onion, coarsely chopped

3 celery stalks, coarsely chopped

1 head garlic, halved

2 sprigs fresh sage

¼ cup fresh parsley sprigs

1 bay leaf

10 whole black peppercorns

4 quarts Chicken Stock (page 315), or canned chicken broth

1. Preheat the oven to 400 degrees F.

2. Rinse the lamb bones well in cold water. Place the bones in a roasting pan large enough to hold them easily in a single layer, and roast until lightly browned, about 30 minutes. Transfer the bones to an 8-quart stockpot.

3. Pour off the fat from the roasting pan, add 1 cup water, and place the pan on the stove over high heat. Deglaze the pan by stirring with a wooden spoon to dissolve and incorporate any browned bits into the water. Pour the juices into the stockpot and add all of the remaining ingredients. Bring to a boil, reduce the heat to low, and gently simmer the stock, uncovered, for 4 hours. Using a ladle, skim occasionally to remove any fat or foam that rises to the top.

4. Strain the stock into a saucepan and reduce at a steady simmer to 2

quarts. Pour into a clean pot or metal bowl and allow to cool to room temperature. Skim to remove any fat that rises to the top. Refrigerate 2 to 3 days, tightly covered, or freeze in a plastic container for later use.

Vegetable Stock

MAKES 3 QUARTS

Here's an all-purpose, all-season vegetable stock, to be enjoyed on its own as a broth or as soup base. It is also a superb stand-in for chicken stock when you're cooking risotto, legumes, or braised vegetables.

1 tablespoon extra-virgin olive oil

3 cups scrubbed and sliced carrots

3 cups sliced onions

1 medium head Bibb lettuce, rinsed
    and chopped

2 cups chopped Savoy cabbage

2 cups well rinsed and sliced leeks

1½ cups sliced celery

1 cup peeled and sliced parsnips

½ cup fresh parsley sprigs

3 garlic cloves, sliced

2 fresh thyme sprigs

2 tablespoons chopped fresh basil

1 bay leaf

1 tablespoon whole black peppercorns

2 tablespoons kosher salt

1 Idaho potato, scrubbed and sliced

2 tomatoes, cored and chopped

3 quarts water

1. Heat the olive oil in a 5-quart stockpot over high heat. Add all the ingredients except the potato, tomatoes, and water. Cook, stirring occasionally, to soften and wilt, about 7 minutes.

2. Add the potato, tomatoes, and water. Bring to a boil, lower the heat, and simmer, covered, for 40 minutes. Strain in a colander set over a bowl, pressing the vegetables to extract the maximum amount of stock. Refrigerate, tightly covered, up to 1 week, or freeze for several months.

Basic Tomato Sauce

MAKES 5 CUPS

This sauce is perfectly good on its own with pasta, and it makes an enriching base for vegetable dishes. We combine the lively acidity of fresh tomatoes with the meatiness of canned plum tomatoes for a well-balanced sauce. If you are seasoning with cheese, we recommend Pecorino Romano as a complement to the sauce.

1½ pounds fresh ripe tomatoes, cored and
    chopped

1 (35-ounce) can Italian plum tomatoes (4
    cups)

2 tablespoons olive oil

½ cup diced onion

1 teaspoon minced garlic

1 tablespoon chopped fresh basil

½ teaspoon kosher salt

¼ teaspoon freshly ground black pepper

1. In a 3-quart saucepan, combine the fresh and canned tomatoes with their juices. Cook over medium heat for 15 minutes, or until the tomatoes are quite soft. Pass the tomatoes through a food mill set over a bowl to remove all the seeds and skin. Set aside.

2. In the same saucepan, rinsed and wiped dry, heat the olive oil over medium heat. Sauté the onion and garlic until softened but not browned. Add the pureed tomatoes and the basil. Cook at a simmer until the sauce thickens, about 30 minutes. Season with salt and pepper. The sauce can be kept for up to 1 week, tightly covered, and refrigerated, or frozen for several months.

Oven-Dried Tomatoes

MAKES 1 1/2 CUPS

Plum tomatoes have won acceptance primarily as an ingredient for making cooked tomato sauce. Their sturdiness also makes them superb candidates for enduring a long, slow day in the oven. These roasted plum tomatoes can be enjoyed any way you've ever used sun-dried tomatoes, but they're even more versatile, since they're a lot less salty.

2 pounds ripe plum tomatoes, washed, cored, and split lengthwise

1 teaspoon kosher salt

2 cups extra-virgin olive oil

2 large fresh thyme sprigs

1 fresh rosemary branch, split

2 to 3 sage leaves

3 medium garlic cloves, peeled and split

1. Place the tomatoes, cut side up, on a baking sheet. Sprinkle with the salt and let sit for 1 hour.

2. Preheat the oven to 200 degrees F.

3. Roast the tomatoes for 5 to 6 hours. The tomatoes are done when they

are dried, but still slightly plump; they should definitely not be leathery, nor as dry as commercial sun-dried tomatoes.

4. Allow the tomatoes to cool to room temperature; then transfer them to a jar or bowl. Stir in the olive oil, herbs, and garlic. Cover tightly, and refrigerate. The tomatoes will improve if marinated for 2 to 3 days before using. They will keep for up to 2 weeks in the refrigerator.

Fresh Pasta Dough

MAKES 1 POUND PASTA

Preparing fresh pasta from scratch ranks among the most pleasurable and satisfying tasks in the kitchen. Readily available ingredients are transformed into heavenly strands of fresh pasta that delight diners. We heartily encourage you to learn and enjoy this simple skill.

A few basics: We've included procedures for making the dough both by hand and in the food processor. While the latter method is quicker, the former has the benefit of giving the pasta maker, over time, a truer sense of the texture and feel of the dough, a sense of how much flour the eggs can absorb, and, ultimately, a more tender pasta. Remember, however, that "tender" does not mean flaccid: fresh pasta, if it is worked correctly during the stretching process, should have texture and "tooth." Once your pasta dough is made, there are again two methods you can use to stretch the dough. The hand method, using the long, dowel-like European rolling pin, usually not more than 1½ inches in diameter, is by far the more demanding skill. We recommend a good-quality pasta machine, either hand cranked or electric, which produces an excellent product.

2 cups all-purpose flour

3 large eggs

½ teaspoon salt

1 to 3 teaspoons water, as needed (if making dough in a food processor)

Olive oil, for drizzling

HAND METHOD

1. Prepare a clean work surface and have at hand a pastry scraper and a fine-mesh strainer.

2. Pour the flour and salt onto the work surface and in the center of the flour, form a well large enough to hold the eggs. Crack the eggs into the well, add the salt, and beat lightly with a fork to mix. With a stirring motion, and pulling the flour from the inner base of the well, use the fork to slowly incorporate the flour into the eggs. When the egg and flour mixture is thick enough so as not to run, push all the remaining flour into the center with your hands and mix to form a dough. When the dough is stiff, and will no longer absorb any flour, move it to a corner of the work surface, away from the remaining flour and small pieces of dough. Clean your hands, and scrape the board clean with the pastry scraper.

3. Place the remaining flour and bits of dough in the strainer and shake the clean flour onto one side of the work surface. Discard the pieces of dough remaining in the sieve, as they will not incorporate into the dough. Place the dough on the sieved flour, and knead with the palm of your hand until it holds together well and is no longer sticky. Incorporate as

much of the sieved flour as the dough will absorb without becoming too hard or dry.

4. Transfer the dough to a clean surface and, with clean hands, knead with a steady and firm motion, giving a quarter-turn with your left hand while you press down on the dough with the heel of your right hand. Knead until the dough is smooth, dry, and elastic, about 5 minutes. Drizzle with olive oil, wrap tightly in plastic wrap, and let rest at least 30 minutes.

MACHINE METHOD

1. Combine the flour and salt in the bowl of a food processor and pulse a few times to aerate. With the machine running, add the eggs through the feed tube and process until the dough begins to form a ball in the bowl of the machine. If the dough is too dry to form a ball, add water by the teaspoon and continue to process.

2. Turn the dough out onto a clean, unfloured board, form it into a ball, and with clean hands, knead as described above. Oil and wrap the dough, and let rest at least 30 minutes.

To cut the pasta:

1. Sprinkle some flour on a jelly-roll pan or cookie sheet and set aside. Set up the hand-cranked or electric pasta machine on one end of a work surface, and lightly flour the surface in front of the machine. Cut the pasta dough into quarters; wrap 3 of the quarters in plastic and set aside. Pass 1 dough quarter through the widest setting on the machine.

Decrease the setting a notch and pass the dough through once again. Decrease another notch, and pass the dough through. On the work surface, fold the flattened dough into thirds, bringing the two ends in toward the center as you would to fold a letter. Flatten the dough with your fingers, return the machine to its widest setting, and pass one of the two open ends of the dough through the machine. Repeat this entire process 5 or 6 times, dragging the dough strip through the flour every now and then, until the dough feels silky and elastic.

2. Now begin rolling the dough through the machine on decreasing settings until 1 notch before the finest setting. Roll the dough through this setting 3 times, until you have obtained a long sheet of pasta that is very smooth and elastic, and approximately the same width as the rollers. Cut the sheet of dough into thirds (each piece will be about 10 inches long). At this point you can either use a long kitchen knife, a circular pasta cutter, or one of the pasta-cutter attachments available with your machine to cut the pasta into whatever shape you desire. Repeat to roll and cut the remaining dough quarters. For long pasta, such as fettuccine, tagliarini, and cappellini, roll the cut pasta around your fingers to make a nest, and then toss gently with flour on a jelly-roll pan. The pasta can then be refrigerated for up to 1 day, until it is cooked, or carefully wrapped and frozen for several weeks. Note that when using the rolled-out dough sheets for anything but stuffed pasta, you can allow them to dry slightly on the work surface before

cutting. For stuffed pasta, such as ravioli, cappellini, and tortellini, the sheets should be kept covered to prevent them from drying, as you will need to fold them.

Mashed Potatoes

MAKES 4 CUPS

Who can resist the creamy comfort of perfectly mashed potatoes? We've found that even the most persnickety diner can be convinced to try almost any new or unusual dish on our menu—so long as it's accompanied by mashed potatoes. These creamy spuds make everything they come in contact with taste better. A few tips for making perfect, smooth mashed potatoes: use a food mill or ricer. A hand-held masher will give you lumpy potatoes, and a food processor will make them gummy and tough. Also, mashed potatoes are always best when they are freshly made. While this recipe explains how to hold mashed potatoes for up to 1 hour, they'll change dramatically if you reheat them the next day. Once you've learned this basic recipe, have fun with some of the mashed potato variations in our chapter of Side Dishes and Condiments.

2 pounds Idaho potatoes, scrubbed and
     peeled
2 teaspoons kosher salt
8 tablespoons (1 stick) unsalted butter
½ cup heavy cream
½ cup milk
¼ teaspoon freshly ground white pepper

1. Place the potatoes in a 2-quart saucepan with 1 teaspoon of the salt and cold water to cover. Bring to a boil, lower the heat, and simmer,

covered, until completely tender, about 30 minutes. Test the potatoes by piercing them with a paring knife—there should be no resistance. Place in a colander and allow to drain well for several minutes.

2. Combine the butter, heavy cream, and milk in another saucepan and heat gently until the butter has melted. Keep warm.

3. Working over the saucepan used to cook the potatoes, pass the potatoes through a food mill or a potato ricer. If you have any difficulty, add a little of the hot milk and butter to the potatoes.

4. To serve, place the potatoes over a low flame and begin adding the warm milk mixture, whipping the potatoes with a wooden spoon or spatula at the same time. When all the liquid is absorbed, season with the remaining 1 teaspoon of salt and the white pepper. Serve piping hot. Mashed potatoes are best served immediately, but if you are unable to do so, or need them for another recipe, keep the potatoes hot for up to 1 hour by placing them in the top of a double boiler, covered and set over barely simmering water.

INDEX

butter:

    brown, Sardinian ravioli with, 70–72

    -tomato sauce, crabmeat-artichoke
        tortelli with, 66–69

buttermilk-blueberry sauce, for
        blueberry–lemon meringue pie,
        284–87

butternut squash, *see* squash, butternut

butterscotch pudding with brown sugar
        sauce, 302–3

cabbage:

    baked sauerkraut, 220–21

    sautéed, 218

cakes:

    almond, 292–94

    banana "cup," 288–91

    lemon–poppy seed angel food, with
        fresh raspberries, 281–83

    poached peach shortcakes, 278–80

calamari, *see* squid

calf's liver with bacon and sage, 190–91

caper-tomato sauce, striped bass with,
        114–15

caramel baked apples, 271–72

cardoon gratin, 222–23

carrot(s):

    beet, and watercress salad, 48–49

    -mushroom *sformato*, 210–11

    sweet-and-sour, 207

cauliflower, roasted, with tomato and green
        olives, 212–13

celery, Swiss chard, and leek *tortino*,
        228–29

chanterelles, roasted lobster with corn
        and, 140–41

cheese, *see specific cheeses*

chicken, 145–53

    Lambrusco, 148–49

    pan-roasted, with Cognac-peppercorn
        sauce, 152–53

    poussin *al mattone*, 154–55

    salt-baked, 145–47

    saltimbocca, 150–51

    stock, 315–16

chicken-fried venison, 176–77

chicken liver crostini, 8–9

chickpeas, in *minestra di ceci*, 37–39

chili and sage–rubbed salmon, 119–20

chocolate:

    dulce con leche crêpes, 268–70

    pudding flan, 300–301

    white, –cream cheese frosting, for
        almond cake, 292–94

chocolate chip-oatmeal cookies, 306–7

chowder, spicy corn, 30–31

chutney, 256–63

    apple-pear, 256–57

    green tomato, 260–61

    plum, 258–59

    quince, 262–63

cipollini, glazed, 203

citrus-yogurt marinade, sea scallops with,
        134–35

clafoutis, plum, 276–77

clams:

    baked stuffed littleneck, 12–13

    linguine with pancetta and, 86–87

    in Michael's *insalata ai frutti di
        mare,* 60–61

    steamed, arugula and, 14–15

coconut-rum sauce, 310

coffee cream, 311

Cognac:

    -peppercorn sauce, pan-roasted
        chicken with, 152–53

    sauce, red snapper with, 128–29

cookies, 304–9

    alfajores, 304–5

    chocolate chip–oatmeal, 306–7

    peanut butter, 308–9

corn:

    chowder, spicy, 30–31

    roasted lobster with chanterelles and,
        140–41

    sweet, fettuccine with gorgonzola and,
        79–80

cornmeal:

    -crusted ricotta fritters, 10–11

    polenta with white beans and chard,
        244–45

country cream, 312

crabmeat, crabs:

    -artichoke tortelli, 66–69

honey semifreddo, 298–99
horseradish-mashed potatoes, 253–54

ice cream, malted vanilla, 313
Indian-style dishes:
    apple-pear chutney, 256–57
    "bouillabaisse," 142–44
    plum chutney, 258–59
    sautéed shrimp Goan-style, 132–33
    -spiced acorn squash, 204–5
    spiced creamed spinach, 216–17
    sweet-hot beet soup, 28–29
ingredients and equipment, xviii–xx
insalata ai frutti di mare, Michael's,
    60–61

jalapeño peppers, in *pennette
    all'Arrabbiata,* 94–95
Jerusalem artichoke:
    pancakes, 224–25
    -potato gratin, 226–27

lamb, 178–85
    chops, baked, 178–79
    olive-stuffed, 180–81
    roast rack of, 182–83
    stew *alla romana,* 184–85
    stock, 317–18
lambrusco chicken, 148–49
leek(s):
    in lemongrass vichyssoise, 26–27
    Swiss chard, and celery *tortino,*
        228–29
lemon:
    -blueberry meringue pie, 284–87
    -garlic steak, Michael's, 163–64
    –poppy seed angel food cake with
        fresh raspberries, 281–83
    -raspberry glaze, 282–83
    -spinach sauce, sheep's-milk ricotta
        gnocchi with, 104–6
"lemonette," frisée salad with bottarga,
    grapefruit and, 55–56
lemongrass vichyssoise, 26–27
lentil:
    and beet vinaigrette, grilled salmon
        with, 112–13

-bulgur pilaf, 238–39
    goat cheese, and beet salad, 52–54
    soup with portobello mushrooms and
        spinach, 32–33
linguine with clams and pancetta, 86–87
liver:
    calf's, with bacon and sage, 190–91
    chicken, crostini, 8–9
lobster:
    grilled, with bruschetta sauce, 138–39
    roasted, with corn and chanterelles,
        140–41
    in *spaghetti all'aragosta,* 88–90

maple-roasted sweet potatoes, 246–47
marinade, citrus-yogurt, sea scallops with,
    134–35
marjoram, zucchini puree with, 206
mascarpone, in Sardinian ravioli, 70–72
mashed potatoes, 251–55, 321–22
    bottarga-, 252
    horseradish-, 253–54
    mustard-, 251
    olive-, 255
"meatballs," eggplant, 15–16
melon and vodka soup, chilled, 36
meringue pie, blueberry–lemon, 284–87
minestra:
    di ceci, 37–39
    di farro, 40–42
mint risotto with eggplant, anchovy and,
    102–3
monkfish *scarpariello,* 130–31
morel mushroom(s):
    sauce, salt-baked chicken with,
        145–47
    in spring risotto, 96–97
mortadella and apple stuffing, 234–35
mozzarella:
    and eggplant "meatballs," 15–16
    in *suppli al telefono,* 18–19
mushroom(s):
    -carrot *sformato,* 210–11
    in *tagliarini ai funghi,* 81–83
    see also cremini mushrooms; morel
        mushroom; portobello mushroom
mustard-mashed potatoes, 251

poppy seed:
   –butternut squash spaetzle, 242–43
   –lemon angel food cake with fresh
      raspberries, 281–83
pork tenderloin, spice-rubbed, 186–88
portobello mushroom(s):
   crostini, 6–7
   lentil soup with spinach and, 32–33
   spinach, and fennel salad, 50–51
potato(es), 248–55
   baked, with roasted onion and sour
      cream, 248–49
   Italian fries, 249–50
   –Jerusalem artichoke gratin, 226–27
   in lemongrass vichyssoise, 26–27
   sweet, maple-roasted, 246–47
   see also mashed potatoes
poussin *al mattone,* 154–55
prosciutto, in chicken saltimbocca, 150–51
Provençal-style olive-stuffed lamb, 180–81
pudding:
   butterscotch, with brown sugar sauce,
      302–3
   carrot-mushroom *sformato,* 210–11
   flan, chocolate, 300–301
puree, zucchini, with marjoram, 206

quail, roast, 156–57
quiche, crustless, Swiss chard, leek, and
      celery *tortino,* 228–29
quince chutney, 262–63

rabbit:
   in *pappardelle al sugo di coniglio,*
      76–78
   sage-fried, 188–89
radicchio leaves, in risotto *rosso,* 100–101
raspberry(ies):
   fresh, lemon–poppy seed angel food
      cake with, 281–83
   -lemon glaze, 282–83
ravioli, Sardinian, 70–72
red snapper with Cognac sauce, 128–29
rhubarb-strawberry pandowdy, 274–75
rice:
   basmati, pilaf, 236–37

in *suppli al telefono,* 18–19
   see also risotto
ricotta:
   fritters, cornmeal-crusted, 10–11
   sheep's-milk, gnocchi, 104–6
   in Swiss chard, leek, and celery
      tortino, 228–29
ricotta salata, in Sardinian ravioli, 70–72
rigatoni with zucchini, tomatoes, and
      cream, 92–93
risotto, 96–103
   with eggplant, anchovy, and mint,
      102–3
   rosso, 100–101
   spring, 96–97
   zucchini, 98–99
roast(ed):
   asparagus, 202
   cauliflower with tomato and green
      olives, 212–13
   goose, 160–62
   herb-, rack of veal, 172–73
   maple-, sweet potatoes, 246–47
   onion, baked potatoes with sour
      cream and, 248–49
   quail, 156–57
   rack of lamb, 182–83
   root vegetables, 208–9
   turkey with apple-cider gravy, 158–60
roe, *see* bottarga
Roman-style dishes:
   braised oxtails, 174–75
   chicken saltimbocca, 150–51
   lamb stew *alla romana,* 184–85
   poussin *al mattone,* 154–55
   trippa alla trasteverina, 192–94
rum-coconut sauce, 310

sage:
   calf's liver with bacon and, 190–91
   and chili–rubbed salmon, 119–20
   -fried rabbit, 188–89
salads, 45–61
   bitter greens, anchovy dressing, and
      cornmeal-crusted ricotta fritters,
      10–11